JUL 03 2017

D0865074

Tracing the Roots of Globalization and Business Principles

Tracing the Roots of Globalization and Business Principles

Second Edition

Lawrence A. Beer

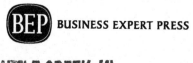 BUSINESS EXPERT PRESS

WILLARD LIBRARY, BATTLE CREEK, MI

Tracing the Roots of Globalization and Business Principles, Second Edition

Copyright © Business Expert Press, LLC, 2015.

All rights reserved. No part of this publication may be reproduced, stored in a retrieval system, or transmitted in any form or by any means—electronic, mechanical, photocopy, recording, or any other except for brief quotations, not to exceed 400 words, without the prior permission of the publisher.

First published in 2011 by
Business Expert Press, LLC
222 East 46th Street, New York, NY 10017
www.businessexpertpress.com

ISBN-13: 978-1-63157-230-2 (paperback)
ISBN-13: 978-1-63157-231-9 (e-book)

Business Expert Press International Business Collection

Collection ISSN: 1948-2752 (print)
Collection ISSN: 1948-2760 (electronic)

Cover and interior design by Exeter Premedia Services Private Ltd., Chennai, India

First edition: 2011
Second edition: 2015

10 9 8 7 6 5 4 3 2 1

Printed in the United States of America.

MILLARD LIBRARY, BATTLE CREEK, MI

Abstract

The term globalization is too often defined by the results it produces, both positive and negative, as opposed to being defined as a socially engineered device naturally occurring as civilization progressed. It is a mechanism to manage the affairs of human beings as they provided for their mutual, but not always equal, attainment of satisfaction. It is therefore a universal instrument that emerged out of the ordered exchange process and is to be found in all cultures. Its growth and maturity were fueled by common denominators of value that are shared across and between social groups around the world and act as a trade agent, bridging and bonding alien territories. As such it began in ancient times and continues into the present, where its prevalence has resulted in a more borderless world with increasing interdependence of nations. The historic commercial activities used in the past form the platform of principles still evident in its modern-day structure.

Keywords

ancient commodities, business principles, competition, cost, economics, globalization, government, international business, market, mediums of exchange, proprietary rights, religion, secular laws, technology, world trade

Contents

Prologue

When I began teaching global management business courses I was struck by the reality that the vast majority of my students had a minimal introduction if not noticeably absent knowledge as to the history of commerce. They also lacked an appreciation of the impact of the commercial imperative on the development of civilization. As most of them were born in the era of modern globalization, with product choices and common brand names for everyday goods coming from a broad spectrum of foreign sources, the assumption that the world marketplace was created in their time was a commonly held conviction. The notion that globalization is a recent occurrence with a decidedly prejudicial depiction as a United States, no less European-inspired event, permeates the presentations of many educators, books and articles, authors, and the public.

The idea that such a system evolved over time and that today's business management principles were birthed in antiquity were concepts my students never considered. I decided that I would open every class with a presentation on the roots of globalization, the emergence of the exchange imperative, and trade as a prime initiator propelling and contributing to societal growth and development. All cultures throughout history at one time or another engaged in cross border trade—what we today call globalization. It is an economic system with overtones of social and political ramifications that links all of us together. Many years later my continuously updated lecture notes for such sessions, coupled with a private research fascination on the contribution of the commercial imperative to civilization, have resulted in this book. Beyond the impetus provided by my students to investigate the subject matter, I remembered vividly my global executive experiences when an understanding of the history of global commerce would have well served my world managerial responsibilities if only such an introduction was given to me during my academic years. Doing business with foreign associates requires a deeper appreciation of how the art and science of working across borders developed, as the processes and principles that emerged still impact the establishment of commercial relationships today. Framed in the era of modern globalization, the current function of both undergraduate and MBA programs is to produce global citizen managers rather than graduates who are specialized in specific disciplines. This new educational pedagogical approach begins with business history or the roots of globalization.

In many textbooks and articles the word "globalization" is defined by the result it produces as opposed to the mechanism it really is. The term is used to describe a spreading economic phenomenon, the increased trend of nations to trade and invest across and between borders at a pace and to a degree not seen before: The growing economic interdependence around the world to signify that the economic good fortune or in reverse, the economic ills, of any one sovereign country could affect all the others. It reflects an interconnected interlinked global marketplace. The word is plainly objective. It describes an exemplified condition supported by fact. The term is not judgmental. Modern globalization is not a perfect economic system; it just exists, and one needs to deal with it. The term, however, has been hijacked by numerous prejudicial agenda-driven groups who have altered the word's simple definition to suit their political, economic, and social agendas. It has been used to metaphorically symbolize problems that a changing environment endures. Some see the phenomenon as capitalism gone globally viral and that the commercial imperative lacks an ethical direction when applied worldwide. Many portray the process as contributing to the widening gap between rich and poor—the haves and have not's. They fail to understand that the original exchange process that evolved into ancient cross territorial trade was never intended to be an equitable system of give and take. Undue advantage and damage has always accompanied relationships of humans since the beginning of mankind.

The word "globalization" should be defined as a universal mechanism that grew out of the naturally occurring ordered-exchange process. It matured on the back of common denominators of shared need values across and between social groups around the world. This meaning properly recognizes it as a socially induced system that is inherent in all cultures fostering social integration. It is a method to help manage the affairs of human beings and a collectively engineered apparatus to provide for the mutual, but not always equal, attainment of basic needs. As such it began in ancient times and continues in the present.

However, students in undergraduate and graduate business programs, as well as owners and managers of corporations, face a career historically marred by the negative overtones that the commercial endeavor has produced.

While the commercial world today and throughout history is not justifiably immune from valid criticisms for its practices and overall conduct, its influence on the development of civilization should not be overlooked. This consideration, along with the desire to acquaint the current business profession with its roots of its principles, provided the motivation for the construction of this book.

The book is intended to provide a historic perception of how the natural process developed, how the commercial world evolved to form the basis for many of our modern business techniques, and how the trade imperative (the precursor of global commerce) influenced the construction of our constantly developing civilization. The gathered material was constructed as a neutral assessment and not intended to portray globalizations as good or bad. However, any inspection into historical accounts must recognize that there will always be the prejudicial filters that are part of human record-keeping activity. The term "history" is derived from the Greek word *historia*, which means information or an inquiry designed to elicit truth. I recall one of my own professors once remarking that history is the version of past events that people have decided to agree upon, and therefore it is always subject to reinterpretation and examination sustained by newly confirmed facts that themselves can be challenged by future observers. It should be noted that the majority of references to history in this book are taken from generally accepted researched writings with many based on the published accounts as offered by scribes of yesterday. Such accuracy is always suspect as early public record keeping was in the purview of territorial rulers who engaged writers to portray their deeds in a decidedly positive fashion, cementing the fact that their historical tenure would always be preserved in the best possible way. Many historic accounts reported years, if not centuries, after the actual events took place relied on storytellers who themselves blended myth and fact to sustain their subjective conclusions. Classical authors did not rely on statistics, as such a collection in antiquity was not officially organized or, when it was available, was deeply suspect. Hence illogical contradictions appear in historic writings. Many ancient historians were therefore careless with details, reckless with chronology, and more desirous of flamboyant rhetoric to attract readers than interested in accuracy. Historian T.J. Cornell perhaps best sums up the danger of relying on historical records reminding us that, "all history contains an element of fiction."[1] In spite of such misgivings, pictures of the past do emerge that are worthy of inspection, examination, and reflective comment. Some theories introduced in the book recount the ideas of fringe historians as historic consensus is always in flux and new discoveries may alter what is presently considered correct. No matter how history is presented, and for that matter debated, to paraphrase the great Greek orator Cicero, in order to gain the maturity of knowledge, one must inquire into the past or the infancy of wisdom will remain.

As history is an unending dialogue between the past and the present, looking backward allows us to better plan for the future and such is the overriding intent of this book: to give current and future managers a better appreciation and understanding of the process they have inherited so they might use it better. Lao Tzu, the Chinese philosopher whose sayings are often recounted as those of Confucius, wrote that "By three methods we may learn wisdom: First, by reflection, which is the noblest, second by imitation, which is the easiest; and third by experience, which is the bitterest."[2]

Globalization is a modern term but the roots of its theoretical inception are deeply buried in antiquity, and hence an inspection into the past, which allows for reflection in the present, is a good way to gather intelligence, perhaps emulate it and in the end use it to combat the harsh realities that occur around us. To put globalization in a time perspective, drawing a mental picture of its progression, think of a stadium and a playing field. In the beginning, ancient times, the participants in the game were few. Most of the earth's population either sat on the sidelines as a supporting cast or in the stands watching the event while experiencing its effects either directly or indirectly. Over the centuries, such bystanders were more and more influenced by the incumbent players and got more involved in the game. They demanded alteration of the rules of the game to satisfy their needs and the participants began to structure their strategic intent and tactical activities with spectators in mind. In the modern fast-changing global environment, the audience has begun to come out of their seats as the appeal to join those on the field and get into the economic game has strengthened. The basic system, however, was created long ago, and over time more and more territorial participants entered the arena as players as opposed to just sitting in the stands.

At the end of 2014, the world population exceeded 7.3 billion and by 2050 conservative estimates predict another 2.5 billion will be added, a 34 percent increase. As the world grows, so will the interaction of its inhabitants as players rather than spectators. The effect of modern globalization in the words of Thomas L. Friedman is a "hot, flat and crowded" world.[3] Metaphorically, what is happening is best illustrated by a lyric from singer-songwriter Don McLean's song *American Pie* (1971): "'Cause the players tried to take the field [but] the marching band/Refused to yield, do you recall what was revealed."[4]

Such a question has been answered. More and more participants are on the global commercial field of play and the stadium continues to fill up. A larger slice of the world's population will now be represented as the era of modern globalization, the unprecedented expansion of trade between and among nations based on ancient principles, takes hold. Emerging nations, the marching band, have made their presence known, and competition with the incumbent players has begun. Ironically, history reveals that the so-called developing nations of today were at one time the early purveyors and in fact the dominant players in the global trade game.

The modern world is, however, a changing, evolving one that students of today, the future executives of tomorrow, will need to engage. While new skills and techniques will need to be engineered to deal with such issues, the lessons of history still form the basis of this educational process. Most textbooks on the subject of international business and/or management devote an introductory chapter describing the globalization process, recounting such development in a series of statistical charts and depicting the growth of international or cross border trade and its financial cousin—foreign direct investment. The data shows that the world has embraced the phenomenon in the modern period, after World War II, at an accelerated pace and to a degree never before experienced. But such a concentration targeting the leap in natural progression, based primarily on arithmetical references in the modern era, does not tell the whole story nor does it allow an appreciation and understanding of how the development of the world was enhanced and fueled by the concept of globalization throughout history.

Commercial history is intertwined with mankind's history and this partnership will continue to shape and influence the future. Knowing where one comes from helps in the construction of the current journey and such is the theme of this book. As well stated in a recent article, "There are already manifold interactions between business history and management studies, but to date they have been tended to be more particular and patchy than general and systematic." A "closer engagement" to "further consideration and discussion" is warranted so that research historians and business theorists can combine to provide a platform of introspection to further the education of international managers.[5]

The study of history is often placed in the realm of humanities in most universities. Business school students, with their desire to learn something that will lead to a job, are more prone to take courses that build specific managerial proficiencies, which directly relate to career opportunities. The traditional pedagogy employed in most programs tends to stress fundamental skill sets within the core dimensions of finance, accounting, marketing, supply chain or logistics. They are all tied together by managerial strategy and cross administrational systems. When economics is added to the instructional mix a measure of history is introduced into most curriculums. However most texts, offering an element of historic prospective, tend to go back only as far as the 18th century and the industrial revolution before leaping forward to the modern era beginning with World War I.

However, to study history is to study and learn about people. It is the language of emotion,[6] events, and response to them. It relates mankind's relationship development. Since the beginning of time people have built numerous systems to help them adjust to human behavior: "The observant person goes through life asking: Where did that come from?"[7] Only by appreciating and understanding the past can we construct the future.

Mark Twain, the American writer, humorist and social commentator, is credited with saying "History doesn't repeat itself but it does rhyme." The saying is not as strong as the dangerous warning issued by George Santayana, an American philosopher, essayist, poet, and novelist, although he always kept a valid Spanish passport writing "Those who do not remember the past are condemned to repeat it." While the events of the past and those that are about to unfold are not in perfect unison there is a lot to be learned from examining them. Today's business managers need to recognize that those that went before them, even in antiquity experienced analogous issues attached to the parallel commercial process they currently engage in. There exists a patterned reference between the past and the present. Therefore today's executives, especially those operating in a global context, walk in the pathways constructed by ancient trade merchants. They were the first cross territorial ambassadors venturing into culturally alien societies but finding a common ground upon which to build relationships. It was called exchange, a globally shared human system as old as time itself whereby all people satisfied their life material needs. To accomplish their uniform goals universal principles of business from a variety of civilizations were devised that are still used today. Hence the conducting of commercial transactions, abet to varying degrees, is found in every society on earth.

This book is intended as a consolidated historic look at how the exchange imperative evolved into ancient cross territorial and then intercontinental trade, the precursor of modern-day globalization. It does not cover all events as such a task is simply too daunting. Therefore the information presented is selective and the presentation style is not built around a precise chronological passing of notable events. Events are approached with references linking historical aspects of the commercial process with sections depicting their modern relevance.

The book begins with a discussion of the prime driver of human relationship the normative ingrained desire, both physical and physiological, to exchange the fruits of one's labors with others, precursor of trade, and its contribution to the development of civilization. It traces the emergence of the trading initiative via early commercial profiles of geographical regions and into the age of global exploration. It then offers an inspection of three areas of the business operational axis—products, infrastructure, and mediums of exchange—to show their contribution to the modern commercial system. Next the influence of the collateral elements of religion, government, and commercial laws is offered.

While many similar concepts lead to the emergence of common principles across the globe, they developed in the context of varying historical events. The text, therefore, presents them from a number of diverging yet intertwined circumstances and references academic disciplines from a different perspective. Because of this consideration, the text may repeat itself if only to stress their importance and influence on the globalization process.

The Second Edition of the book expands on the basic premise of the first one. To provide managers with a historical prospective of the process that came to be known as globalization and the appearance of universally applied business principles. Even in the short period since the original was published more and more research has emerged tracing the exchange process to thousands of years before transactional records were kept. Archeological expeditions have unearthed artifacts indicating that global trade was more wide spread and linked more geographical distant groups than previously thought hence Chapter 3 has been augmented to reflect such considerations. The ancient trading activities of countries including Russia, Brazil, Korea, the Caribbean and others are added while a deeper examination is offered for countries initially profiled. The first global products as presented in Chapter 5 are enlarged to include additional items that throughout history economically defined an era. All the other sections have been updated where appropriate to reflect new information.

All authors, whether they write non-fiction or fiction books, have a recurring theme they wish to portray. It is kind of an internal personal driver that motivates them to put something down on paper. In my three books on the subject of international business beginning with ethics, this one on globalization and the last devoted to cross-cultural management my underlying premise is to show the reader that the world is more the same then different. There are connecting rods of similarity despite the factors of separation in value determinants that underscore the diverse application of ethical behaviors and cultural identities. The system of exchange as explored in this book unites us all. It supports a natural ingrained desire to reach out and touch others, itself the catalyst of human development. It is an inherited human trait, a common denominator that is universally applied. Every society on earth has practiced exchange as far back as recorded history. The process is a sacrosanct social contract that has evolved into the modern term globalization. Even when the activities of ancient peoples were not chronicled the remnants they left behind show evidence of trade between indigenous groups and alien territorial societies. Global managers would be well advised to keep such consideration in mind as they venture out into the world. While they will encounter variations in socio-economic conditions and culturally induced value systems they need to keep in mind that there is a shared common thread, the exchange imperative. The merchants of old realized this phenomenon and the commercial traders of today merely follow in their footsteps. It is a shared legacy. Tracing the roots of globalization and business principles truly parallels the development of civilization on earth.

This book is dedicated to my children and grandchildren. May they learn from the past as I have, use such knowledge in their lives, while making sure they pass it on to those that follow in their footsteps.

Lawrence A. Beer,

July 15, 2015

Acknowledgments

I am deeply indebted to the editors of international collections at Business Expert Press (BEP) for their supportive encouragement along with their valued guidance and suggestions. Professor Gary Knight of Willamette University early on recognized my possible pro-business prejudice as a career senior executive before joining the academic ranks and gently prodded me to present a balanced portrayal of commercial history and its influence on civilization. His input in constructing the Second Edition of the book is deeply appreciated. Professor Michael Czinkota of Georgetown University kindly advised me to put a human face on historic examples to better illustrate the influence of business organizations and their sometime partnership with government and religious institutions, as well as their products and services on the social environment. Tamer Cavusgil of the University of Georgia, even before my association with BEP, encouraged me to put down on paper my ideas on international business subjects and I am forever thankful for his friendship and continuing supportive guidance.

Introduction

The commercial managerial process is twofold: First, it provides strategic planning for institutions; second, it creates relationships within and without organizations to assist in achieving such goals. To arrive at these conjoined considerations requires managerial decision makers to acknowledge that everything has a history, nothing evolves in a vacuum. This axiom is especially important in conducting business on a global scale. Given the extensive degree and scale across the world, commercial process requires an introduction into the roots of globalization.

The lessons of the past can be instrumental in planning for the future. Knowing how strategic business principles came to be established between people in alien territories is a vital complement to the educational skills and abilities the modern manager must possess. The concepts used today in all business disciplines developed from a myriad of ideas, techniques, and applications composed by ancient civilizations from around the world as they dealt with the creation of a workable exchange system. Because they emerged in a more simplistic world, one can cut through the minutia and concentrate on the core problems they addressed as the basic issues faced today are the same fundamental considerations before. Even modern analytical models confirm the strategic decision making of ancient merchants.

In the modern era of globalization, bringing diverse groups of business people together into a cohesive global unit has never been so important. This managerial function demands an inspection into their historic commercial relationships with each other. While the world is today more technically universal, it was constructed on a human historical foundation. Appreciating this base, on which all was built, allows one to reach new levels of accomplishment.

As a young export director I began to travel the world for a well-known U.S. company working with local distributors, licenses, joint venture partners and embedded subsidiary managers. Charged with generating increased foreign revenue I was eager to get into the nuts and bolts of every day commercial opportunities. Armed with a portfolio of product knowledge, economic statistical data and competitive intelligence I was often stymied by the seemingly reluctant get going attitude of my associates. After a period of getting to know each other many would finally say to me, *as you Americans are fond of saying let's get down to business*, and I felt better. This often heard statement always echoed in my mind. It tended to solidify the misnomer that the *doing of business* was either invented by Americans or that we were the true protagonists of the activity, especially in modern times. The term globalization was in fact first used in the U.S. to portray the global growth of American commercial interests. The word tends to be used to solidify the predisposed notion that world business revolves around US companies when in fact this basic proposition is false with one collateral exception.

The opening of the northern western hemisphere continent to the rest of the world was due to a commercial imperative while the country's founding and growth was fueled by mercantile interests as practiced by the rest of the world. The *doing of business* was not an American innovation. The process of exchange, trade between the peoples of the world was a practice as old as mankind. It was an inherited human activity that propelled the growth of civilization around the globe long before the United States of America was born. As I reflect back on the statement by my worldwide associates that initiated the personal satisfaction of a young businessman that he was finally getting down to doing his job I can't help but realize that it was said *tongue-in-cheek*. (A *figure of speech* used to imply that a statement is humorously or otherwise not seriously intended, and it should not be taken at face value. It may also signify contempt for another's attitudes.) My associates had a longer history of doing business then I could ever imagine. It was ironic that to placate me they acted as if my way, the American way, was the only business way. When I look back and realize my naiveté, and hence my presumptive attitude, I am embarrassed. This book should help set the record straight. It is therefore dedicated to all my foreign colleagues who never humiliated me by reminding me that I, as an American, was a neophyte in a world that had been practicing the art of business since the dawn of time. All I had learned about doing business was originated by their ancestors with the concept of globalization a practice instituted before the so-called discovery no less colonization of my own country.

My own international executive experience taught me that in constructing the globalization of my own company's interests a key element to keep in mind is that different territorial and hence cultural groups were always combining. It was a practice that has always existed. U.S. firms and their managerial cadre are the new guys on the block. We are interlopers in a system that others used centuries ago and we need to be respectful of what came before our entrance into the global commercial club. I am mindful of a phrase that should have been uttered by my business colleagues around the world during my executive tenure days: "You guys didn't invent business, the world has been practicing it since recorded history. We do know something about it. Sometimes we even forget this consideration but you shouldn't."

Commerce expanded around the globe, joining societies in the ancient world into unsophisticated by arguably economic alliances as well as economic conflicts. The remnants of these historic events are still in evidence today. How ancient merchants manipulated the emergence of the commercially globalized world provides lessons for the modern inheritors of this never ending process.

When taken together, a simple conclusion emerges. Globalization is the historic story of the spreading and widening of the natural human exchange process, a commercialization of the basic need for reciprocity between people. It is a factual testament to John Donne's quote, "No man is an island unto himself";[1] the desire to connect with others is at the core of humanity.

The more salient points of the book can be summarized as follows:

1. The process of exchange is a natural, inborn human trait that no other species on Earth emulates. The primeval basic desire of all men to exchange the fruits of their labors or specialized abilities for those of others is a natural social condition of the human psyche. It is part of our social ritual that continues in the present day as the prime impetus to bring people together. This was first evidenced in the process of collective action in adjunct with survival instincts when

men worked together to protect themselves from the harshness of their environments, and even each other. Such fundamental societal individual behavior resulted in the barter system, the division of labor, and expanded when the idea of creating a surplus beyond one's immediate needs was realized and the excess offered for trade. The same fundamental commercial onus exits today.

2. Every society trades and the cross territorial experience contributed to the development of civilization. Merchant traders were the first ambassadors of cultural change and their influence continues to this day. Their activities provided for, and still account toward, the impetus for physical infrastructure development and technological advances even in the modern world. As merchants crossed over through new territories, creating intercontinental paths on land and water in their pursuit of the exchange of goods, they provided the avenues for swapping not just foreign resources; their activities propelled the growth of a cross-cultural dialogue that in turn furthered intellectual progress. On the rails of commerce the world grew as ideas, inventions, and religion-based philosophical beliefs were also transferred, borrowed, and copied in the process.

3. Ancient merchants introduced the principles of business that are still in use today, from rules of commercial engagement to the creation of institutions that carry them out. Universal marketing methodology as well as international sales networks and logistics were historically practiced along with the creation of global strategic alliances using repetitive middlemen transactions; all of these tactics are still employed in the present.

4. All religions, as a social behavioral instrument, recognized the need to incorporate in their teachings the element of rightful exchange of things between people and their doctrines still in use today contain such directional guidance. At times the Church even participated in the trade affairs of nations and was an active partner in commercial exploration of the globe.

5. Governments, in varying degrees, have always supported the commercial process. From the creation of standardized measurements to the establishment of mediums of exchange to the enactment and

enforcement of laws, state regimes have, and continue to be, a collateral factor in the world of commerce. Their foreign policies not only reflected the importance of the financial resources it provided, but their combined influence on the world stage has altered history to the benefit and detriment of people. Such joint considerations still exist, and their interplay directs the lives of the world's population.

Wisdom comes from appreciating how and why things developed. It is as important as the end knowledge provided by them. Understanding commercial history is a valued mechanism that global executives should have in their managerial educational skill collection as it often provides the key to unlocking the complicated, multifaceted global world. Managers who study the past will be better prepared for the future. In too many textbooks and articles the word "globalization" is defined by the results it produces as opposed to the mechanism it really is. The term should be used to describe a universal instrument that grew out of a naturally occurring, ordered exchange process. Its maturity was fueled by commonly shared denominators of value across and between social groups around the world. Such meaning properly recognizes it as a socially induced system that is inherent in all cultures and acts as a binding agent across and between cultures. It is a method to help manage the affairs of human beings, a socially engineered apparatus to provide for the mutual but not always equal need attainment. It began in ancient times and continues in the present. Its scope and degree in the modern era of civilization have resulted in a more advanced borderless economic world as demonstrated by the interdependence of nations and exemplified by increasing traverse territorial commercial trade and investment around the world.

Herman Melville, the American novelist is quoted as saying:

"Our lives are connected by a thousand invisible threads, and along these sympathetic fibers, our actions run as causes and return to us as results."

Every day billions around the world perform the act of exchange. The beginnings of the process in antiquity are the roots of globalization and its continuance into the modern age are merely its branches. The world is interconnected. It is a system constructed for human kind to exist and hence a valued component in the growth and sustainment of civilization. Its origins and effect are therefore recorded as part of our globally combined history.

PART I

Exchange

The Natural Social Imperative

An author's conclusions or reflective summaries are normally reserved for insertion at the end of a book. But I have always been impressed by the writing style of Pulitzer Prize writing author Jared Diamond who offers the reader an insight into what he has learned in his introductory chapters.[1] Let me follow suit and share my own thoughts, as a number of amazing concepts came out of my research and editing of this book. Overall, the essential contention of this book is that globalization incites and magnifies humanity's strengths while exposing its weaknesses. It thereby acts as a prime provocateur for the growth and development of civilization. Built on a system of multiterritorial, economically inspired social mobility, it facilitated cross-cultural relationships, thereby engineering not only the exchange of products but also the sharing of ideas and talents through competition, which alter the human experience and continue even today. Modern business principles were born out of this process. More specifically, the text attempts to show that, first, the exchange process is a man-made event. It originated everywhere on earth and no specific society or specialized civilization can take credit for its invention, as it is a unique human trait shared by all. While other species on earth do in fact horde or store food resources for future use, share their kills in the field with other hunters, bring back to the pride or nest their finds for the benefit of others, and engage in a division of specific labors for collective survival, only man trades.

Second, without the exchange process, the world would have never progressed. Civilization would not have evolved. Hence, the two are intertwined with trade, the golden thread in the tapestry of civilized development. Exchange fuels men's actions toward each other and is fundamental to the establishment of relationships. It rewards specialized individual abilities within the context of a group. Trade allows for society to be organized and brings us together.

These two conceptual considerations led me to examine the research of anthropologists, archeologists, and the writings of historians in regard to the importance of the element of cross-cultural exchange in their inspections. While these scientific and scholastic fields report on finding ancient physical artifacts, products, or goods from other territories or societies, usually pottery shards and other detritus objects as evidence of foreign trade, they do not always discuss the influence of cross-regional and even intercontinental associations in respect to the evolution of mankind. Answers as to where, when, how, and by whom advancements in civilization were made require inserting the trade factor into the examination of life on earth. It is a key factor, an important link in the appreciation of how people developed in settlements around the world.

The numerous merchant transactions that accompanied cross-terri-torial trade produced a myriad of interpersonal relationships and with it the transfer, sharing, and borrowing of knowledge and ideas on living. Sometimes, the process of information exchange is hidden or its iden-tity masked; it does not have the physical properties to evidence itself in the surviving ancient artifacts, as rarely were philosophical thoughts or advanced technological skills written down and preserved. They were passed on orally or via demonstration. We tend to attribute learning to the group that first offered it to us, forgetting that perhaps they learned it from others. For example, the Arabs are credited with inventing Western-style mathematical numerals, advancements in chemistry, and star navigation. But what if they learned these from Indian traders crossing the Indian Ocean who had in turn first learned them from the Chinese with whom they also traded? Each time a new discovery from antiquity is made, evidence is found in the cross-contaminated nature of cultures due to the trading phenomenon. This makes it more and more difficult to determine where anything first began. In my research, I observed that every society at one time or another had contact with alien societies. Even a seemingly isolated island always attempted to reach out to another remote island. For others, the desire for foreign contact stretched out from their singular territorial land borders, while still others crossed continents and eventually circumnavigated the globe. Often we see only two sides of a trade link and forget that it is part of an elongated sequence that is connected to all the others, an interlocking elongated series. Each link dispenses and receives information not just from the links on either side that it is attached to but from all the other links in the chain. When you touch one you are really touching all the others, essentially forming stepping stones across the world pond, each influencing the other.

Third, most of the modern-day basic business concepts, commercial instruments, organizational models, legal regulations, and the administration of institutions involved in profit-making activities were developed and used in antiquity. They have not changed dramatically but have merely improved due to technological advances. While on the subject of technological improvements, it should further be noted that the motivation behind new inventions that have bettered mankind over history are either traceable to the commercial imperative or owe their spread across the globe to the business imperative. The need for, and the investment in, developing them arose out of entrepreneurs whose visionary understanding provided the value incentive.

Fourth, the exchange process begot cross-territorial trade and emerged into what we now call the globalization phenomenon. This mechanism contributed at all times in the history of mankind to the advancement of civilization even if such an apparatus came with pluses and minuses. It has opened new areas and brought people together, offering the bounties of the world to an ever-widening audience. But the process also depressed and robbed people of their human freedoms, did not result in shared equal economic returns, and destroyed natural environments. The process is not perfect as it emanates from man who himself is not perfect. All one can do is recognize its creative and destructive forces, hoping that future business managers strive to make it a positive component in the sociopolitical and economic system it initially helped to create.

Globalization is the final chapter in the spreading and widening of the natural human exchange process, a commercialization of the need for reciprocity between people. It has been going on since mankind first engaged in a bartering transaction wherein the fruits of one's knowledge, physical labors, or both in respect to their interaction with the varying environments around them, allowed them to swap or replace the products of their skills and abilities with those of another. In the process, a materially measured worth was assigned to each man's harvesting, alteration, or both of the earth's bounties and a relative value was established between the parties. While the principles first used in the exchange process have evolved over time into a more mature and sophisticated system, the conceptual imperative remains the same. People are connected and they need each other to survive and progress. Exchange is the bedrock on which civilization was constructed. It is the socially induced phenomenon that allows for growth and change. It has been with mankind since the beginning of time on earth and will remain with us in the coming millenniums as we search the stars.

CHAPTER 1

Globalization Takes Root

History is a maiden, and you may dress her however you wish.

—Chinese proverb

History can be approached from numerous vantage points. I have chosen to clothe her in the context of commercial imperative. This distinctive garment shows off history's greatest accomplishment—the development of civilization—with the threads woven from the remnants of the vital exchange arrangement. The process of exchange or bartering, where one thing is traded for another, is perhaps the oldest social system known to man. With the exception of man's survival relationship with nature and the establishment of the family unit through sexual attraction, it represents one of mankind's most basic instincts. It may have predated ancient organized religion and even forms of early social order, government, in many cultures. Called the *splendid exchange* by author William J. Bernstein,[1] the principle of trade is at the cornerstone of the development of civilization. Its influence on global societal development via the emergence of the commercial profit imperative as it evolved from the simple exchange process has been both progressive and destructive. Nonetheless, it is hard to argue that it has not been a prime component in the history of mankind, possessing both good and bad elements.

Jeffrey A. Tucker, a guest blogger for *The Christian Science Monitor*, relates a simple purchase in a grocery store with the familiar refrain "thank you, you're welcome" as evidence of the "essence of exchange and core magic of what happens … trillions of times every day all over the world."[2] He calls this process "a system of mutual benefaction, unrelenting and universal," increasing a sense of personal if not social welfare. Tucker cites the teachings of St. Thomas Aquinas, who described the action of exchange on its own as a "means of increasing the well-being of all people" and that the "mere fact of exchange-based human associations" enhances social wealth. Tucker also mentions the 16th-century Spanish theologian Bartolome de Albornoz, who wrote that "buying and selling is the nerve of human life that sustains the universe," as it unites the world, joining distant lands, people, and ways of life. In his conclusion, he observes that "the market is rarely given the credit it deserves for helping humanity improve its lot,"[3] as it enforces cooperative interaction, a socially worthwhile event.

While these comments contain religiously infused, socially based platitudes for the exchange process are noteworthy and appear in the doctrines of other spiritual organizations, the ethical actions of the commercial practice are not without critical opposition. Buddhist teachings encourage followers to engage in the *right livelihood*. In Christianity and Islam, their scriptures contain a condemnation of interest or usury while Jewish law talks of earning money in a kosher or right fashion. All religions advise people to be honest in their dealings with others as they recognize that life is a series of constant reciprocal arrangements with one's fellow men. Therefore, prodding them to do so in an equitable fashion promotes harmony and social order. A more detailed analysis of the interplay between religion and the exchange process is presented later in the text, but as religious institutions evolved to assist in providing social orderliness and direction, their acknowledgment of business as a subject of interest, worthy of comment, is indicative of its influence on daily activities and the development of civilization.

Historic ventures in the name of economic improvement, the quest for wealth, and dominance by one nation over another have resulted in wars triggered by trading disputes, no less the outright conquering of lands and the colonization of their people to merely appropriate them for slavery and plunder their resources. Name almost any war throughout history and one uncovers that the underlining, if not the key motivational intent, has a financial or wealth-creating incentive to it. Throughout human history, commercial exploration, as further presented later in the text, and at times partnering with governments and endorsed by religious organizations, has resulted in destructive consequences for those involved.

There is no purity of the marketplace as created by the exchange or trade process. Mankind is flawed and the mechanisms he creates to help manage his life contain the human errors. However, the commercial system, as during its beginning in antiquity and continuing today, has allowed mankind to sustain their lives and improve their lot. It is the lifeblood of civilization; its nurturing agent supplies the world with its necessities. Its by-products gave the world the impetus for developing language, record keeping of written documents, mathematical systems, and a multitude of inventions and advancements in science while providing the capital funding for the arts to name just a few of its beneficial properties. Perhaps, the best way to describe the effect of exchange initiative on civilization is to compare it with water in the formation and maintenance of life on earth. Like all forces of nature, it brings both the good and the bad. Rain nourishes crops and replenishes rivers and streams while refilling our precious water reservoirs. At the same time, its overflow washes away valuable land and can destroy the social settlements placed around it. The exchange process both gives and takes like any other natural occurrence. In its wake, it sets up social stratification—that is, those who are abundant and those who are needy (i.e., the well-to-do and the poor). It is not an equal system. The capitalistic system, a branch of the exchange process, is an economic model for creating wealth but not for its equal distribution. Hopefully, all observers and commentators can at least agree that the concept exists and that the business students of today, the managers of tomorrow, will live in the tide of modern globalization created by the trade waves of those who have gone before.

As this book was being composed the intent behind the text presentations was clear. The book argues that the ancient economic process of barter or the exchange of one thing, be it a product or service or even knowledge, for another thing, evolving into the trade initiative with the substitution of mediums of exchange (money) for tangible or intangible things and culminating in modern times as a fundamental factor in the globalization phenomenon, has throughout human history influenced and propelled the development and growth of civilization. The book is not intended to be a history of economic thought nor is it a review of the history of socioeconomic models. It is not an elongated position paper in praise of or in condemnation of free-trade principles or the capitalistic system. Whether one subscribes to these ideas or to an engineered or managed trading theory or the socialistic approach or a communist-type handling of the means of production or any other definition of economics one cares to apply, the operative underlying connecting word in all systems is trade and its actionable results. Ha-Joon Chang, in his book making a case against free-trade orthodoxy, although balances his perspective, reminds the reader of the simple fact that "the importance of international trade for economic development cannot be overemphasized."[4]

The investigation presented in the book is intended to acquaint business managers with the effects of their institutional actions—their commercial operations—on the human social condition known as civilization. The power and reach of the commercial imperative have always impacted mankind—sometimes as a positive force and sometimes as a negative force—but its significant relative positioning in the expansion and maturity of civilization should not be dismissed or relegated to a minor fragment in the inspection of history.

Business history is too often regarded by mainstream historians and business school economists as a rather narrow area of study, with little intellectual merit. A number of scholars even doubt if the subject really deserves classification as a separate and distinct subdivision of history. Others feel that it is best delegated to a subsection of the science of economics or placed in the context of other social sciences from anthropology to archeology and the subtexts of cultural determinations that are embedded within such areas of study. The *Journal of Management Studies* has announced that it wants to theme a special issue devoted to business history in order to encourage a discussion among scholars as to the advantages of a closer engagement between business history and management studies, a collaboration that the editors feel is worthy of further deliberation in the academic arena.

For business managers who must conduct their responsibilities and obligations in today's commercially expanding world, acquiring an education of their heritage as influential social interlopers in the establishment and continuing growth of the human condition is valid. Knowing how their ancestors impacted the world gives them a greater understanding of their role in the continuing process as they assume such mantles of responsibility.

Globalization Defined

We will never really know who invented the word *globalization*. The term could have rolled off anyone's lips as it constructs itself naturally in the

English language by combining the word "global" with the standard suffix *ization*. It would obviously be used to convey the process when things, events, or systems expand beyond a constrained territory or recognized border to *become global*, signifying a wider influential reach or something along these lines. According to the *Oxford English Dictionary*, the word globalization was first employed in 1930. It is defined as "the act of globalizing," from the noun "global" meaning "pertaining to or involving the whole world," "worldwide" or "universal." This publication's *Dictionary of Economics* denotes it a process by which the whole world becomes a single market. This means that goods and services, capital, and labor are traded on a worldwide basis, and information and the results of research flow readily between countries. It entered the *Merriam-Webster Dictionary* in 1951 as the development of an increasingly integrated global economy marked especially by three prime factors: free trade, free flow of capital, and the tapping of cheaper foreign labor markets. The term was widely used in academe by economists and social scientists by the 1960s. The *Cambridge Academic Content Dictionary* places the world in the social studies category defining it as the development of closer economic, cultural, and political relations among all the countries of the world. The common theme in all definitions is the recognition that the word denotes a continuing developmental process, a perpetual state of being as opposed to a single act or event. This would mean that globalization has been occurring, hence it has a history and will continue to evolve, and hence it has a future. If something has a past then it seems natural that one can look to trace the roots of its existence and how it advanced. This is one of the objectives of this book.

One should not confuse globalization with other terms that play off the global reference such as Marshall McLuhan in 1962 analyzing the impact of mass media on society creating the phrase "global village" to describe the result. Many in the business scholastic field attribute the actual printed use of the world to Theodore Levitt, a former professor at the Harvard Business School. His concept that business was becoming globalized, which Mr. Levitt defined as the changes in technology and social behaviors that allow multinational companies such as Coca-Cola, McDonald's, IBM, and Sony to sell the same products worldwide, first appeared in a 1983 *Harvard Business Review* article "The Globalization of Markets."[5] He said, "Gone are accustomed differences in national or regional preferences." Although critiqued by some for exaggerating the idea, the recognition that companies actually had to balance persistent national cultural patterns with the general trend toward embracing global brands, was a growing phenomenon. Levitt said that the "world is flat" more than 20 years before Tom Friedman used the term.[6]

Some economists refer to the word to denote a historical stage of accelerated expansion of market capitalism, like the one experienced in the 19th century with the Industrial Revolution. Many academics place the term within the perspective of modern times, describing it as a fundamental transformation in societies because of the recent technological revolution, which has led to a recombination of the economic and social forces on a new wider or extraterritorial dimension. Almost everyone everywhere wants all the same things they have heard about, seen, or experienced via the new technologies but a similar driving motivation occurred in the past. Because the word globalization began to appear in scholastic circles, no less in the literature, in the last 50 years, the misapprehension is that it describes a current wave or trend in a time framework. It is rarely used to portray an ancient time when, in fact, it was, and still is, a process that has been continuing since man began to exchange things with his fellow men over increasing distances.

The term *globalization* as a social engineering phenomenon that emerged in the early 1960s, with some attributing the new word to an article in an undistinguishable magazine.

It was used to describe a coming period in world commerce and economic conditioning when the timeless integration of global markets would have a more important social impact than ever before. The scale and degree of movement to an interlinked world, while always occurring, were beginning to move to such a critical mass that the phenomenon was worthy of developing a term to characterize the event. Once created, such designations became subject to further identification and examination. Researchers penned numerous articles while international business textbook writers incorporated the idea into their opening chapters to explain and comment on its effect. In short, whether one depicts the phenomenon as a positive or negative force, it gets a lot of attention as it is the dominant economic system in place today and for the near future.

The current antagonistically disapproving use of the term is well exemplified by the title of a recent book using a dictionary approach. Called *Globalization: n. The Irrational Fear That Someone in China Will Take Your Job*,[7] the authors debunk the often misguided contention that international trade, the mythical interloper in one's life, is a domestic, economic, and destructive force. They argue that there are limits to the effect of outside agents bestowing material advantages on some national markets to the disadvantage of others. The book dispels such misunderstandings by showing that countries control their own economic fate and that global trends can both aid and hinder economic progress. The authors, aided by U.S. statistical abstracts of occupational employment in various industries since 1983, demonstrate that overall job growth has been strong and that in areas where losses have occurred, they have been in low-level positions with the primary culprit being automation and not job movement overseas. In their introduction, the authors dramatically demonstrate that a search on Amazon.com would turn up more than 4,000 results that have the term globalization in them and that the New York Public Library contains close to 500 books devoted to the subject with more to come. Chapter 1, "It May Be News, But It Isn't New, A Brief History of Globalization," confirms that the phenomenon has a history but states "it is hard to say precisely when it began."[8] The Roman Empire is offered as a starting point but because it did not cover the entire world, such a time frame is dismissed. The British Empire after 1815 is considered but dismissed, as international trade was insignificant during its origination as the far-flung global colonies were created to basically service Britain and not other nations. The authors settle on the late 19th century when barriers to international trade were reduced and new technology was shrinking the world with increased efficiencies in communication and transport coupled with increased cross-country immigration.[9] Such considerations resulted in a key determinant, the diminished economic power of historic national rivalries according to the authors who themselves cite Norman Angell's timeless book *The Great Illusion* as the theoretical engineer of the concept.[10] Hence globalization, if defined as a decline of national economic influence and the emergence of an independent global force built on a worldwide interconnected system, but allowing for bumps in the coordinated structure due to world wars and the great 1920 depression, would be considered a modern 19th-century phenomenon. According to Bruce Greenwald and Judd Kahn, it really began its ascent in the 1950s.

What these learned authors fail to account for in their brief history of globalization primarily is that technological advances have always been part of mankind's desire to reach and touch others with continuing progress, always being made to tie the world closer together (see Chapter 6). That the economic power and prestige of nation-states in antiquity to effect trade outside their borders were always augmented by independent merchant traders who partnered with sovereign countries to pursue international commercial ventures. Today these merchants, in the guise of multinational corporations (MNCs), are challenging the global strength of the nations they once serviced. Dan Rodrik opens *The Global Paradox* with a chapter titled "Globalization in History's Mirror" with a profile of the beaver trade in the Native American territories of 1671.[11] He follows with references to the Hudson's Bay Company and East India Company, the mercantilist chartered trading companies of that era, noting that they operated with "statelike enforcement powers … imposing their own rules over foreign populations in distant lands."[12] Rodrik seems to indicate that such quasi-government-public enterprises, the forerunners of today's modern MNCs, were the provocative agents for the beginning of globalization. While learned authors on the subject of globalization chose varying periods in history to mark its emergence, there is no doubt that its roots were planted in ancient times. What we see today are its mature trunk and branches—the continuance of its development. It is not a modern-day birth no matter which specific group of events and parties is used to illustrate its time line.

The term is used most commonly to define a more globally integrated system of economic interdependence among nations as reflected in increasing cross-border flows of (a) goods and services, (b) capital, and (c) know-how as fueled by advancements in technology shrinking the world via more connected communication and transport mechanisms. Using a historic time portal, globalization can be profiled as a process of intensification of cross-border social interactions due to declining costs of connecting distant locations through advancements in technology affecting transport and communication. It is further actuated by the increased transfer of capital, goods, and people between and through sovereign territories. This process has culminated in the modern era with the transnational interdependence of economic and social actors, an increase in both opportunities and risks, and intensified competition.

Today globalization is accelerated by a myriad of factors. Government-driven and financially based decisions, as exemplified by reductions in barriers for trade and more liberal privatization and deregulation policies, have allowed for increased flows of foreign direct investment (FDI), capital, and related services. Political upheaval—such as the removal of the iron curtain and the independence of former Soviet Union states, partial transformation of communist China into a more open economy, and the growth of emerging nations—has contributed to the faster pace of modern globalization. Rapid technological advancements in respect to information processing and enlarged communication highways via the Internet and wireless devices using satellite transmissions, coupled with more efficient transportation mechanisms, have allowed for faster and more efficient connections between and among dispersed global supply chains. Sociopolitical developments have always accompanied international trade, allowing for increased migrations, creation of new identities, and the spread of human knowledge between and across social groups. The quickness of these developments has propelled the modern phenomenon we call globalization, but its beginnings are firmly planted in and have evolved from the ancient exchange imperative, which contained elements of all these considerations.

Globalization also possesses a social opportunity ingredient. It slowly eats away at isolation, integrating people, and thereby changing people's ideas and relationships, reshaping the world just as it has been doing for thousands of centuries. It is a reengineering of the global economic system, with repercussions that would influence the sociopolitical climate around the world, and a time when the economic good fortune or, in reverse, the economic ills of any one sovereign would impact others—the coming of a more interlinked borderless world.

The term *globalization* ushered in a whole new genre of book offerings, most notably the popular best-selling book series by Thomas L. Freidman, as noted earlier, beginning with *The Lexus and the Olive Tree* published in 1999 to *The World Is Flat* in 2005 and the most recent update *Hot, Flat, and Crowded* in 2008. The newly coined word became a touchstone for its overriding notion that the world was expanding both economically and socially with more players in the game and more spectators being affected by a new structure. At the same time, the world was shrinking as technological advancements in communication and transportation made it easier to reach out to one another. Thomas Friedman summed up such a novel world force by concluding that globalization, as he defines it, has replaced the Cold War as the prime international socioeconomic political system and is neither a trend nor a fad.[13]

One of the problems with the term *globalization* is that by first being coined in the latter part of the 20th century it has taken on a meaning associated with more recent events that seem to justify its emergence. Globalization is an action word to describe a writer's interpretation of a mounting trend that was beginning to affect the world like never before and perhaps reengineer the global economic system with repercussions that would influence the sociopolitical climate around the world, as Friedman's conclusion suggests. In essence, the word was to exemplify the growing interdependence among nations, a time when the economic good fortune or in reverse the economic ills of any one sovereign nation would impact other nations to a degree never before experienced. As noted earlier, the actual start date of the phenomenon is subject to numerous interpretations. It is often portrayed as a collection of modern historic events within the opening chapters of most textbooks, critical and supportive essays, and journal articles on the subject of international business treating the subject as a modern and perhaps 20th-century proceeding. They all too often describe the phenomenon as duly emerging from the decline in governmental barriers to the free flow of goods, services, and capital as driven by industrialized nations after World War II and fueled by dramatic advances in technology, most notably communication, information processing, and transportation.[14] These two macro-events and changes in the political economies of a number of nations in the latter part of the 19th century certainly contributed to the strong emergence of modern globalization, resulting in a linked and more integrated world. But the process did not begin in recent history; it was only altered with more fuel-efficient components added at that period. Some textbooks in their opening chapters provide a triparagraph historical retrospective[15] while others use a page inset[16] to give the reader a sense of the developmental process extending back to the ancient world. But such limited inspection is deserving of an increased introspective.

The start date for globalization is subject to numerous conclusions. Mike W. Peng offers a good insight into this academic discourse, describing three approaches. He first considers the arguments of perhaps agenda-driven antiglobalization parties who view it as a new phenomenon that originated in the late 20th century with the dual result of technology coupled with "Western hypocrisy designed for MNEs [multinational enterprises] to exploit and dominate the world."[17] His second approach contains a historical commercial signature as he references the existence of the multinational enterprises (MNEs) starting 2,000 or 8,000 years ago back to the Assyrian, Phoenician, and Roman Empires.[18] The third proposed initiative cites Joseph Stiglitz's pendulum degree definition, stating that globalization is a "closer integration of the countries and peoples of the world that has brought about by the enormous reduction of the costs of transportation and communications, the breaking down of artificial barriers to the free flow of goods, services, capital, knowledge and (to a lesser extent) people across borders."[19] All three of Peng's proposals on the emergence of globalization have an economic pedagogy to them that is constructed on the commercial imperative, which of itself is tied to the simple process called trade, a fundamental practice built on exchange—the handmaiden to mankind's overall civilized development. Friedman's reference, as noted earlier, that it has replaced the Cold War marks the event in a modern time period, the late 1960s. But in his second book on the subject, Friedman slightly alters this view, suggesting that there are three great eras of globalization, a theory accepted by many scholars. The first was in 1492 with the voyage of Christopher Columbus, the second was from 1800 to 2000 (including the Industrial Revolution), further changing the world but interrupted by the Great Depression and World Wars I and II, and the third being the modern current era as individuals from every corner of the world are being empowered,[20] leading to a flattening of the world. Alan Beattie offers a growth-layered definition with the base level, the first great era of globalization, between 1880 and 1914, or also the age of what some historians called High Imperialism—the apotheosis of the dominance of European colonial powers over the rest of the world[21] followed by the Industrial Revolution and the modern era.

Globalization as defined by economic statisticians, and typically illustrated in a series of factual charts in most textbook opening chapters, uses a series of quantitative trends to portray the rapid growth of cross-border trade (volume and production) as well as foreign financial investment (FDI flows) along with changes in percentages of world output and exports as supportive evidence that a more integrated world economy has developed. A time frame beginning around 1950 and running to the present is the normal periodic reference.

While statistical data to define globalization do offer valid examples of its financial affect, the term is more complex than objective numbers portray. The word needs to contain a subjective human face to really define what is happening. Anand Giridharadas offers such an insight by describing the polar opposites of the phenomenon's impact on the Indian society.[22] He notes the reaction of some in this caste-conscious nation to view the process as reducing people to their specifically assigned global economic task, stripping them of their humanity just as their traditional socially ordered system did to their individual dignity. On the other hand, he uses the same measurement criteria—historic caste classification—to show that it has allowed Indians to imagine a revolutionary realization that perhaps their lives may not be controlled by fates (kismet) and prescribed roles (karma). Globalization has brought opportunistic ambition and with it self-invention that allows servants to become masters of their own destiny. He uses the example of rural townsfolk demanding reliable electricity so that they can use the Internet and satellite television, today fundamental necessities in their lives, where before they would humbly accept the historic interruptions as part of their place in society and as not to be challenged. These opposing viewpoints of the effect of globalization on the human condition may be appropriate to describe the dual reactions of people in many of the emerging nations around the world.

Friedman's book collection uses advances in technology around the mid-1960s (presumably the Internet as the prime motivator) as factors that propelled globalization. He sees an economic flattening of the world where more and more participants will be entering the global commercial arena because they have more equal access to the same information. Some theorists even dispute the whole idea of globalization. In an article by Alan Rugman and Chang H. Oh,[23] the authors deconstruct Friedman's globalization theory and base their definition of true globalization on the global reach of MNEs. They use *empirical realities* to show that MNEs do not operate globally but in fact regionally; hence, true globalization, a process that encompasses the whole world per their testing criteria, does not exist.

I find myself disagreeing with the offered definition proofs to portray globalization and propose that the phenomenon, if tempered by the term *known world*, actually occurred throughout the history of man while quantitatively and qualitatively growing in size and influence. The concept is well characterized by many historians like Michael Rostovtzeff, observing that the differences between the ancient economy and the modern economy are differences of scale, not of kind, a restatement of the Stiglitz pendulum degree definition.[24] As defined by William J. Bernstein in *A Splendid Exchange: How Trade Shaped the World,* "Globalization, it turns out, was not one event or even a sequence of events; it is a process that has been slowly evolving for a very, very long time."[25] Globalization is not a definable destination with a precise beginning and end result but rather a term that portrays the journey. It is not a singular condition in time but a process that happens in steps. Such progression continues to this day and will continue to play out. Like water it will appear in many forms, from liquid to gas to a frozen state and perhaps back again, but it will always contain its base element—that is, the exchange imperative, the golden thread that binds mankind together with each other and the environment. The process of globalization is likened to a tree with the phenomenon rooted in ancient trading activities via the bartering system, the emerging stem, developing into the trunk during the age of discovery as the world is explored, and finally growing branches as it continues to spread out and touch all areas of the globe in the modern era.

Exchange Nourishes Civilization

The study of business at the university level does not contain a prestige equal to the other scholastic degrees. It is often relegated to a secondary or tertiary status, as the disciplines involved do not always qualify as life sciences nor liberal arts that contribute to the development of life on earth and the human condition. While the subject of economies is often considered closer to a scientific inquiry and hence worthy of scholastic inquiry, the disciplines of commercial management and the history of its growth across recorded time do not receive the academic prominence they should. The reason for this prejudicial view is that business, while recognized for providing people a system to receive the necessities of life, is not seen as a contributor, no less a supporter, of civilization. Nothing can be further from the truth.

The study of trade (i.e., the commercial imperative) is deeply intertwined with the development of civilization. The simple fact is that the exchange process, the grandfather of today's modern globalization, was a prime ingredient for the growth of the world's society while being responsible for many of the collateral improvements of the human condition and at other times a destructive force. Trade allowed indigenous peoples to exchange products and services among themselves to foster their lives and was the impetus to venture outside their domestic territories in search of new resources. The desire to explore new lands and engage new societies was and still is inherent in the exchange imperative. It is a process that is fundamental to the survival of mankind as well as the underlying driver to integrate with others and learn from them. When trade broke down, it was also one of the prime drivers for making war on those who would not share in an equitable arrangement the bounties of their land with others. It should be noted that other conditions do result in armed conflicts as the pure greed of man and his desire to dominate others are strong provocateurs. Trade, as sections in the book illustrate, was the onus for the development of linguistics and the emergence of common languages, as well as the recording of events and activities. Deeply ingrained in the study of archeology is the recovery and classification of the remnants of the past having a commercial base. Trade influences the sciences of anthropology and sociology as they are part of the study of the human condition. The emergence of mathematics (weights, measures, and calculations) and astrology for directional application has a direct correlation with the exchange desire and the trading process. It not only motivated the quest for thousands of inventions and processes in a variety of fields but also allowed for such advances to be shared with others.

Commercial operations and their applied decisions manipulated politics and governments, thereby becoming a prelude to wars that changed history. It was intertwined with the spread of religion around the world and is reflected in the teachings of spiritual texts that recognized that part of securing social order required addressing how exchanges between people should be regulated. Many of mankind's early laws to control ancient societies had at their core principles of trade and the recognition of property rights. The commercial imperative was instrumental in the organization of the exploration of the world's oceans and land masses. It is responsible for cross-cultural exchanges and for the modern phenomenon called globalization. While such considerations paint a positive picture of the exchange process, they also harbored negative and destructive events. As noted earlier, it was a motivator for war, enslavement, and geographical redistribution of people for commercial gain. It has partnered with tyrants and repressive governments to meet its materialistic goals to the detriment of numerous societies across the globe. It has been accused of unethical behavior, creating a world that promotes the rich and keeps the poor entrenched in economic hardship. The process has been blamed for repressing the freedom of workers (i.e., to assemble and redress the wrongs) and for creating labor conditions that are unsafe and harmful. Its activities are condemned for the destruction of the natural environment that affects the entire global population. No wonder business has been labeled as an immoral pursuit without any redeeming social value that destroys mankind's altruistic responsibilities and duties to fellow men, as the profit motive trumps all other considerations. No wonder such activity is portrayed as evil and devoid of charity and caring for others.

Whether in the final analysis the commercial imperative is characterized as good or bad, its impact on the world cannot be underestimated. Hence, an inquiry and therefore understanding of its role in the development of civilization is right for inspection and reflection. Students learning the various disciplines of commerce in order to become better future managers need to know that their ancestral brethren, the traders and merchants of ancient times, helped transform the world. As much as the reign of any regional royalty, the gifts bestowed on society by masterful inventors and scientists; the inspirational writing of great philosophers; the works of accomplished composers, painters, and sculptors; and the creativity of skillful architects and endowed craftsmen (those involved in the commercial process) also contributed to altering societies around the world and in many instances fostered and supported their efforts. Merchants were instrumental in spreading the words of the great religious prophets beyond the abilities of their own clergy. They walked beside the great conquerors from Alexander the Great to Genghis Khan, helping to sustain their empires as well as those royalties around the world. Businessmen have supported democratic as well as totalitarian governments in the sustainability of economies under their respective political systems.

Trade: The Incubator for the Growth and Development of Civilization

Civilization is defined as an advanced state of human society in which a higher level of culture science, industry, and government has been reached. According to Ian Morris, it is a process of

> social development—basically, a group's ability to master its physical and intellectual environment to get things done. Putting it more formally, social development is the bundle of technological, subsistence, organizational and cultural accomplishments through which people feed, clothe, house and reproduce themselves.[26]

When used in a broader sense, with trade advancing the state of human society by providing a breeding ground for the developmental process, ancient commercial activities fueled the pursuit of proactive positive change, acting as a forcible element for social progress, the attainment of basic necessities. Civilization therefore is linked to an economic derivative. It began when a certain surplus of resources was built up and people began trading the excess after their immediate needs were satisfied, a reference to mankind's change from daily foraging and hunting to harboring his collected. Seed cultivation in agriculture was the first step. Instead of gathering naturally available resources, organized planting of crops developed. This led to the harboring of seeds to plant for the future as opposed to planting everything and eating everything that grew. Seed modification followed as some yielded better results than others, thereby producing a potential excess over consumable need. From such a consideration, the idea of using the surplus developed, which in turn could be exchanged. The domestication of wildlife from fowl (chicken) to sheep, goats, cows, pigs, and horses begot herding, and recultivation of the stock, as opposed to stalking and killing, followed.

Such activities acted as a prelude to the exchange process and the eventual bartering of what was not immediately consumed, which was followed by the intermediary commercialization process that gave rise to the profit incentive. The first recorded state-sponsored public storage of surplus grains organized by governmental decree is to be found in ancient Egypt. The idea was also cultivated in the Jordan Valley around 9300 BCE as evidenced by archeological findings of clay storage chambers (about 10 ft. wide and 10 ft. tall), which were presumably constructed by regional administrators in conjunction with private individuals.[27] Such granaries, underground silos, were initially constructed with the goal of surviving periods of bad harvest for the collective good, itself a symbol of civilized social behavior. However, such a practice during good harvests gave rise to the trading imperative: the selling of the surfeit, which was not required to sustain the local population. The concept of surplus—that is, the accumulation of things in excess of current and projected needs as an ancient stimulus for the commercial trading function—is a principle still driving the mercantile practice today. Many companies got their start in the export process from selling redundant domestic inventory to new foreign markets. Even surplus-seasonal goods that do not move in periodic climate influenced regions and are rerouted abroad to other hemispheres, offering multinational firms a more year-round global sales experience. The new bathing suits that do not sell in the summer in the northern hemisphere find a revolving market in the upcoming southern hemisphere as their temperatures warm up. If cross-cultural social integration or internationalization—the crossing of national boundaries—has contributed to the growth of civilization on earth, then certainly the provocateurs of such human endeavors were the merchants of old. Their commercial pursuits paved the way for mankind to venture beyond their home territories, resulting in linkages between different societies, with the relative contributions of each furthering the development of the others. If civilization is the culmination of the human learning curve, such a process was advanced on the commercial pathways constructed on the ancient trading imperative. As these activities occurred long ago, the term *globalization* in its most generic content is not a current phenomenon but merely the branches of the roots planned earlier in time. The globalization directive has been around for centuries and has taken numerous forms, expressed in terms of worldwide systems including political, economic, cultural, and technological to name just a few. But when added together, the result is civilization. Even when characterized from a fiscal accounting monetary perspective, the concept pays tribute to an ancient heritage. Globalization is simply the economic philosophy in vogue now but it is not a new concept. It is merely a part of the natural evolution begun when man exchanged the fruits of his labors with his fellow men, maturing into the cross-territorial intercontinental trading process, which affects most of the world today. In the end, modern globalization is just a phrase to describe a period of advanced civilization—a part of mankind's cycle on earth when cross-border trade was reaching new heights and as such a piece of human history on earth.

People without Trade

Jared Diamond, in his book *Collapse: How Societies Choose to Fail or Succeed*,[28] uses the failure to trade as one of the cornerstones in the eventual disintegration and disappearance of historic societies, the fall of their civilization. Such a conclusion, although well sustained by this Pulitzer Prize–winning author, requires one to hypothesize on events in the past and does not allow for a purer scientific investigation, a living example. However, the proof supporting the theoretical hypothesis that a society becomes more civilized and does not die but perhaps lies dormant can be exemplified by examining an existing group whose growth has been stymied by its desire not to develop an exchange process either among themselves or with foreign entities.

Daniel Everett, a linguistic anthropologist, studied and wrote about an Amazonian tribe called the Piraha (pronounced *piria*) in his book *Don't Sleep, There Are Snakes*.[29] Their semiclosed society, with the exception of the occasional contact with foreign parties along their territorial river bank, has not altered their tribal cultural existence, nor has it made any progress in their daily lives. They have little knowledge or no inclination to commercialize their lives, no less change them. An investigation into their culture reveals that they do not possess any of the universally recognized values consistently found in other groups around the world that would form the basis of an exchange-related society. They live and act in the present with no concept of the past or future. Their daily actions are organized to support a moment in time. When they are hungry, they forage and gather or hunt and fish, consuming immediately all that is taken from the environment around them. If such activities are not performed, they simply do not eat. As such they do not horde, stockpile, or keep supplies. Everything that is made is used up at that moment. Their skills and abilities are for their immediate self-consumption only. If baskets are needed for the collection of edible substances, they make them as needed and dispose of them thereafter. Their homes are seasonably moved and the old ones discarded. They wear the same clothing from day to day and possess no ceremonial or special occasion garments. Accumulation of material wealth is not represented in their culture. The only remnants that are kept from day to day are basic tools, metal cooking pots, a knife-like sharpened instrument, and bows and arrows to allow for a daily subsistence living. They view things, the personal possessions of others, as not related to them in any significant way. Commitments for the future do not exist—couples unite; and by simply choosing to live with one another, or not is how their marriages are formed and dissolved. No promises of any kind are offered or given and no remedial form of obligation or its modern concept of a contract is in their nature. There are no written laws and even when a tribal member commits a bad thing against another it is normally accepted and forgotten. If a really bad thing is done that could hurt the entire tribe, the offending member is ostracized from the group—the supreme punishment. There is no common supernatural entity, nature or entity that has influence over their lives, although each tribal member does relate to an inner spirit they mystically see in their minds, which exercises some influence over internalized actions but not in their relations with others. No chief or leader emerges in the communal group and no shamans or so-called Western witch doctors live in the community except for the theatrically gifted native who entertains the community from time to time, although the natives refer to him in the spiritual characters he mimics in the spirit show, as opposed to his real name.

The Piraha do not record anything, as this could not be used as a reliable reference or the process would involve the later acceptance of a historic event or past transaction they actually had not experienced. Remember, they live only in the present. Stories cannot be handed down once the original party to an event dies. So, technically, they as a people have no history, everything is in real time. Symbols may be used to designate a concept or idea at that moment but not a remembrance of a past deed or thought. Knowledge for the Piraha requires eyewitness testimony. Transmission of thoughts and ideas is not subject to peer review. The test of knowledge is not that it is universally accepted as truth by everyone but that it has value for singular individuals in their daily lives. They have no counting system, no exacting words for all or part of a thing, as they live in a numberless environment. As no common measurement system exists, they do not bother to record a thing's worth or value. In the quasi-exchange transactions they enter into with foreign traders on a periodic basis for the same goods, the transaction always results in differing values, to the disadvantage of the Indian tribe.

They simply do not think in terms of value maintenance. They have no regard for, nor concept of, personal property. They do not exchange items among themselves: There is no barter value system. Instead, they just ask each other to share when something is immediately needed. Repayment is only offered if the other party requests their aid, but this is not viewed as a thing in return but part of their social responsibility. Therefore, there is no medium of exchange and no intermediary article of value has emerged in the tribe. When dealing with foreigners, they have adopted the practice of barter but without the collateral process of bargaining or value haggling, thus failing to assimilate the concept of a product's value that others have into their lives. They do not borrow or incorporate this culturally induced concept into their daily exchanges with each other. The repetitive contact with foreign people and their material goods is always considered as a new, singular event. Hence, anything learned does not make its way in the lives of the Piraha. They never truly assimilate themselves, resulting in their failure to alter or change their ways. New things introduced to them are used and discarded; and if it never shows up again, there is no loss of value or benefit. It is almost like their tribe has Alzheimer's disease permeating their people. Any contact, therefore, with the modern world has little or no effect on them. The Piraha therefore do not venture out of their territory in search of resources or even utilize the special skill sets of those not in the tribe. They do even acquire new abilities from outsiders but only rely on homegrown historic skill sets. The author relates a firsthand event that demonstrates this point. The natives see a canoe they call "Brazilian" and are intrigued by its design and worthiness, but do nothing. The author who lives with them arranges for one to be built in their presence, trusting that they will learn from the experience. They participate in erecting this new water conveyance, watching and helping. But when it is finished and given to them as a gift, they simply use it; they do not attempt to build another and offer no value in return. It is just accepted as a new thing in their lives, which, when it loses its utility, will eventually be discarded.

There is no discernable division of labor in the tribe and all perform the same activities, although the women forage in the forest and the men hunt and fish. This is the extent of the recognition of differing skill sets—it is more of a social gender order. While some members are admired for their superior abilities in such activities, as in "he is a good fisherman," jobs are not separated, which would allow people to do what they do best and hence trade with others for what they do best, thus developing a mutual reward system. They do not exhibit the principle of competitive advantage, a key element in the exchange imperative. The Piraha have not emerged from their primitive existence. Their cloistered existence has not changed and their civilization has not developed. While their belief or value system is certainly a prime motivator to this phenomenon, their negative desire to develop an exchange-based society, the precursor of the trading imperative, whether within their own culture or in a continuing rule-based system with others outside their community, is a most interesting observation. It is evident that to sustain the hypothesis of commercial dealings, the eventual economic system emerging from the process of reaching out and touching others in a simplistic exchange procedure is a major contributor to the growth and development of civilization. Without the cultural imperative to trade, nothing moves forward and human progress is stymied.

CHAPTER 2

Tracing the Roots of Globalization

From the dawn of civilization, man has always reached out and touched others to sustain their needs and to improve their lives. International trade, both in ancient times as well as in the modern era, allows one to take resources from places of abundance to insufficient areas. The mutual benefit derived from the exchange process has enabled societies to both survive and prosper. Cross-territorial movement and the engagement of those apart from us have resulted in both the destruction and building of civilization, both intertwined like the yin and yang of human interaction as well as all things. It is because of the trading imperative canvas that the historic development of the world has taken place with the semifinished picture today titled globalization. This social harmony phenomenon as depicted in the cartoon (Figure 2.1) is the prelude to modern globalization. A universal societal system called economics is the prime propelling agent of change and the prime ingredient in the development, sustainment, and growth of civilization.

Economics

The Greek Land-Management View

Economics, like many of our modern-day words, is based on a combination of two Greek activities prevalent in their lives. The development of the term evolved over time to describe a field of study, the science of production, distribution, and consumption of goods and services leading to the material welfare of society. The *eco* in economics is taken from the Greek word *oikos*, which refers to one's environmental habitat, household, or family estate—the physical space that provides subsistence.

Figure 2.1 *What is economics?*

Source: Reprinted with permission of John L. Hart FLP. © 2011.

This beginning root is paired with the Greek word for managing, caring, or stewardship roles over such property called *nomos*. When used collectively, they describe methods or a series of valuable lessons, a colloquial *rule of thumb* for the wise maintenance of one's physical surroundings to enable one to live. The two root words appeared in unison to form the title of a thesis by the Greek author Xenophon called Oikonomia, which is perhaps best translated as "The Household Manager," a guide to managing one's estate. It was an early reference to the *Farmers' Almanac*, itself an annual periodical first used on the plains of the Midwest to aid farmers in their seasonal and daily chores as well as offer homespun advice on their lives. The word usage was further expanded when it was referenced by the great philosopher Aristotle to describe the inspection of the public management of resources, a process or science he called *oikonomika*. In the Greek way of organizing their lives, they tended to extract from small-scale, domestic administrations and extrapolate the hierarchy of magnitude from the ordinary household organization to learn how to control larger and more extensive factors of production for the common good or welfare of the state.[1] It is not surprising, therefore, that the term *economics* continues to describe the extended commercial ventures of men as they organized their activities to encompass wider horizons, from managing their estates to the exchange of goods across territories. It was inevitable that localized household-based activities would emerge into larger enterprises as the marshalling of trained labor began to specialize and new skills were acquired, the technology imperative. Add to this transition the discovery and use of expanded extracted raw materials and the addition of more capital assets, all spread across domestic regions and then across borders; and the growth of economics was fueled and globalization began.

The Greek influence on commercial activities is evidenced not only by their trading expeditions and administrative or organizational structures to carry out such ventures but also by their contribution to modern terminology and business strategy. As noted earlier, the word *economics* is based on Greek roots with the concept of commercial management originating in prescriptions for the maintenance of the household or family estate. Writing in *Economics*, Aristotle sets out basic principles in regard to business investments and their manageable sustained return. Although the language of the day is organized around property (real estate as the asset) and the manager is portrayed as the head of a household, any chief executive officer (CEO) running a company today would be wise to follow the tenets expressed as quality objectives or strategy:

> There are four attributes which the head of a household must have to deal with his property. First, the ability to acquire. Second, the ability to preserve what is acquired: if he doesn't have that, there is no not benefit in acquiring. It's as good as balling bilge-water with a colander, or the proverbial wine-jar that sports a hole. Third, he must know how to improve his property. Fourth, how to make use of it. After all, those latter two attributes are why we want the ability to acquire and preserve.[2]

While early Greek philosophers were mindful of the need to create economic-based patterns in their lives, their sentiments also questioned the true values in life. Many writings were constructed around themes advising one to be mindful of a life filled only with measurable material values; a basic principle tenant found in almost every religious doctrine. Such an idea is well summarized by the playwright Euripides (480-406 BC) BCE): "The company of just and righteous men is better than wealth and a rich estate."[3] Long before the religion-based pronouncement linking hard work with God's work on earth, as exemplified in the

Protestant work ethic (see Chapter 8), the concept was rooted in Greek philosophy.

As translated and recounted by researchers, Hesiod (circa 700 BCE), a Greek poet, admonishes his brother to embrace work and eschew idleness to please the gods and fellow man. He writes,

> Gods and men are angry with the man who lives idly,
> Let it be dear to you to set in order tasks that will be well arranged,
> So that your barns be loaded with seasonal production.
> Out of labors men become rich in sheep and wealth,
> and engaged in labors they are much dearer to the immortal gods.
> Work is no cause for blame, but idleness is blameworthy.
> And if you work, soon an idle person will envy you as you grow
> Rich, for virtue and glory wait on wealth.[4]

A shortened version aimed at extolling men to associate growth and improvement of their society with commercial effort was written by Epictetus (55–135 BCE) in *Discourses*. A stoic philosopher with roots in slavery, he said "Never look for your work in one place and your progress in another."[5] Even in the ancient world, the art of commerce not only was delivered by a series of admonishments aimed at the overseer or manager of operations but also was treated as a science that could be codified into economic ideology. Take, for example, the basic rule of supply and demand, the quintessential element in the pricing of goods, especially commodities and the future market. Note the principle as applied to the grain industry and customers in ancient Greece (from Xenophon's *The Household Manager*):

> You are saying ... that our father was a lover of agriculture ... no less than merchants are grain lovers. Because of an intense love for grain, wherever they hear there is the most grain merchants will sail after it ... then acquiring as much as they are able, they transport it through the sea ... they do not offload it at random wherever they turn out to be, but wherever they hear that grain has the highest price and people are valuing it the highest, conveying it to these people they put it on market.[6]

Plato, in *The Republic*, summarized such an exemplified lesson rather succinctly with his observation that an excessive increase of anything causes a reaction in the opposite direction.[7]

So important was the commercial imperative to society and the sustained development of the Greek civilization that the philosophers, poets, theatrical writers, and commentators of those days devoted many of their morally induced writings to the process of exchange—commerce. Using the activities of merchants as base examples, codes of acceptable behavior were introduced, and much later such axioms of living made their way into religious teachings as well as secular laws.

When one acknowledges the Greeks as suppliers of the root words for the term *economics* and the initial development of its principles, it must be remembered that it was devised from the management of the family estate. Many of the intellectual thinkers of those their days looked at the political economy through this narrowly extended lens of the prime wealth-producing entity of the day, the self-sustaining farm as an economic model for the whole society. But such a platform of inspection acted as an insulting mechanism from the concept of spontaneous market order, resulting in a philosophical disconnect from commercial activities in the mercantile real world and the assent of the collateral craft business taking place around them. It earned the commercial process the scorn of the intellectual elite. The result was that philosophers strongly believed in systematic administrative coercion, the ability of the state to impose a social utopia by the exertion of their power. That anything related to the general society could only be achieved through the artificial and deliberate actions of its organizer, the government.

The most eminent and distinguished philosophers of ancient Greece as represented by the SPA gang (Socrates, Plato, and Aristotle), as listed by their appearance in history and linked influential thinking, did not grasp the growth of the free-market process around them nor the relationships of men occasioned by such self-regulating activities. They underestimated the importance of a spontaneous but disciplined market system coming out of the daily efforts of the general population as such economic direction contrasted with their cloistered estate-based agricultural pursuit: the proper way for a Greek to earn a living and contribute to society. Socrates was always looking for virtue in one's life and had an inbuilt disdain for the constant accumulation of more material wealth, specifically through entrepreneurial profit. In essence, he was anticapitalist with little use for trade and he did not completely appreciate the relatively influential strength of the self-sustaining market order in determining public exchange values. While Plato was a champion of private property rights, the protective driving force behind capitalism, he condemned usury, not appreciating its use as a capital acquisition tool, and did not appreciate the effect of the cost of money on consumers, savers, and the investment initiative. Aristotle saw the process of commercial exchange as a behavior based on proportional reciprocity as opposed to market pricing. He was therefore critical of entrepreneurial profit and dismissive of merchant traders. In agreement with Plato, he felt interest (*tokos*) as an unjustified generation of making money on money as opposed to its more equitable use to merely determine commonly accepted exchange value for things and services.

These famous ancient Greek philosophers did not see the commercial exchange process in a favorable light. Their philosophy is perhaps best rooted in the oral poems of Hesiod, who deduced that because of the scarcity that time, labor and production of goods need to be efficiently allocated and that the state therefore should publicly administrate or organize economic activity. Due to his depiction of the plight of the independent small farmer in his verse "Work and Days," he is sometimes regarded as the first economist, although the poem is based on a dispute between him and his brother over their inheritance. In contrast to the SPA elitists were the Sophists, professional teachers who took a fee for instruction as opposed to public philosophers. They were best known for teaching the skill of persuasive argument (i.e., advocacy of either side of a dispute), which led many to criticize them as proponents of deceptive rhetoric. It is interesting to note that the first lawyers were thought to come from this assembly of educators. Sophists felt that one did not have to be of aristocratic birth to teach *arête*, or the application of excellence in the management of one's affairs and especially in the administration of a society; rather, such an ability was not an inborn qualification but the result of training. This group felt that if an action is advantageous to the individual, then it is good and that the interaction of such pursuits by numerous parties formed a positive societal environment and sustained a working sociopolitical economic system, essentially a market-based society. They therefore sympathized with the concept of commercial trade; the profit motive and the entrepreneurial spirit as such were in line with their basic outlook, a distrust of government to direct economic affairs and in favor of individualism as the cornerstone of a good society.

While the Greek Olympic festivals were held to honor Zeus every four years, featuring athletic competitions, the games, which were protected by military truce, attracted an audience composed mainly of the aristocracy, the landed gentry, and controllers of wealth. Such an international event (various Greek states along with bordered foreign entrees) allowed for the convergence of common interests, both political and economic, a sort of ancient networking. Today the games are global, reaching more households and potential customers than ever before. They are underwritten by the vast advertising revenues supplied by the large multinational corporations to televise the event while the trademarked names and logos of globally marked products adorn venue sites and the athletes themselves. The commercial interests visited on the games of antiquity now dominate the event in the modern era. The same principle that overshadowed their original premise, the exchange imperative, today has evolved into international trade through globalization.

The Indian Social Approach

While in the West Greeks began to explore a system of economic management of their resources, a similar if not wider social approach emerged in the East. Somewhere between the second and fourth centuries CE, the *Arthashastra* by Kautilya was constructed. This massive treatise guiding secular social behavior in India, and not originating from a religious inspiration nor proclaimed as a specific code of laws, was composed of 15 books combining strategic policies for rulers of the domain. Often referred to as the *Rajarshi* (symbolic of a wise and virtuous king), the writings also set out relationship obligations of the masses.

Many scholars have attempted to translate the word *arthasastra* in order to define its expansive doctrine on ordered civilization. It has been referred to as "science of politics ... material gain ... political economy."[8] In academic and business circles, it is synonymous with economics, with

Kautilya (*aka* Chanakya) being considered the world's first management guru. Many of its underlying principles still form the basis for the policies of governments and commercial institutions in India today.

Portions of his writings have been compared to the strategic positioning and tactical actions proposed by Sun Tzu in the *Art of War* (Chinese), Miyamoto Musashi's *The Five Rings* (Japanese), and Machiavelli's classic *The Prince* (Italian); all of these have been converted into lessons for managers.[9] *Arthashastra* is often referred to as the science of wealth and it contains a number of propositions on economic theory as well as commerce. The text recognized that international trade or globalization could increase total wealth using the concept of comparative advantage by explaining that a country could benefit from exporting some goods as well as importing others. It commented on the process of wage determination, noting that their value should be proportional to time spent, the specialized skill set involved, and the amount and price of the output produced. The idea of a progressive tax system was even proposed for both a sales tax and personal income tax. Those products being considered luxury and those individuals earning a higher income should be assessed assed at a higher tax rate.

Radhakrishnan Pillai, director of ATMA DARSHAN, a management services firm, refers to the teaching of the *Arthashastra* (alternate spelling) in his promotional literature, calling it the "7 Pillars of a Business," using it to profile and explain the use of CEO leaders (king), executive managers (ministers), the market (the country), head office (fortified city), the financial division (the treasury), one's labor team (army), and consultants (allies).[10] Such a modern application of a commercial organizational structure is based on institutional management of a society to form an economically based model to foster the exchange imperative.

While the *Arthashastra* is not a legal code per se, it sets down principles of expected behavior by a nation's citizens. In *Book IV, The Removal of Thorns*, a number of chapters are devoted to the treatment and obligations of those in commercial ventures as Kautilya believed in the building of a society on sound economic policy.[11] Chapter 1 is translated as "The Protection of Artisans" and features specific references to numerous segments of specialized labor such as weavers, washermen, goldsmiths, scavengers (miners), physicians, and even bands of musicians. The recognition of these groups as prime contributors to the nation's welfare and its economic growth is evident while the reference to them is a fore-runner of the establishment of the craft guilds of 16th-century Florence. Chapter 2 is referred to as "Protection of Merchants" and includes portions related to their dealings as well as explicit reference to traders dealing in both local commodities and foreign produce differentiating the profit percentages attributable to such varying territorial activities. *Book III* has chapters devoted to recovery of debts as well as rules regarding slaves and laborers.[12] This ancient text on the construction of a society is laced with commercial attributions noting its importance in the civilization process along with basic principles that supported early legal regulations to define the obligation and responsibilities of those participating in trade trans-actions. It is virtually a blueprint for the creation of society with strong references to the value of those parties engaged in the exchange process as necessary contributors to its positive development.

An Early Chinese View

A passage quoted from the Chinese historian Sima Qian (also called Ssu-ma Ch'ien), as referenced in the book *China's Economic Transformation*,[13] relates a profile of the sociopolitical and economic times of the Han dynasty that followed the Qian reign around 206 BCE and shows that a functioning market economy existed.

> There must be farmers to produce food, men to extract the wealth of mountain sand marshes, artisans to produce these things, and merchants to circulate them. There is no need to wait for government orders: each man will play his part, doing his best to get what he desires. So cheap goods will go where they will fetch more, while expensive goods will make men search for cheaper ones. When all work willingly at their trade, just as water flows ceaselessly downhill day and night, things will appear unsought and people will produce them without being asked. For clearly this accords with the Way and is in keeping with nature.

The paragraph depicts an intended capitalistic society that works without governmental decree controlling the division of labor and allocation of resources but one that relies on the law of demand and supply to create ordered employment based on need satisfaction. It essentially is a blueprint for civilization based on *the way*, the natural order of man to maximize self-interest within a value-induced system of exchange without guided interference. The concept seems to be an early depiction of the *invisible hand* mechanism driving the marketplace. As Gregory Chow comments, the passage "provides a clearer and simpler description of a market economy" than the theory introduced centuries later by Adam Smith in his *An Inquiry into the Nature and Causes of the Wealth of Nations* (popularly known as *The Wealth of Nations*).[14]

Chow in referencing Qian relates his commentary to the original teachings of Guang Zhong, offering the following proposition:

> Each man has only to be left to utilize his own abilities and exert his strength to obtain what he wishes When each person works away at his own occupation and delights in his own business, then like water flowing downward, goods will naturally flow ceaselessly day and night with being summoned, and the people will produce commodities without having been asked.[15]

Sima Qian was a free-market advocate commenting on entrepreneurship and the rise of the private sector in long-distance trade, previously in the domain of the imperial court, as the process of looking for and taking advantage of opportunities, which he saw as a good thing. In his book *Guanzi*, Zhong, who lived from 725 to 645 BCE, introduced his theory of light and heavy to explain the changing value of things in the marketplace. He describes the self-regulating process as follows: when a good is abundant, it becomes *light*, and its price falls. When a good is *heavy*—not easily movable and therefore locked or kept away from the marketplace—its price rises. His example, while not using the exact terminology, is the precursor of the pressures of supply and demand on economics. Zhong, in essence, not only appreciated the constant movement of the market to determine the relative value of things but also applied his theory to money. He proposed that when money, the acceptable medium of exchange in a society, is light, its value would fall and the prices of goods they bought would therefore rise—that is, there would be inflation. In today's modern jargon, it is referred to as the quantity theory of money. Mixing philosophical motivation with its effects on societal economics, Zhong felt that one's quest for profit, material gain, or wealth accumulation would drive one to make the right choices without the need for any outside guidance or intervention by administrative forces—the government. He believed that the principles of light and heavy, coupled with the profit incentive, would create free-market efficiencies—a theme later seen in the writing of Adam Smith 2,400 years thereafter. During the same era as classical Greek thought was born, spanning the period from the sixth to fourth century BCE, comments on economic philosophy continued to emerge. Chuang Tzu, who generally opposed strong governmental administration of society, was said to have felt that good order in a kingdom results spontaneously when things are left alone. He adhered to the conclusions of Lao Tzu, a central figure in Taoism, that government inaction is interference in life and is appropriate because it limits the ability of individuals to flourish in the pursuit of their desire for contentment. The defense of individual liberty leading to a laissez-faire, free-market approach to economics tends to be in contrast to the traditional Greek desire for governmental structuring of the commerce.

Early Muslim Thinking

The Arab-Muslim region was greatly influenced by Islamic religious teachings, given that all life is controlled by reverence to its determinations. Abu Hamid al-Ghazal (1058 to 1111), a theologian of Sunni thought and philosopher, offered commentary on the role of economics in society. While deeply supporting the Islamic doctrine, he held that mathematics and science could be applied with dual rationales to life's spiritual choices. Such a consideration allowed him to acquire a deep understanding of how markets act in a coordinated rhythm to create economic activity as well as how specialization and division of labor affected the commercial landscape. He recognized the role of voluntary, impersonal market forces, a veiled reference to *the way* in ancient Chinese economic literature and later referred to as the *invisible hand* by

Adam Smith. The following statement provides the essence of al-Ghazali's position: "Man's inability to fulfill all his needs alone persuades him to live in a civilized society with cooperation; but tendencies like jealousy, greed, competition, and selfishness, can create conflicts. Therefore, some collective arrangement becomes necessary to check those tendencies."[16] His use of the term "collective arrangement" refers to a system organized by market forces.

In al-Ghazali's work called *Ihya*, in a chapter titled "Ethics of Business/ Trade/Work Practices," he discusses a prime tenet of the Islamic approach to commercial transactions, an equitable exchange of value with no fraud in the pricing of goods. While he recognizes *use value* as the basic determinant of fair and proper criteria, he also mentions market-determined prevailing prices as a collateral condition to be taken into consideration.[17] While expressing some disdain, although not condemnation, for profit seeking, he recognizes the motivations for the sources of profits as well. Profits are viewed as the return to risk and uncertainty, as traders and businesses bear a lot of trouble in seeking profits, endangering their own lives and those of others during the perilous voyages taken in the pursuit of such activities.[18] However, al-Ghazali is critical of *excessive* profits. His comment on the use of money reaffirms the concept of usefulness again as the prime value consideration, as he feels that dirhams and dinars, the coined currency of this period, are not needed for themselves. They are created to change hands and to establish rules for exchange with justice and for buying goods that are useful.[19] Incidentally, al-Ghazali also talks of *prevailing wages*, similar to the position of St. Thomas Aquinas and his idea of *just wages*. Both philosophical commentators viewed the meaning of their alternating terminologies (*prevailing* and *just* price) as reflecting a joint concern for distributive and commutative justice. They combined a market-accepted value assigned to products and compensation for services along with a moral component. Their writings underscore the establishment of a price that benefits both buyer and seller, one that meets their mutual needs. If such value is achieved, then no ethical issues emerge and the parties have treated each other with equitable respect.

It is interesting to note that all the early philosophers, in both the Eastern and Western cradles of civilization, knew of and discussed the concept of the free market as a way of establishing value in the process of exchange: that demand and supply are evident factors in the systematic workings of societal economies. The principle of a spontaneous free market to set exchange values and the influence of capitalism via trade on the process were equally developed around the world. Today, the integrated system to manage the activities of men first required in antiquity is now played out on a worldwide stage, morphing the original term into the two broad categories: microeconomics and macroeconomics. These two areas of inspection and research are merged with or expanded to include their cross-effect on social conditioning and culture, as well as political structure, and eventually, the development of civilization.

Birth of Exchange

People have always woven a web of connections and interactive interwoven exchanges leading to modification or replacement of existing activities through adoption or outright transfer of the new ones. Regardless of what period of time in human history is examined, this economic phenomenon has existed. One of the elements of economics is finance, which itself is in fact the foundation of human progress, the essential backstory behind history.[20] The constant development of civilization was propelled by the locomate channelization between societies, which served as the birth process of what we today call globalization. It is therefore not a new event. Its roots are older than recorded history. All that is practiced today can be traced to yesterday. Although the study of history is imperfect, always told through the eyes of distant observers, it is nonetheless a valuable tool to help unravel and reveal how things came to be. Sometimes they also assist to understand how ideas, in response to need, evolved so that their modern use can be appreciated.

It is important for today's students and parishioners of global management to more fully recognize that they literally walk the pathways first encountered by their commercial ancestors. The Anglo-Saxon root word *trada*, from which the term *trade* emerged, means to walk in the footsteps of another. Much like their ancient relatives, the businessmen of today impact the world around them, even in the modern age when the world is deeply interconnected via technological advancements in communication and transport, shrinking the globe to reach out and touch society. The main force behind such integration is commercial cross-territorial trade and its collateral element: increased direct foreign investment from the preliminary outsourced supplier stage to the more embedded project contract level and on to the solidified greenfield or brownfield (acquisition models) presence in an alien territory. At all graduated phases of international expansion, the impact on the home and host-country civilizations are felt. The issues faced by antiquated traders and their influence on the social, political, and economic environments of their times are mirrored in today's world as mankind continues to exchange one thing for another and build on the past to shape the future. The past events presented in this book are by no means revolutionary. Readers may, like combative business historians, arrive at varying and perhaps opposite conclusions. The perceptions as to the development of civilization and its intertwined relationship with the commercial imperative as a contributing driver to the process may not be acceptable to other historical commentators as empirical evidence drawn from antiquity is not exacting. Archeologists, anthropologists, and sociologists all have different opinions on how mankind developed. If the dual thesis of this text has any merit, it will be in the hopeful generation whose further interest in the subject is to create a greater appreciation of the trading initiative and its influence on world society and its historic advancement of the commercial principles still in use today. Not all events are presented in chronological order as certain aspects of them, being reflected in later periods, are linked together to illustrate their effect on the development of civilization and the commercial imperative shared by many societies at varying times. Therefore, the hypothesis of this manuscript is to illustrate two basic propositions that managerial practitioners and students should be introduced in the study of global business: (a) the commercial imperative contributed to and influenced the development of civilization, and hence the history of the world; and (b) many of the basic tenets of modern business can be traced to ancient trading practices, which, despite being used in a more efficient scale and exercising a wider degree of influence today, remain the same. It is difficult to determine the exact moment in time when the first organized business actually ventured beyond its recognized border to solicit opportunities with citizens of a true alien land. The simple act of barter brought man out of his cave existence, providing an enhanced reward system for life's activities.

While bands of people bound by a common tribal heritage certainly traded goods with other clans, venturing out to people separated by land masses and water obstacles whose specialized resources or talents bestowed on them unique and different entitlements was indeed a most remarkable journey.

Anthropologists working alongside archeologists comparing the dig sites of prehistoric men, Neanderthal and Cro-Magnon, have concluded that cross-tribal trade may have begun with the latter group on the evolution scale of mankind thousands of years ago. While the Neanderthal relics were made from local resources, those of the Cro-Magnon contained artifacts bearing raw materials from territories hundreds and perhaps thousands of miles away from their native habitats. The simple conclusion is that prehistoric men practiced the trading imperative as part of the natural order of mankind as they progressed.

Because no records of actual exchange transactions across and between territories were maintained in the caveman era, the artifacts found in different locations, some across vast distances, are relied on to prove such movement of goods. Perhaps, the first extensive trade networks that extended beyond local neighbors were constructed via waterways. Navigation of the Nile, the Tigris, and Euphrates, as well as the Yellow River in China, provided a natural highway to move goods. The domestication of camels around 1000 BCE gave rise to the use of commercial caravans to transverse extensive land routes. Historians believe that what might qualify as the first documented cross-continental or global trade occurred between Mesopotamia and the Indus Valley in Pakistan around 3000 BCE. In the third millennium BCE, Sumerian craftsmen in Mesopotamia created farm implements and other objects made of glass and bronze from raw materials not found in their region. Researchers believe that clearly a widespread network of contacts abroad is in the background, above all with the Levant and Syria huge distances away, but also with Iran and Bahrein, down the Persian Gulf. Before 2000 BCE, Mesopotamia was obtaining goods—though possibly indirectly—from the Indus Valley. Together with evidence of documentation (which reveals contacts with India before 2000 BCE), it makes an impression of a dimly emerging international trading system.[21]

This practice has been recorded throughout history. When alien groups met for the first time, the ceremonial exchange of goods was part of their mutual greeting, and trade became the initiator of socialization between them. Hence, anthropologists define globalization as a connectivity of individuals and institutions across the globe, as opposed to economists, who view such activity in a more limited financial framework: a global market where institutions engage in the flow of goods, services, and assets across national borders.[22] The former characterization more closely identifies globalization with the development of civilization and recognizes its unique contribution to the socialization of man on earth. The simple act of buying and reselling with the inherent value in the ongoing commercial exchange, as opposed to pure singular localized barter, had its base in the ancient world. These original seeds of modern-day globalization were planted long ago and provided the rails on which societies first engaged cross-cultural diversity as they learned about their differences. Such antiquated trade routes were the communication high-ways for the transfer of newinventions, varying religious beliefs, differences in artistic styles, languages and social customs as well as the physical manifistations of peoples styles, the raw materials they used and the goods they bought and sold. All were transmitted and redistributed by people moving from one place to another to conduct business.

In *The Shape of Ancient Thought: Comparative Studies in Greek and Indian Philosophies*,[23] the author argues that Eastern and Western civilizations have not always held separate, autonomous, and metaphysical schemes but have in fact mutually influenced each other as evident in their key mutual philosophical paradigms. He attributes this phenomenon to the ancient trading imperative and on examination states.

> The records of caravan (cross territorial trading convoys) routes are like the philosophical stemmata of history, the trails of oral discourses moving through communities, of texts copied from texts ... What they (commercial exchange documents) reveal is not a structure of parallel straight lines—one labeled "Greece," another "Persia," another "India"—but a tangled web in which an element in one culture often leads to elements in others.[24]

While this book is primarily devoted to the crossbreeding of philosophical outlooks, other aspects of culturally shared characteristics due to the transversal of territories by such ancient traders are noted in examples of traditions and customs that were carried in the minds, actions, and practices and left in the footprints of such commercial ventures.

Trade across cultures is "perhaps the most important external stimuli to change," notwithstanding military conquest, that the world has and will ever see.[25] Trading centers were the impetus for creation of nation-states around which countries were born: "Trade communities of merchants living amongst aliens in associated networks are to be found in every continent and back through time to the very beginning of urban life. They are the most widespread of human institutions."[26] These ambassadors from other tribal lands, the first conveyors of cultural diversity, were tolerated because they provided a useful service but they may have also acted to allay fear and prejudice of the unknown. They may have been pioneers of cross-cultural understanding and the unforeseen initial promoters of world exploration. As merchants stopped to rest in trade route towns, they not only traded goods but also shared stories and customs from their homelands, contributing to the spread of knowledge and exchange of ideas across societies. Professor Charles Standish, director of the Cotsen Institute of Archaeology, has been excavating the shoreline of Lake Titicaca on the shared border of Bolivia and Peru for years, locating evidence of trade between ancient people in the area. He feels that interregional trade is one of the key factors in the development of civilization, as we know it.[27] This University of California, Los Angeles UCLA archaeologist also offers two additional factors affecting the development of people into civilized groups. He lists war and specialized labor along with the cross-territorial exchange process as the three most influential predecessor drivers to the advancement of a society anywhere on earth.

The Exchange Imperative Grows Up

As previously noted, one of the prime characteristics that separate *Homo sapiens* from all other species on earth is the exchange or trading imperative, beginning in one's own clan and then conducted with strangers from alien lands. This exclusive activity practiced by human beings to exchange natural materials hunted or collected, as well those with added merit due to specialized labor activities conducted on them, is as old a practice as mankind itself. Adam Smith, the father of global economics, in *The Wealth of Nations* (1776), recognized the gains of mankind from exchange and the division of labor. He felt that the prime propensity to *truck* (an old English term meaning to transact), barter, and exchange one thing for another is common to all men and is to be found in no other race of animals on earth. Such an inbred characteristic sparked the ancient trading imperative, and created the desire to venture into foreign lands in search of new resources and items of unique special-ized skills applied to them. Laurence Bergreen, writing on the travels of Marco Polo, comments on the endorsement by this famed explorer that those he encountered "do great trade" and such activity "virtually defines their humanity."[28] The attributed observation suggests that even if man is savage in his practiced customs and traditional beliefs, as Polo used his European environment as a criterion for acceptable civilized behavior, the fact that they exchange goods with others is their common linkage to humankind. This natural ingrained practice to trade by humans evolved over history, resulting in the current integrated world economy. Even when a later intermediary medium of exchange value was used, like gold, silver, precious stones, or salt, the process continued. With the advent of specie (coins), paper currency, and documents, the trading process flourished. The use of money, *trust inscribed* on metal or paper, allowed for a unit of accounting, a storable and portable value.[29] The process of a mutually acceptable exchange assessment made the trading process a more workable system and thereby contributed to the commercial imperative, which influenced, propelled, and shaped the development of civilization around the world. Modern globalization is merely another act on an ever-evolving progressive stage that began with the inherent natural desire of man to trade with others across territories and find methods to make the process more universally efficient. In its current configuration, globalization is but a period branch.

The term *globalization* is often banded to a language of inflation, suffused with prejudicial grammar that tends to mask and often obliterate rather than illuminate its heritage. The result is a paralyzing debate. Today it is maligned and portrayed as the demonized imperative of inequality around the globe and a beacon for groups sighting environmental destruction, the loss of national sovereignty, and cultural imperialism. It has also been praised as the process that has and will create jobs for millions of workers in developing nations, allowing opportunities they never would have had and both fostering economic growth for such depressed areas and contributing to more democratic reforms in repressive countries as free-market factors and open borders emerge.

However, is globalization new or is it merely a natural extension of man's unique primeval trait to trade with others and therefore act as a prime catalyst in the creation of civilization and world development? Globalization is not an event whose happenstance was engineered with plus and minus agendas but rather progressed in a normative fashion over a vast time scale. The road to today's interlinked and therefore "borderless world," a phrase first used in the title of a book by Kenichi Ohmae in 1990,[30] was constructed on the ancient paths first traveled by peoples of all territories. Examining commercial history reveals the great influence it has had and will continue to have on mankind. Such investigation is the crucial element to understanding it, before commenting on its constructive or destructive tendencies.

Theories of the Development of Civilization

Some researchers consider the interior of Africa, using the Darwinian theory of evolution to explain the emergence of *Homo sapiens* and the beginning of societies. Other research suggests that the appearance of human beings on earth was initiated in four cradles of civilization across the globe. Support for this consideration is based on the fact that these culturally grouped societies monopolized the power and resources of the ancient world as evidenced by the archeological remnants that have and are still being recovered. This research suggests that the process began in four regions of the globe: (a) the Nile River basin (Egypt, Mesopotamian planes of Asia region); (b) Babylon, (c) the Indus region of India; and (d) and further to the east on the banks of the Yellow River in China. Researchers cannot always agree on which of these harbors of civilization first appeared or if a singular one in Africa may have begotten the others.

Although the exact geographical point of the first humans on earth may continue to be a debated mystery, the question of how civilizations evolved around the world has produced a number of theoretical conjecturing. The following three conceptual ideas are often circulated to explain the human evolutionary cycle and the creation of civilizations across the globe.

Spread Theory

The development of civilization on earth, by many anthropologist accounts, began in 7 million BCE on the African continent and spread northward into the Middle East and further to the east across Persia, India, and China in about 1 million BCE. It then branched out into the northern Mediterranean and the European zone in 500,000 BCE, snaking its way to the Western Hemisphere around 11,000 BCE via Asian land bridges (see Figure 2.2). Given such a time line for the spread of humans around the world, pockets of civilization emerged. But could they have been, in turn, linked by ancient trade routes as the points of connective contact among them? Was the motivational impetus for the emergence of individual societal development based on mankind's desire to reach out and explore alien territories for new resources to improve his lot in life?

Remnants still exist of the first true land routes across the Middle East. Ancient paths like Egypt's King's Highway or the Persian-constructed Royal

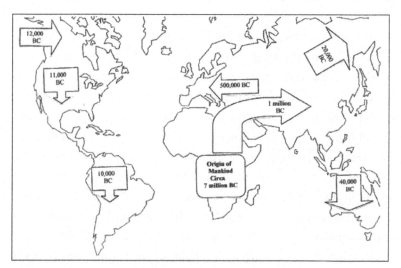

Figure 2.2 Spread of mankind across the globe

Road have been uncovered across modern-day Jordan and into Damascus, Syria, Iran, and Turkey and from there to numerous points in east. As mankind discovered boats, travel on the Nile River and later navigation of the Mediterranean seacoast became a natural path for movement of goods across territories. Later on, as larger and more seaworthy vessels came into use and knowledge of monsoon wind patterns emerged, crossings from East African costal ports to India and Asia progressed. With advances in cartography, astronomy, and navigational instruments like the magnetic compass (discovered by the Chinese), all points on the global compass were finally synchronized even in ancient times. While mankind moved around the earth initially seeking more fertile resources for survival as hunters and gatherers, the joining of societies into a primitive systematic economic existence was attributable to the exchange process. To state it simply, man learned that he did not have to physically move to another location to obtain the bounty of varying environments and enjoy the skills of other inhabitants in them, but he could trade with them and remain in one place. The concept of globalization, albeit in its infancy, was born. We are the inheritors of this principle today but on a greater scale and to a higher degree of cross-territorial integration. Along the positioning axis depicting the spread of humans around the world were the pockets of civilization that were perhaps initiated. A basic consideration worthy of inquiry and inspection may be insinuated from Figure 2.2. As mankind branched out from a central core, the interior of Africa, he probably did so with the prime imperative to locate new sources to sustain life. He did leave remnants of his society in the old territory while establishing colonies of new habitation and continuing to join the original settlements with the explored virgin areas. This connective impetus was the process of exchange, the trading principle, the umbilical cord that held regions together. As each new region grew, it in turn matured and perhaps eclipsed the original civilization. Mankind also ventured out to other lands, creating, perhaps, the multiple pocket theory.

Multi-pocket Theory

Some believe that civilization developed in selected areas independently of others and not from a common core or ancestry in Africa. Many researchers subscribe to the multi-pocket theory—composed of four regions as found in Egypt, Mesopotamia, India, and China. Some anthropologists feel that the initial cradles of civilization should also include Crete, Mesoamerica, and the Andes as simultaneously emerging with the first four generally accepted areas of first human development (see Figure 2.3). The theory is based on the human condition prompting people, wherever they were, to exhibit like characteristics and shared instincts to create similar methods to cope with life. Initially, contact with others outside of their territories was severely limited and adaptation was a factor of the local environment and the intuitive nature of mankind to work in his given environment. The world grew up in pockets, which were first composed of clans and tribes that locally banded together to survive the physical situation and also the attacks of each other. Each separate society along varying time lines initially developed independently, with interaction and exchange restricted to their internal boundaries. In essence, each civilization developed from a whole cloth with the threads of others originally

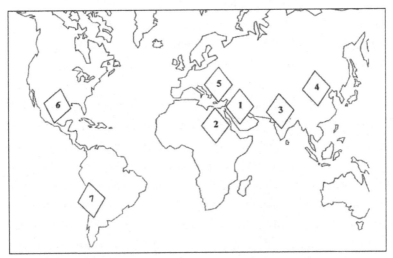

Figure 2.3 Pocket theory of civilization development (four cradles of civilization and others)

1. Mesopotamia (Sumerian) civilization (ca. 3500–1500 BCE); later the Akkadian, Babylonian, Assyrian, Chaldian, Persian, Hittite, Anatolian, Canaanite, Phoenician, and Israelite.
2. Egyptian civilization (ca. 3000 BCE); later the Nubian, Kushitic, and Ethiopic.
3. Indus Valley civilization (ca. 2500 BCE); later Indian (Aryan, Mauryan, and Grupta).
4. Wei and Shang civilizations (ca. 1500 BCE); later the Chinese dynasties (Chou, Chin, and Han).
5. Crete/Minoan civilization (ca. 2500 BCE); later Mycemeam, Hellenic, and Hellenist (Greek).
6. Mesoamerica (Olmec) civilization (ca. 1200 BC); later Toltec, Mayan, and Aztec.
7. Mesoamerica (Chavin) civilization (ca. 900 BCE); later Andean, Chimu, and Inca.

having no impact in them. Eventually, however, even these separate civilizations began to move beyond their seemingly independent domestic regions with the same impetus employed in the spread theory, a desire to seek out alien lands and to use both natural and man-made resources through the social connecting process known as trade.

Whether people subscribed to the spread theory (the geographical systematic movement of earth's population across land masses) over time or the multi-pocket theory (autonomous conclaves emerging in various areas around the world), they shared the same umbilical cord—the desire and need to trade for each other's resources. The process of commercial exchange is the midwife that allowed civilization to grow. It was the catalyst in ancient times, as well as in the modern era, for globalization.

Mythical Master Theory

Other propositions about the development of civilization consider the emergence of a prime civilization that subsequently was the *engineer* of other civilizations. Such a theory defers from the spread theory in that one nucleus of civilization created all others as opposed to borrowing and learning from other regions and suspends consideration of the multiple pocket theory as only one superior society is responsible for the creation of multiple civilizations. A cult of antediluvian writers considers the mythical kingdom and/or lost continent of Atlantis as the master civilization, consisting of half-god and half-human citizens. Such theoretical reasoning is based on the dialogues of the Greek philosopher Plato, "Timaeus," written about 360 BCE and the supposed tale of Critias relating a 9,000-year-old story recorded on inscriptions on columns in the ancient city of Sais (Egypt). While most of the debate on Atlantis has been relegated to finding its exact location, no less its actual existence, it is interesting to note that all provocateurs of this unique historic account have a number of common links in their descriptions of the legendary civilization.

Common to all believers in the Atlantis story is that they all conclude that this Bronze Age Kingdom attained its wealth and status from trading outside its shores. They built a colonial-type empire using their superior technology to construct a mighty fleet that sailed the world harvesting the natural resources of foreign lands. In doing so, they set up outposts around the globe that became the foundation for the independent societies that emerged after the demise of the home kingdom, which was destroyed by some natural disaster. The prime contribution therefore of this mythical society was the construction of additional civilizations originally built on their expanded commercial trading ventures.

Even in the world of historical fiction, the importance of the exchange imperative across territories provides the impetus for human progress on earth. It should be noted that many critics of the Atlantis theory, while not abridging the idea of a great trading empire, feel that the legend is based on a Western prejudicial theory or the Europeans' biased view of the world. Investigators of classical literature, like James Romm, a professor at Bard College, have proposed that Plato created this fictional kingdom as a literal symbol to illustrate his ideas about the divine verses, human nature, ideal societies, and the gradual corruption of human society if it fails to follow his numerous dialogues on proper behaviors. Such conceptual developments are all found in many of his works. Atlantis was a fictional vehicle to get at some of his favorite themes by setting them out in an entertaining format.

Within the mystical mantra of a singular, superior entity giving birth to all others is also the notion that beings from another planet, solar system, or somewhere in the vast universe brought their advanced knowledge to earth, sharing with us numerous geographically isolated societies. The theory was popularized in 1968 with the first printing (4 million sense) of *Chariots of the Gods? Unsolved Mysteries of the Past* by Erich von Daniken.[31] It presented the hypothesis that technologies and religions of many ancient civilizations were bestowed on them by space travelers who were welcomed as astronaut gods. These ideas have been largely rejected by historians and scientists but even under this fiction of civilized development it would seem that differing prizes were bestowed on separate groups and that through the process of exchange these gifts were more evenly distributed across societies. Hence, even in the mystical sense, the process of international trade allowed for commercialized exchange, with the process acting as a key contributor to the development of civilization on earth.

No Man Is an Island: The Philosophical Interloper

Inherent in all the previous theories of the development of civilization on earth is the observation that "no man is an island, entire of itself," written by John Donne in *Devotions Emergent Occasions*.[32] This often-quoted passage was directed at advising man that he is not alone and that his theological soul requires others to inhabit his life. The quote, however, is apropos as its expanded connotation beyond the inner spiritually directed self-examination expresses well the idea that people are not to be isolated from one another but rather that mankind is interconnected and interdependent. We are naturally social creatures and have the need to interact with our environment, which includes our fellow men. Through the ages, mankind has instinctively banded together for survival against both the forces of nature, beasts, and earthly climatic changes and attacks from other human beings. Safety in numbers is a proven hypothesis. Being part of a larger physical group, which is the tribal instinct, an individual is proportionally less likely to be the victim; thus one's continued existence is inherently interlinked with others. This principle produced the first prehistoric clans, then settlements, and later evolved into the creation of towns in the cradles of civilization. However, the concept that one could produce absolutely everything that was needed or desired (a self-sufficiency mind-set) began to be challenged. Early farmers began to realize that they could barter their agricultural surplus for other foods as well as tools and pottery as local seasonal markets developed.

The citizens of larger cities began to also appreciate that they could acquire the goods they did not produce locally from other regions and specialists called merchant middlemen willing to make long-distance journeys were introduced.

Man learned that different environments yielded varying resources and that the skills and abilities of men to adapt and flourish in the world around them are not always equal. The division of labor was recognized. While such dual consideration has been the basis for armed conflicts, it has also produced a positive, more peaceful side: the process of exchange or barter in the ancient world. In the end, man either trades or makes war to survive and grow—the yin and yang philosophy of the social animal: human beings.

The development of civilizations or the history of the human race is in direct correlation with the natural urge in all societies. No matter where they first originated to exchange the fruits of their resources as enhanced by their intellectual applied labor, man has always reached out and touched others to sustain their needs and improve their lives. The capacity to trade with others is therefore intertwined with the development of civilization. Mankind learned from others, especially those societies closer to one another, and developed faster due to the exchange not only of raw materials and things made from them but also of ideas and shared knowledge. The platform for such valued exchanges was the trading imperative. It provided the system for improving the lives of all who engaged in the practice.

Darwin and the Exchange Imperative

The concept of exchange being a natural progression and hence a mechanism that drives the evolution of mankind and the construction of civilization may be considered a restatement of the economic abstract of Charles Darwin's concepts as related in his famous 1859 treatise *The Origin of Species by Means of Natural Selection*.[33] The progress of species on earth from plants to animals to mankind is a process of adaptation. Those that pass on their survival traits will evolve into stronger versions by acquiring those characteristics that allow them to continue to better themselves. The mechanism in man, his survival transformation, is embedded in the exchange process—seeking out new resources and others with added skills and trading with them to improve his lot. Those who are successful in creating a system of exchange will progress, and those who fail will not survive.

In Darwin's later years, after his voyage on the Beagle, which took him to faraway lands and sparked his insightful discoveries on which he based his initial theories, he solicited the opinions of animal and plant breeders all over the world. He learned from such inquiries that successful breeders selected those variants having characteristics of *commercial value* while less exchange-worthy varieties were denied the opportunity to breed and hence began to disappear. Artificial selection of this type, a system based on marketable or profitable results, produced cows giving greater quantities of milk, horses of greater running ability, and so on. An economic justification is introduced in the natural selection process but at the heart of the formula is mankind's desire to improve and progress—itself a natural motivation.

Herbert Spencer (1820–1903) was reflecting on the ideas of social evolution and progress prior to Darwin's publication but his thought-provoking concepts lacked a label. With the coinage of terms like *adaptation* and *survival of the fittest* applied to social thought, the term *social Darwinism* emerged. The concept can best be described as the benefits of cooperation and community for human evolution. Mankind learned in his earliest years that banding together with others promoted survival. Whether group tasks were undertaken for protection from predators (other men or beasts) or foraging and hunting for sustenance, advancement of men's skills later evolved into divisions of labor, in short, collaboration among men and the need for a systematic society based on the mutually beneficial exchange of services or jobs. Political economists have described human evolution as tribe members who first performed identical activities for themselves and then progressed to a system whose members severally engage in different and varied actions toward each other. The individual producer of any one thing is therefore transformed into one of many parts of a separate working unit that benefits all under the exchange umbrella. From such primeval and natural recognition developed the trading imperative as tribes or clans bartered among themselves and then ventured out to extend the process to those in other territories (the roots of globalization).

The idea of social Darwinism evolving into the classic trading system of mutual beneficial exchange, which was later identified with David Ricardo, the early 19th-century economist who analytically studied the concept of competitive advantage, has its base in ancient tribal activities. Assume that tribe A is capable of both hunting and fishing but its prowess or time efficiency is best devoted to hunting. Tribe B is not as proficient as tribe A in either activity but is better at fishing. Ricardo concluded that both tribes would benefit (eat better) if tribe A transferred (sold) game to tribe B in exchange for fish.

Both groups would win in the barter process; and perhaps even more so for tribe B, which has less efficient skills. Ricardo's theory lies at the heart of the strong support on behalf of those modern economists who prize the benefits of globalization, which itself has a conceptual base in the early history of mankind.

The theories of Darwin and Spencer on the evolution of mankind define a process that continues to influence our lives today. Their ideas have matured into and form the basis for a modern social framework we call globalization. Fueled by evolving technological advancements, it is causing the world to contract and become one at a pace and to a degree never before experienced.

Two books on the development of the world—*Globalization and Culture* by Jan Nederveen Pieterse in 2003[34] and *Creative Destruction: How Globalization Is Changing the World's Cultures* by Tyler Cowen in 2002[35]—comment on the integration effect of globalization and culture, the two queens of civilization, with the trading imperative being the influential and necessary handmaiden.

It is not the intent of this observation to judge the positive or negative effects of globalization. Some argue that cross-territorial trade destroys authentic local culture and diversity, making the world too universal, whereas others consider it the molder of civilizations, as trading initiative ideas were exchanged, allowing the world to grow up and have more choices. No attempt is made to evaluate the process in all its manifestations as such inquiry and resulting conclusions are best left to historians.

The focus is to examine the simple premise that globalized trade is a natural and evolving inbred human trait, our socially induced DNA, which has been with us from the beginning of recorded history and perhaps before. The intent of the material presented is to conduct an examination of the historical trading stages on which globalization emerged so that proponents and opponents of the phenomenon might find common rooted ground on which to launch a more meaningful and less emotional discussion of the issues facing all of us in the future.

Trade and the Theory of Collective Intelligence

While pure physical survival caused groups of people to band together, the collective nature of humans also produced another phenomenon that drove the creation and progression of civilization: the notion of collective intelligence. This concept is defined as the sharing of group intelligence that emerges from the collaboration and competition of many separate individuals. The process enables humans acting in unison to progress to a higher order of complexity, and possibly harmony, by using the dual mechanism of integrated differentiation and collaborative competition, which results in the development of civilization. It is a form of networking. Matt Ridley's article "Humans: Why They Triumphed" argues that "the answer lies in a new idea, borrowed from economics, known as collective intelligence, the notion that what determines the inventiveness and rate of cultural change of a population is the amount of interaction between individuals."[36] He also added that trade and the urbanization that came about due to the exchange activities of intermediary merchants in ancient times being centralized in commercial centers (and later centralized institutions) were and still are "the grand stimuli to inventions, far more important than governments, money or individual genius."[37] He points out that even agriculture, the oldest form of human collective labors (hunting and gathering were individual ventures), was invented where people were already living in dense trading societies. Ridely concludes that "trade is to culture as sex is to biology" and that "exchange makes cultural change (its progressive advancement) collective and cumulative," thereby allowing civilization to take root and grow.[38] W. Brian Arthur makes the case that almost all new technologies evolve from combination of other technologies with such new ideas emerging from swapping or exchanging one thing for another—the trading imperative.[39]

In antiquity, the commercial process was the chief agent of cross-cultural exchange. The trading initiative was the original rails on which collective intelligence first traveled. And as collective intelligence was itself a prime contributor to the development and progression of civilization, it naturally follows that trade was its midwife.

According to Don Tapscott and Anthony Williams, in order for collective intelligence to take shape, and thereby drive civilization, a mass collaboration system containing four principles needs to exist.[40] The first two require an *openness* and a *sharing initiative* to be in place—a desire to form collaborative associations in order to produce significant gain improvements. While in ancient times people were more reluctant to engage in such freedom, they more closely guarded their knowledge or know-how and raw materials, modern commercial enterprises, especially multinational corporations (MNCs), have embraced this key characteristic. They are driven to find the most knowledgeable venues and engage in partnerships via strategic alliances with those parties processing such advanced intelligence resources. The third principle, *peering*, leverages varying divergent organizational skills to improve a product or service and/or gain cost efficiencies. The process called outsourcing or third-party contracting is used by today's MNCs. The last principle, *acting globally*, constantly searches for connections around the world to gain access to new markets and to take advantage of the extreme global value chain, the placing of their value-producing activities in the best available geographical locations to gain a competitive advantage over rivals has become a more common practice. While ancient merchants practiced these concepts as they expanded their geographical territories for new and exotic products, the modern age of globalization has ushered in these principles at a pace and to a degree never seen before in the history of mankind. As in the past, and still today, the global trading initiative fostered and embraced the idea of collective intelligence, itself an influential contributor to the development and growth of civilization. On the early trade routes, middlemen merchants erected varying ideas, inventions, customs, and beliefs, which were exchanged between distant regions. While the modern communication era, dominated by the Internet, has replaced such historic avenues, business still acts as an ambassador of knowledge and information flow.

Globalization, the Human Social Phenomenon

Robbie Robertson constructs what is the best explanation of the social imperative called globalization that has always touched mankind with no definitive time frame nor relative incident or episode in history to mark its beginning:

> If we simply focus on globalization as a modern strategy for power, we miss historical and social depths. Indeed the origins of globalization lie in interconnections that have slowly enveloped humans since the earliest of times as they globalized themselves.

In this sense, globalization as a human dynamic has always been with us, even if we have been unaware of its embrace until recently. Instead we have viewed the world more narrowly through the spectacles of religion, civilization, nation or race. Today these old constraints continue to frustrate the development of a global consciousness of human interconnections and their dynamism.[41]

The inherent desire to engage others in trade, and the natural extension across foreign territories, is at the nucleus of globalization. Human beings possess a unique trait, the capacity to exchange that is ingrained in our DNA. The process of trade has been characterized as an intrinsic human impulse in parallel with the basic need for food, shelter, sexual intimacy, and companionship.[42] As Adam Smith observed, no other class of living organisms trades one thing for another, no less developed an artificial common intermediary value to replace the actual physical things exchanged. While many animal and plant species may create a surplus storage of collected or hunted food, such harbored extras are not swapped for other materials. The fundamental exchange consideration, the forerunner of the commercial trading initiative, is one of the cornerstones of the development of human civilization. Out of such vestiges of dealing with others across territories, the world grew up and societies were formed, laws were constructed to guide associations between people, and the process of cross-pollination of ideas furthered civilization. The contemporary phenomenon is merely the maturation of activities on a greater scale and to a wider degree but nonetheless a continuance of an ingrained human desire.

The world grew up on the paths first traversed by merchants and it continues to do so. Many of the practices, principles, and techniques used in business today were initially birthed in the exchange process and through time the ancient commercial trading initiative produced many of the progressive business policies and laws used today.

Modern business orientations—the current guidelines used to enter new markets and sustain activities around the world—were constructed centuries ago. An inspection of the process that produced such practices allows one to reflect on his or her usage and application, producing a better result in the modern age of globalization as they are continuously applied. These suppositions do not suggest that a new paradigm be developed to research ancient trade. The literature certainly exists. What it does aim to invoke is a greater understanding of its effect on cultivating civilization and hence its impact on mankind. Seen from the perspective of the economic theory of the firm, the business firm is conceived of as a "nexus of contracts."[43] But when placed within the science of human relationship development the same theory is applicable. We are always making agreements, assuming cross-obligations with others. Human interaction is a series of social contracts and the actionable result is the exchange process.

Trade: The Determiner of Societal Growth or Demise

In the Pulitzer-Prize-winning novel by Jared Diamond, the author relates a meeting with a man on a beach in New Guinea, who asks a question concerning the development of civilizations around the world. The text that follows attempts to answer the riddle of how the fates of human societies brought the world to its current state. However, what is on the mind of the inquiring young man, asking with a "penetrating glance of his flashing eyes," is a very specific question: "Why is it that you white people developed so much cargo and brought it to New Guinea, but we black people had little cargo of our own?"[44] Within the context of the story the term "cargo" seems to be a code word for the development of the human intelligence factor as measured by mankind's handling of the world around them. It is the key cipher in determining the advancement of some societies over others. It is against this backdrop of inquiry that Diamond summarizes his book in one sentence. He states, "History followed different courses for different people because of differences among people's environment, not because of biological differences among peoples themselves."[45] The adjustment and reaction to varying geographies influenced numerous societies around the world to develop differently with the products of their own culture. The author's metaphor for products, guns, germs, and steel became the title for the book, and through their development he proceeds to show how they affected the fate of all earth's civilizations. The scope of Diamond's text tracing the history of mankind should be a mandatory reading for all university students no matter what their major or the disciplinary skill they wish to acquire, as the insights provided into the development of mankind touch all accumulation and use of knowledge across varying cultural environments. In the context of my early global executive career, coupled with my later instructional responsibilities and research activities as a college professor of international business, I have read and reread the first Diamond book, *Guns, Germs and Steel*, as well as his second, *Collapse: How Societies Choose to Fail or Succeed*, in order to understand and appreciate the world around me. In both books, it is through the prism of mankind's management of his environment and relationships with others based on the exchange of such resources that world history is examined, events explained, and conclusions drawn.

For years I have endeavored to give my students studying global business a historic prospective of the development of civilization, applying my own inspectional filter: the process of exchange—that is, the forerunner of the commercial trading imperative. Using this inspectional tool, I have found myself taking liberty with the applied definition of the word *cargo* as used in the inquiry of the young man from New Guinea. I define cargo as denoting the freight of a ship—the commercial designation of goods for trade in transit. This alternative application of the term may be one of the keys to unraveling the mystery of how the world grew up, why certain civilizations advanced, and why others melted away or simply were absorbed by stronger ones.

All cultures, no matter when or where they geographically emerged, had a common designation; they participated to varying degrees in the exchange process. The intertwined transfer of tangible property (things) and intangible assets (ideas or proprietary knowledge) was the key to sustaining and improving life. It was this motivating human desire to acquire the new and different that propelled civilizations forward or held them back, eventually leading them to grow or die off.

Some societies were limited to an interchange in their own clans or between groups within their known tribal territories while others ventured out of their geographical comfort zones, commuting with alien cultures. This key motivational inspiration provided the impetus for some societies to sustain, expand, and grow while for others their isolation stunted their ability to acquire new resources and skills; hence, failing to reach their full potential. Those who used peaceful contacts with others, in a positive manner, enhanced their own civilizations and benefited from cross-territorial commuting.

Mankind throughout history, and as Diamond's books have shown, has learned that different environments yield varying resources and that the skills and abilities of men to deal with such external factors for the maintenance of their lives are not always equal. Such recognition has laid the basis for conflict and war between groups as man reached out to acquire that which his environment did not allow him to accumulate using his own devices. But the desire also resulted in a more productive side, the process of transfer and the bartering of what one environment and its people could produce (whether resources or acquired intellectual skill of others). In modern times, we call the second of this interrelated philosophy, war being the first, the trading imperative, and its resulting modern phenomenon—globalization. Diamond acknowledges this concept in both his books. First, within his discussion of an influencing factor, he calls the diffusion the immigration of people among the continents.[46] Simply stated, the movement of people with their things and ideas—the transfer of tangible and intangible assets across regions—is in fact the prime definition of globalization. To illustrate the importance of commercial trade to foster the development of civilization Diamond asks the question of why China, the most advanced society on earth, lost its lead of thousands of years to late-starting Europe. His answer to this question was that the development and support of a merchant class, which allows some of the market-driven characteristics of capitalism to take root, and a form of patent protection for new processes were factors the Chinese left out of their society.[47] They failed to encourage privatization of commerce, supported some open-market provisions, and provided fundamental regulatory protection of invented assets that could be turned into wealth creators. While trade has been shown as a prime ingredient in promoting the development of civilization, its loss or demise according to Diamond's second book is a significant contributor to why civilizations disintegrate. As Diamond constructed his five-point framework, explaining how societies chose to fail or succeed, his exemplified research concluded that a decreased support of one's friendly neighbors allowing for the imports of essential trade goods is one of the contributing factors. A good trading partner reduces the risks of a weak society from collapsing and disappearing while the disruption of the trading process between social groups by dual hostilities or raiders can destroy civilizations.[48]

Did the Market Economy have Ancient Roots? No!

Did people meet or gather in some sort of a marketplace for the ancient purpose of bartering or exchanging goods and therefore socially create a market economy? Does history support such contention? Not all economic historians believe that such a classification was evident throughout civilization. Instead of an economy being ruled by social relations, some feel that the economy ruled social relations and resulted in a different structured system in ancient times than is still evident today.[49]

A market economy is one in which the allocation of resources and the division of labor applied to them in turn construct the prices and wages (their assigned value), which are influenced and further determined by supply and demand. A market economy is not planned or controlled by a central administrative authority. It is free of imperial or governmental influence, a monopoly, or collusion among commercial institutions as well as other external interferences. Freedom for the value of things to fluctuate, move up or down, is based on open-market conditions.

Karl Polanyi, an anthropological economist, feels that the role of markets and their freedom to self-regulate by influencing financial outcomes was marginalized in ancient economies because they were simply too far apart from each other. Essentially, the markets themselves were localized and insulated; so the ability to affect conditions across areas was severely limited. He feels that the prime commercial motivator, the profit incentive, did not play a significant role in economic systems of ancient civilizations.

Early societies were driven more by the establishment and maintenance of social relationships than by wealth accumulation via self-interested individuals. Polanyi in his researched observations concludes that the transactions of early humans, the primeval urge to trade, were conducted to enhance their social standing, social assets, and social claims as opposed to personal gain.[50] He based his hypothesis on his examination of tribal or clan societies, where everything is shared collectively, and hence the maintenance of social ties is paramount. Against this societal structure all obligations in the community are reciprocal and hence personal gain does not come into the value equation. The exchange of equal worth between members of the society is the chief responsibility, with the failure to reciprocate resulting in a loss of status and possibly extrication from the group with little prospect of survival in the environment by oneself. The idea of acting in a way where a personal value advantage was achieved in the exchange process would be detrimental to one's social obligations. All were expected to behave in the best interests of the community as a whole. Polanyi deduced that the principal activities of early humans as hunters or gatherers were for the mutual benefit of the whole group in which they lived and not for individual or immediate family enrichment. As they were dependent on the tribe for survival, the safety in numbers theory, they would do nothing to upset this conditional necessity. Implied trust and confidence with strict allegiance to the continued existence of the group would forbid them from acting independently, to have more than their rightful share of the collective environmental bounty—all was to be shared. Redistribution in tribal societies was determined by the chief or headman. Hence, wealth in the ancient world was explicitly controlled. It was not subject to free-market conditions—supply and demand.

This is an interesting concept, as the idea of globalization as rooted in the commercialized exchange for profit incentive may not have been produced by the connectivity of individuals and institutions across the globe that we see today, and the phenomenon is in fact truly a modern principle. Perhaps, the rationalized connection linking ancient cross-territorial trade to the wider form of capitalism is a mistaken presumption. If societies in ancient times were truly collective with the socially accepted premises to share the traded fruits of their labors with such dispersal delegated to an authority as Polanyi suggests then the notion of globalization as rooted in ancient trade is a wrong conclusion. However, if "capitalism is a better instrument for the creation of wealth than it is for the equitable distribution of its benefits,"[51] and if the prime goal of the ancient exchange system was a fair and even-handed distribution of the trading exercise among a group, the emergence of the commercial private merchant and the cross-territorial trading initiative would never have evolved. We see, however, from historic records that early trade did in fact produce such players and that although they often plied their trade under the authority granted by regional overlords (i.e., the designation of the Kings Highway or Royal Road from Tanis in Egypt across the Sinai through Jordan to Damascus, Syria, and onto the Euphrates as well as other points in the East) who either taxed or participated in their profit endeavors, they were not economically equal—the crevasse between the poor and the rich has always existed. The great pharaohs of Egypt, the early emperors of China, the historic kings of Europe, and the numerous territorial lords of the old world knew they had to placate their citizens by providing for their economic means of survival, a quasi-collective imperative, to retain their wealth, social power, and control. The idea that civilizations developed in antiquity were motivated to share for the common equal good does not seem to be sustainable, as social status and prosperity are intertwined. Notwithstanding cross-territorial war as an agent of wealth accumulation, cross-territorial trade was the next best campaign to attain riches and social affluence in both the old and modern worlds.

PART II

Trade

A Historical Perspective

When businesspeople talk about history, many discussions cite Henry Ford, the great U.S. automobile industrialist, who is credited for his statement, "History is bunk." Many senior executives echo Ford's remark in their strategic planning and decision-making circles as they proclaim the need to chart new courses of action, reminding their shareholders and organization teams that the world is changing and so must they. But if one takes the time to review his entire statement given in an interview published in the *Chicago Tribune* on May 25, 1916,[1] his words demonstrate that we can understand nothing except through the application of the surrounding context. What he actually said was, "History is more or less bunk. It's tradition. We don't want tradition. We want to live in the present and the only history that is worth a tinker's damn is the history we make today."[2] Ford's commentary was given in the middle of World War I and his reference was to the dangerous devotion to the customs of the past preventing one from grappling with the present environment. He was pointing that European leaders knew history, yet they still blundered into war and their mistake was relying on tradition as a guide to the future. Ford's point was that beliefs and customs based on ritual thinking is the problem, not history. Ford would probably agree that if one studies history, one would learn something valuable. Still many quotes negate looking backward before proceeding forward.

John Nance Garner, vice president of the United States from 1933 to 1941, the period just preceding World War II, purportedly exclaimed that the lessons of history are worth a pitcher of warm piss. The value of studying history is even questioned in our modern cultural music, as evidenced by the song *History Will Teach Us Nothing*, made popular by Sting in 1987 from the album *Nothing Like the Sun*.[3] On the other hand,

Confucius wrote, "Study the past, if you would define the future."[4] This profound observation was echoed by Winston Churchill centuries later when he stated, "The further backward you look, the further forward you see."[5] The study of history is like looking in a car's series of mirrors. Unless one plans on backing up they are rarely useful. But if one wants to pass a car ahead of them as the driver negotiates the competitive traffic conditions around him they become useful environmental assessment tools, as the combined overhead and side rearview mirrors contribute to a 360° view and a safer, more carefully orchestrated future maneuver. Today's global managers need an introduction to business history as it provides a valuable foundation of reference to understand and appreciate the framework that the modern world is constructed on. How the world commercial system developed, the players involved, and the political, social, and economic nuances it handled over time provide the clues to handling today's complex global environment. While history does not always repeat itself its lessons provide for a better understanding for the managers of tomorrow. The Chinese have a saying: "If you don't have an old man, go out and buy one." The past is a valuable alley for appreciating the present. It is the parchment on which the history of today is written.

A historical business view of the ancient world reveals that many areas of the globe were in fact touched by the trading practices of ancient merchants and they all had a hand in establishing a number of the guiding principles that modern-day managers continue to utilize. Today's managers work in the modern era of globalization. To successfully lead their far-flung geographical enterprises, they must become good global citizens. They would be well advised to heed the 1,400-year-old refrain attributed to Socrates when he declared he was neither an Athenian nor a Greek but should be considered a citizen of the world.[6] The Greek-inspired philosophical idea that while one's feet should be planted in a specific country, one's eyes should survey the world shows us that, even today, managerial knowledge and understanding must encompass a broad view. It needs to include a historical perspective of how trade relationships around the world developed as it is upon such prior associations that the current ones will be based. How commercial models, trade systems, and business approaches were first used provides a platform of appreciation on which the current principles can be better constructed and used.

CHAPTER 3

The Beginning of Recorded Trade

Before examining the beginning of recorded trade as practiced by specific recognized civilizations around the world, it is important to keep in mind that the present continues to reflect the past. All of the essential products and services that people required to survive, grow, and prosper have always, and will continue to be, supplied, through the process of exchange. This system devised by mankind has existed from the beginning of human time on earth. Having begun with the simple activity called barter in antiquity, one thing for another, the mechanism man devised to satisfy his mutual need satisfaction continues today. This coordinated integrated effort over history has risen to a level, an unmatched scope and scale, not seen before; and we call it globalization. The ancient exchange between two people has morphed into, and been replaced by, groups of commercial institutions called multinational corporations (MNCs) or the more refined term transnational corporations, the actions of which are controlled or regulated to a degree by national governments and states acting in unison. These global-reach organizations are also influenced by the mandates of the consuming worldwide public as well as nongovernmental and religious bodies.

Before the advent of the word globalization, the term applied to a growing worldwide commercialization was international business. Before that, it was called by varying regional names including conjoined land masses or bodies of shared waters like the Mediterranean. Prior to such geographical classification jargon, it was referred to as cross-territorial trade where such demarcations existed even earlier as exchange with foreigners.

When Did Trade Begin?

Whichever expression is used, the process itself, trade across distances, began epochs before formal kingdoms or nation-states existed. Archaeologists figure out how past civilizations lived from a variety of unearthed sources, sometimes the tiniest of clues that reveal the relationships ancient people had with each other. They continue to uncover artifacts from excavation sites that indicate that the material composition, the skilled construction of relics, or both could not have been locally obtained; they had to come from territories not just adjacent but from areas requiring their transport from faraway lands.

It is difficult to arrive at a specific period in human history when long distance cross-regional trade first began. Researchers are continuously discovering signs in digs that suggest exchanges of land-based resources occurred earlier than once thought. Using more sophisticated DNA analysis from an archeological site off the Isle of Wright, scientists have determined that wheat was imported into the British Isles 2,000 years before there was evidence of domestic cultivation. Deposits of sediment cores from the excavation site date the find to 8,000 years ago, while agriculture was unknown in Britain until 6,000 years ago.[1] The discovery proposes that trade between English hunter–gatherers and the Neolithic farmers of southern Europe, where the crop was already grown, occurred via some form of an aquatic vessel as this would have been the only way that wheat could have reached these isolated communities. The only other method of transport, the wind carrying seeds across such distance, has been strongly discounted. It is also interesting to note that although a period of 2,000 years separated the importation of wheat and its local cultivation, the idea contributes to the first leg of the product lifecycle theory of economic progression wherein products are initially imported and that at a future time they may be produced locally via a learning curve, which in modern terminology is called licensing.

A tool-making workshop, with artifacts dating all the way back to 25,000 BCE, was unearthed at Grotta Sant Angelo in the Abruzzo region of Italy.[2] It has been surmised that such an extensive workplace would not have been constructed just in ancient times for just local supply but for the production of implements for distribution on a wider scale—being sent to distant locations. Obsidian mined in Corsica during the late-Neolithic period, circa 6000 to 3000 BCE, has been found hundreds of kilometers away. Its transport over such distance could only be attributable to the resource being valued and exchanged for something in return.[3] An archaeological team recently uncovered evidence of an ancient harbor on the Red Sea that was used for international trade. While records from around 2490 BCE indicated that the Egyptians traded down the coast of Africa and into the African interior to a land called Punt, the physical evidence of the location of their embarkation remained a mystery. This discovery confirms the Egyptians' ability to take long sea voyages as scholars were traditionally skeptical of such consideration.[4]

Scientists in Denmark have concluded that recently unearthed glass blue beads were buried alongside women's bodies from the Bronze Age. They were originally crafted in an ancient royal workshop for King Tutankhamun as similar globules have been found in his solid gold death mask as well as in the inlay of the plaited false beard placed on him at burial. Given the short reign of the Egyptian boy king, who died in 1323 BCE, it would place the voyage of these artifacts to this northern European region some 3,400 years ago. Such a find raises the possibility that contact between these very distant regions occurred thousands of years ago. Historic scholars feel that perhaps such rare exotic glass ornaments were brought by emissaries as gifts or tribute to another kingdom or they were traded by merchants traveling in search of bartered treasure. In ancient times, the opening of trade routes between regions was first accomplished by envoys or agents of the imperial household. They arranged for the mutual safe conduct of merchants, appointed by rulers to conduct business outside their territories, who would follow. This very old method of new market entry, via introduction at a foreign palace of rare and exotic items from the home country, is a market penetration principle still practiced today. Those who had access to the royal court would in turn wish to emulate what they saw the monarchs having, approving of, or both, as it raised their stature in the kingdom. Products entering a new market would therefore carry the prestige of these initial users. In turn, others just below their social stature would imitate them, and so on. The idea is to entice customers called influential first movers, those at the top of the consuming pyramid, to become patrons of imported products. They in turn act as inspirational motivators for the next tier of customers with each succeeding level of the population following the lead of those above them as distribution is spread out and the market is totally saturated.

A simple artifact, like a metal coin, can also act as an indicator of very early cross-territorial trade across vast distances. A tiny copper coin dated to the Iron Age, almost 2,300 years ago, was found in Saltford, a town between Bristol and Bath in Southwest England. At such time no forms of coinage were being used in the British Isles. The engraved markings on this ancient regionally used medium of exchange value bears an image of a horse's head on one side and the Carthaginian goddess *Tanit* on the other. The find suggests that merchant trading links between Britain and the originally founded Phoenician North African port of Carthage may have existed thousands of years ago. Only eight of these coins have ever been found and interestingly all were discovered on ancient trade routes.[5]

It is also prudent to keep in mind as the beginning of recorded trade is presented that the exchange process contributed to the advancement of the civilizations profiled in this chapter. As previously alluded to, archaeologist Charles Standish offers three factors affecting the development of people into civilized societies. He lists war, regional trade and specialized labor as factors "that keep coming up as predecessors to civilization."[6] The inclusion of the exchange imperative across territories that not only included indigenous products but the cross-offering of unique craft skills and abilities of particular workforces, made it necessary for people to form group associations, the precursor for socialization and hence civil advancement.

Civilizations and Recorded Trade

The four cradles of civilization (the Indus region of India, the Mesopotamian plane of Asia, the Nile River in northern Egypt, and the Yangtze river basin in China) created "rising empires [that] imposed a stability that occasionally resulted in greater interaction between states and peoples ... the most striking example [of which] is trade."[7] Traveling on the back of the exchange initiative is where people were first brought together. Their interaction resulted in environments where "ideas were tested, challenged, and in many instances changed."[8] Trade became a conduit for the birth and advancement of civilization.

The catalyst for such was brought about by the exchange via commerce, which was orchestrated by merchants who introduced new concepts to the lands where they traded and who carried them back to their home societies. Many scholars reason that the collection of peoples in selected areas of the world—that is, the cradles of civilization, also including the Mesoamerica, the Andes region in the Western Hemisphere, and Crete—possessed distinguishing features that suggested they all had independent origins (a rebuke perhaps to the Atlantis legend as the prime purveyor of other civilizations). However, those civilizations located close to each other, such as Mesopotamia and Egypt, soon came in contact with their respective rulers and the land around them with each civilization seeking to learn as much as possible about the present or potential resources to be found in its neighbors' territories.[9] The human desire to acquire the new and different was achievable either by war or by trade, with the latter imperative harboring a more lasting and less violent impression.

Urban growth, which spawned pockets of expanded communities, was built around trading centers whose administrators were admonished to create stability and permanence—a key requirement of the merchant state and a necessary ingredient in the establishment of the social progression into civilizations. The commercialization process or the exchange of alternating embedded goods between people may have been the prime component that helped knit together an area to an intercontinental community. Trade fostered the emergence of civilization centers and propelled the development of societies as opposed to a stagnated group of independent lands with limited growth potential. The creation of the first socialized locations such as villages or towns, the early vestiges of cities, tended to bring people together for worship to pay group homage to their ancient gods and later to pay allegiance along with tribute in product or service to regional rulers. Such gatherings from the fields and woods to a common stage ground soon evolved into trading pilgrimages as agricultural produce and hunted animals not consumed for basic sustenance—the surplus of their life's daily activities—could be exchanged or bartered for goods from those who pursued and offered varied items. This may have been the beginning of the first division of labor leading to the concept of comparative abilities. From such beginnings, specialized artisans developed the ancient field of pottery making, tool crafting, and creating other useful farm implements.

The Western World

Mesopotamia: The Earliest Society

Mesopotamia is an ancient Greek term, which describes a geographical designated location. It literally means *the land between two rivers*. Historians and anthropologists use it to describe the region between the Tigris and Euphrates rivers (the Mesopotamian Plain) and it is the site of the first primitive written records dating about 8000 BCE. It took until 3500 BCE, however, for the symbols to become coherent markings composed of 1,200 different characters, representing numbers and identifying names and objects of personal possession. The ancient Sumerians, who lived in the region, called their system of writing cuneiform and it was created on clay tablets. The earliest use of such written language was to record the quantity of cows, bolts of cloth, simple tools, and other implements—record keeping. Such personal property or named asset identification name was listed with assigned numbered quantities. It had two basic uses: to assign the property to the rightful owner and to assist in the exchange process between a buyer and a seller through bartering. A system of ownership and the ability to qualify and quantify objects being exchanged is at the root of the commercial process. Transactional contracts used such designations to establish the legal arrangements between parties. Those schooled in ancient literacy, known for being skilled in the practice of accounting or recording keeping at such time, provided a valued service to royalty and commoners alike. Such scribes were given a special status in early societies. They were perhaps the first professional white-collar workers, the forerunner of the modern-day accountant profession, as the majority of ancient populations were delegated to manual labor (blue-collar jobs). Today's commercial contracts exhibit many of the rules first used by these ancient scribes. The parties to legal instruments are always stated as the rightful owners of the property to be exchanged while the descriptions of the transactional property are carefully defined and quantified in order for contracts to be valid. Out of this region came a ruler, Hammurabi, who is best known for his monolith code regarding family, land, and commerce (including the ownership and exchange of slaves). It is the oldest known code of secular laws in 1800 BCE. One of the chief tenets of this first set of laws governing society was severe punishments for purposeful malfeasance or fraud in the exchange of property, both land and items (see Chapter 9).

The early Mesopotamian civilization in the Near East, established in 3500 BCE, was primarily made up of agricultural products, the trade in which was essentially local. But the artistic or skill-induced products of the era were commercialized on a broader transcontinental basis via far-flung networks of interregional connections. Objects made from precious and base metals, semiprecious stones, hardwoods, and other exotic raw materials were carried to Afghanistan, the Indus valley, eastern segments of the Mediterranean, and even central Anatolia with merchant traders returning from such destinations with bartered items of equal creative content and design. An intermediary basic unit of value for transactions in the form of silver strands or coils of a standard weight, as opposed to goods, was introduced in the ancient Mesopotamia region around 2100 BCE. By snipping off measured segments of the standardized metal piece made of silver, the proper amount of worth could be established between buyer and seller. This value apparatus combined a medium of exchange with a measurement device. This ancient system to communize transactions between diverse societies based on a commonly accepted denominator of value, which could also be quantified, was the first practical financial step in globalizing trade.

During the Assyrian and Babylonian realms of 1900 BCE, trade by authorized crown merchants dominated the cross-territorial process but it began to shift to self-employed entrepreneurs in the latter half of the period. The introduction of intermediaries to transactions as opposed to two familiar singular parties increased the expansion of the trading process between distant nonassociated individuals while contributing to the formation of the profit incentive in the procedure, value to be made on the transactional or distribution supply system as opposed to that inherent in the property being exchanged.

Birth of the Merchant Intermediary

Cross-territorial trade in this ancient civilization, and perhaps repeated in other societies of the times, was made possible by the use of carriers who moved between distant locations in return for service payments.

Therefore, two principals wishing to engage in the exchange of divisible goods but who were unwilling to travel and personally associate with each other would utilize the services of an intermediary, a courier. A bit of trust entered into the process as both the courier and the principal on the receiving end needed to be motivated (offered further inducement) to complete the trade transaction and not abscond with the goods they held at any point. To assure completion, the courier would make a fixed finite number of trips between the principals carrying loads of ever-increasing values, augmenting the trust factor and adding to the profit incentive. In the first period, couriers received a rent or fee based on such values from both buyer and seller but as the operation grew, these middlemen began to trade on their own account, increasing their utility and flexibility, as they did not have to wait to be engaged but could take advantage of changes in trade patterns for specific merchandise. They also began to recognize that a suitable profit could be made in the exchange intermediary process and that their knowledge as well as their long-distance risk taking was a valued enterprise unto itself. From these two considerations, the idea of the impersonal middleman merchant was born. Sometimes, these trade couriers would invite a group of investors to put up capital to be placed at their disposal, as opposed to goods in the original scheme. Such arrangements colloquially then known as a money-bag or *naruqqu* contract would be established, the forerunner of the modern venture capital model. The concept was born out of the idea that these ambitious commercial explorers did not always possess the money to fund their trading expeditions that the monarchy held; hence, such capital-raising techniques via trade partnerships offered to interested parties were made popular. Technically, it was referred to as a *naruqqum*, named after the legally recognized document creating them.

These agreements contained precise shareholder rights and recited the obligations of all the parties involved. With the expectation that protracted journeys over vast stretches of land and repetitive trading exchanges needed to take place to secure a profit, the arrangement was to last for extended periods, normally 7 to 12 years was anticipated and some were even written for longer terms. Such early documents even provided for the appointment of professional managers to oversee the multiple exchange process with periodic reporting to the partners along with the strict maintenance of records for partner inspection. Both concepts were employed by public corporations throughout the eras of globalization that followed. Thousands of years later, the corporate capitalism of the ancient world was enlarged by the creation in 1602 of the Dutch East India Company (Vereenigde Oost-Indische Compagnie, or VOC), which used the same principles of ownership and managerial construction that the ancient merchants had created. The VOC, as it was colloquially referred to in the 1600s, is considered the world's first large joint-stock company. Created under the auspices of the Dutch Republic, the state obligated the numerous trading companies created to take individual benefit of the Asian trade boom to merge into a single commercial organization or their trading privileges would be withdrawn.

The objective was to create a mercantilist-induced monopoly with private participants sharing in the profits without the state's interference in return for a modest tax dividend. However, the governmental certification of the newly created entity—the right of the state to grant a charter, the legal right to organize and operate as a public company (as well as the financial return due the granting authority), and a tax on profit—provided the basis for the modern incorporation process (see Chapter 7).

The companies placed in this new category of commercial enterprise, while able to control their capital investment and far-flung foreign activities, were required to adhere to uniform guidelines and practices, a precursor of the state's role in regulating private enterprise. This was a bridge model for nations to integrate private institutions into their imperial global territorial conquests and colonial policy as well as impose rules of conduct over their operational procedures. The concept also served as a blueprint for future relationships between governments and private enterprises. It is also a principle used by transitional economies, albeit in reverse, dismantling communist-style state-owned institutions and moving toward privatization.

The emergence of South Arabian civilizations on the desert margins of modern Yemen around 900 BCE was based on their mercantile ability to carry frankincense, myrrh, and other prized spices to consumers in Mesopotamia and on to, via intercontinental trade merchants, a wider audience (see Chapter 5 and the subsection on the incense and spice trade). Such trade connections introduced the advanced ideas of the north, which included a version of the Canaanite alphabet along with religious symbols and sculptural styles. It allowed this ancient civilization to advance beyond its limited capacity and it was the trading initiative that brought new ideas and the knowledge of others to them.

The early land caravans constructed by these traveling cross-continental merchant agents were the predecessor of East–West trade, which is later referred to as the Spice and Silk Roads. These early merchant traders formed commercial colonies at major trading stations along the routes they had traveled that became self-governing *karums* (independent municipalities), some of which were instrumental in forming a governmental entity that later evolved into city-states.

Trade across Persia was mainly carried out by transient merchants moving from east to west through the early Incense Road, and later, the designated Spice and Silk routes. The Persian Empire itself was a primitive station for such business activities with numerous conflicting trading criteria until Darius the Great brought reforms to the commercial process. During his reign, a carefully constructed system of common weights and measures was introduced as well as the use of coin as a medium of exchange to replace the difficult and cumbersome barter structure. Up until then the kingdom was beholden to numerous imported measurement systems and confusing foreign value methods, which made cross-regional trade difficult. These two innovations in the transactional system helped unify the population while economically propelling the Persian Empire into a stronger civilization.

Egypt and Near Eastern Trade

While Egypt, in the days of the almighty pharaohs, expanded its monarchy on the back of its warrior armies, the continuing strength of its empires was based on the exchange process as war victories secured trading corridors into conquered lands and those bordering them. The early Egyptian economic policy was akin to a command-type structure equally employed by the overlords of most ancient kingdoms. The state in the personage of the pharaoh was ruled by divine authority. The countrywide authority of the royal house under kings and queens continued even under the domination of Egypt by the Achaemenid Persian Empire and well into the post-Hellenic period after Alexander the Great conquered the land. Upon Alexander's death, the Ptolemaic system was installed, and the Egyptian economy remained one of the most controlled economies in ancient times. It resembled centuries-later communist societies in the Soviet Union and post-Mao China, which planned all labor activities. The city of Alexandria was primarily founded for regional commercial reasons, that is, to take the place of Tyre in Phoenicia, which the Macedonian army had destroyed. The massive harbor at Alexandria was built to accommodate the extensive merchant fleet used to export the agricultural surplus of Egypt provided by the Nile River. During the Ptolemic era, Egypt was the world's supreme grain merchant, a position it retained for centuries, culminating with it for being the chief provider of grain to the Roman Empire. Agents of the king administered the exportation of millions of bushels every year, which in turn were routed through the offshore distribution centers in Rhodes and Delos and from such intermediate locations to international markets around the globe.

Almost all Egyptian land was decreed royal land, and only with governmental permission could one even fell a tree, breed cattle, or alter the selection of cultivated crops in the field. Royal lands were let out with property leases that often included the leasing of cattle, seed, and tools. In return for the privilege of working such lands, farmers had to plant whatever the yearly official schedule required while also sowing each planted crop meticulously as specified by authoritative planners as to season and even specific dates. All resource use was recorded and decisions as to their expenditures (economic use) were state directed. This command economic system did not account for the individual domestic needs of the local farmers, laborers, or artisans, nor did it recognize the idea of the indigenous marketplace to set supply and demand values. Farmers faced severe punishment if they planted without permission, while craftsmen were limited in the moving of their activities to another district. All land was periodically surveyed and all livestock and crops constantly inventoried with precision, while the conduct of all business operations was administered by legions of royal inspectors.

The weaving industry was carefully monitored to assure that all looms were working efficiently. Precious olive-oil production was totally in the hands of the state, and it was illegal for individuals to own, no less operate, a press for their private benefit. Even the quasi-luxury spice industry (as certain spices were required for food preservation) was supervised, with factory workers strip-searched at the end of their production shifts while the raw material supply network was closely guarded. Barley for beer distilling could only be purchased from the state, and the brewer operated under license with profits going to the royal house. In essence, all essential industries were state monopolies, and those outside of such objective control were subject to heavy taxation. Commercial enterprises paid not only a percentage of their sales but also were assessed on their asset holdings. The exchange of salt was taxed while a tax on dike construction and pasture grazing land was required. Those operating public baths were charged one-third of their revenue while fishermen gave up 25 percent of their catch and wineries paid 16 percent of their sales. High import duties to protect local industries were utilized with foreign olive oil subject to a 50 percent tariff and then only saleable to the state at a fixed price, the result of which was limited competition with the locally produced inferior grades. Foreign merchants desirous of doing business in the kingdom had to first exchange their foreign metal-based values for the locally acceptable coins to engage in local commercial transactions.

While the economy, and hence the market condition, was ostensibly controlled to benefit and supplement the financial well-being of the royal house, the public image portrayed was to sustain the welfare of the common man by protecting the kingdom from famine, which, short of war, was the most destructive social force in the ancient world. By planning all output and placing all assets and labor used under a common, unified, and directed system, the result was a monopolistic nationalization of the means of production under the guise of state socialism. A similar rationale was introduced centuries later by those promoting communism.

The need to control cross-border trade and promote export was necessary to implement this command economy. The King's Highway was a testament to such processes and was enlarged to stretch across the Sinai Peninsula, through Jordan, into Syria (Damascus and Palmyra), and onto the Euphrates. Its outer, eastern edges later developed into the Silk Road (see Figure 3.1).

The ancient Egyptians engaged in cross-territorial trade with their neighbors that offered them rare and exotic resources not found locally.

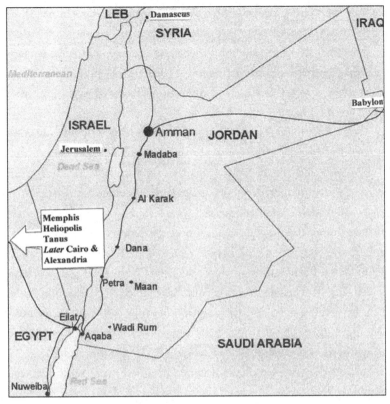

Figure 3.1 The King's Highway

They went in search of gold and incense from Nubia and they imported oil jugs from Palestine. The Egyptians even outsourced the production of pottery from artisans in the land of Canaan. Quality timber not found in Egypt was brought from Byblos while the North African area of Punt offered gold, aromatic resins, ebony, ivory, and a host of wild primates that amused and excited local audiences. Tin and copper for the domestic manufacturing of bronze were taken from Anatolia. The much prized blue stone lapis lazuli, which adorned the jewelry of wealthy Egyptians, was shipped from distant Afghanistan. From the Mediterranean, olive oil produced in Greece and Crete made its way to the ports of Egypt. The bartered exchange offered by Egyptian merchants consisted of grain from the rich Nile agricultural basin, uniquely crafted finished goods like linen, papyrus, carved glass, and stone objects along with products that passed through their middlemen trading activities, which originated in other neighboring regions. This ancient society was fully engaged in the import–export process, as their intercontinental trade spanned three continents: Africa, Asia Minor (Turkey), and Asia (China).

Being in a strategic geographical position the Egyptians were perhaps the initial go-between facilitating the exchanges of commodities from East to West and the first users of routes from Baghdad to Kashmir that ended up in China.

Thousands of years later, these routes would be used by the governing decedents of Alexander the Great and the Roman Empire.

Not only did the Egyptians use the 4,000-mile Nile River as an irrigated agricultural basin but it was also their chief merchant water highway for their domestic economy and for developing foreign trade routes off their shores. Recent archeological findings dating back to 3,800 years support the contention that ocean trade was practiced in the Red Sea region by the Egyptians. Remnants at dig sites in the Wadi Gawasis have yielded ship timbers, deck beams, and hull planks—as well as limestone anchors, steering oars, and hacks of marine rope—all fittings for deep seagoing ships. Such relics may help to give factual credence, previously thought to be a mere legend like Eldorado in the American southwest or Atlantis off the entrance to the Mediterranean—Egypt's trade with the mysterious Red Sea realm called Punt. The land of Punt was considered by the Egyptians as a place of exotic treasures, described as an "emporium of goods for both kings and gods."[10] Thousands of years later, a similar reference would be made by Marco Polo as he described the riches of the East in terms of opulent products the West had ever seen in his best-selling book based on his 17 years in the service of Kublai Khan, the grandson of Genghis Khan and the ruler of China.

The allure of Punt for the Egyptians indicates that it not only was a producer of rare resources—such as the incense known as *antyu* and myrrh resin, along with ivory, ebony, and gum resin—but also possessed a strategic position, which allowed trading ventures with the surrounding area for the skins of, as well as the living specimens of, giraffes, panthers, cheetahs, and baboons. Even dwarfs and pigmies were taken for the amusement of the pharaoh's court. The exact location of Punt is still a mystery but is approximately placed on the African eastern coast and possibly south of Sudan or lower Ethiopia. Punt had its own trading empire that certainly reached into the heart of the continent. The trade process allowed Egypt to benefit without directly exploring these areas,

enabled interior tribes trading routes, and connected such primitive societies to the outside world, which created a stepping stone of connected
exchange across a good part of the continent. Through these separate
but linked geographical locations, a commercial web was established
that enabled ancient societies to extend themselves with the export of
their resources and receive the beneficial resources of foreign exploration without actually visiting them or relying on war and colonization
of other territories to achieve similar goals. This is an early example of
the modern extreme global value chain using intermediary parties and
nations.

The Egyptians also recognized the need to develop better methods to
support the expanding commercial activity that went beyond the mere
exchange between knowledgeable parties, a reasonably efficient method
when mostly basic necessities were first traded. When activities surpassed
ordinary daily life, commodity exchanges spurred the development of the
middlemen or merchants for such transactions.

These commercial agents used ostraca (i.e., small pieces of pottery
or other materials on which short inscriptions can be found) to record
mundane rudimentary records of transactions among distinctly nonroyal
people, the general population. These agents acted like public scribes
(the forerunner of notaries) to authenticate and validate transactions that
could, if need be, be lawfully adjudicated before royal dispensers of justice,
itself a rudimentary court system for commercial complaints. Through
a royal decree, standardization of measurements for common weight
and dimension was introduced, for the bushel and other containers as
previous vessels for the transfer of commodities weighed irregularly and
scales were scarce. Precious metals in a fixed weight were struck, thereby
creating a common intermediary of acceptable value (the forerunner of
payment in specie). Even a code of commercial goodwill and honesty was
proclaimed in the name of Egypt's revered sun deity:

> Do not move the scales, do not change (altar) the weights nor (and)
> do not diminish the fractions (parts) of the measure (bushel) ...
> Do not make (create) a bushel of twice its size (that contains two),
> For then you are headed for the abyss (lest you will near the abyss).
> The bushel is the Eye of Re. It abhors (loathes) him who trims
> (defrauds).[11]

As early Egyptian society recognized the need to admonish those in commercial trade to do business with integrity, the merchants of the day also introduced the concept of credit while laying the basis for the modern legal doctrine of replevin (i.e., recovery of goods in another's possession). If payment was delayed until the other party could produce or deliver the required value, then one party could recover back its own goods first delivered in the transaction. Such a concept is noted in the following translation:

> The scribe Amennakht, your husband, took a coffin from me and said: I shall give you the ox as payment. But he has not given it to this day. I told Pa'akhet. He said: Let me have moreover a bed and I shall bring you the ox when it is full grown grow. I gave him the Bed. Niethre the coffin nor the bed (were paid for) to this day. If you (want to) give the ox, let somebody bring it. (But) if there is no ox, let somebody bring (back) the bed and coffin.[12]

Even in this period, loans were made between private individuals. For negligible amounts, an oral declaration was sufficient but for larger amounts rudimentary language was placed on evidentiary materials like pot shards or clay tablets, as exemplified by the following inscription of an ancient "I Owe You" (IOU) or an informal document acknowledging debt and not a negotiable instrument on display in the Victoria and Albert Museum in London, UK:

> Owed by Apahte, son of Patai; 30 pieces of silver.
> Written in the year 28[?], on the 30th of Mesore.

Many of the commercial credit principles and even the instruments of debt itself in today's world were developed in antiquity and represented part of the exchange imperative that mankind always has required.

In the centuries that followed the great Egyptian Empire, the caravan trade progressed across the region using the pathways first plied on the royal roads, as these routes came to be known as they carried the pharaoh's exchange agents. Some of these roads like the King's Highway (connecting the biblical Jordan kingdoms of Edom, Moab, and

Ammon) were traversed by land caravans traveling from Egypt, Sinai, Jordan, Syria, and ending at Euphrates. However, the cross-continental trading imperative stretched further east through India and into China while also moving west into the Levant corridor (Mediterranean and Aegean Seas) while merging southern routes germinating in the Red Sea and Arabian territories. Many interconnecting routes provided for much wider territories to be incorporated in the trading chain.

Early African Trade

Most anthropological studies have determined that numerous ancient indigenous African tribal societies traded with each other. They bartered for each other's localized resources and craft skills in the adjacent territories settled by them. While there is no doubt that these ancient tribal kingdoms made war on each other, as opposing rulers sought to gain the wealth of others, it was trade that brought them the greatest sustainable material reward. Their leaders quickly learned that the fortunes of war could easily turn with the previous winner vanquished in the next conflict. Commerce was a better alternative. This was especially true when the involvement of people living on the continent in long-distance merchant trade linking them to the wider global commercial chain began to take place.

The tribes that inhabited ancient West Africa south of the Sahara Desert embraced caravan trade with the Berbers of North Africa, who in turn moved merchandise into the Mediterranean basin. These early African tribal leaders tended to be conciliators rather than warriors. Gold from the region was exchanged for something even more prized: salt from the Sahara as extracted from both mining and evaporation. Salt was a multifunctional necessity in antiquity used as a flavoring agent, a food preservative, and for retaining body moisture (see Chapter 5's subsection on salt for an in-depth presentation on this first global commodity).

The ancient sub-Saharan African city of Timbuktu was one of the greatest cross-continental trading centers for more than 400 years. It was located on the southern edge of the Sahara about eight miles (13 km) north from a bend in the Niger River in what is today the West African nation of Mali. The city area rose to prominence in the late 13th century;

it began as a seasonal camp used by Tuareg nomads during their treks to north and south of the continent. North African merchants who plied their main trade across the West to East coastal commercial arena began their transactions with local miners who extracted salt in the desert, carrying this valuable commodity to the city, where intermediaries would transport it on the river to a world hungry for the resource. In exchange, gold was offered and the wealth of the city attracted rising commercial interests, causing it to develop as a strategically important location on the trans-Saharan caravan route. Merchants from Wadan, Tuwat, Ghudamis, and Agula mingled with those traveling from Morocco gathered to exchange gold and slaves as well as North African clothes and horses for the Saharan salt of Taghaza.

Timbuktu became well known as a religious and educational site due to the expansion of Islam, which itself was due to the power and prestige of the Muslim merchants who made the city their home, even though the Tuareg ruling their desert nomadic empire continued to control the city. At the end of the Mandingo Askia dynasty, which itself lasted from 1493 to 1591, the metropolitan area was the intellectual and spiritual capital in southwest Africa, rivaling other great cities of the era around the world. It housed the prestigious Koranic University with its scholars who had trained in the holy city of Mecca as well as Cairo, thereby attracting students from all over the continent. Besides funding a renowned educational institution, the wealthy merchant class saw the erecting of three great mosques. Even the Mali sultan, Mansa Musa, constructed a tower for the magnificent Great Mosque of Djenne, the Djingereyber, as well as a royal residence for himself and other municipal offices to assist in the administration of the city founded on trade.

The city as a prime trading center declined in strategic geographical value for goods transiting the East–West cross-continental African land highway when the Portuguese showed that it was easier, faster, and more profitable to place merchandise in the hulls of ships and to sail around the southern coast of Africa than travel the old desert caravan route that intersected Timbuktu. The city was further destroyed during the war between Morocco and Songhai. Today, the architectural remnants of its glorious days are long gone and it exists as a mud-built shady town with its connection to the modern world only accessible by camel and river boat.

Centuries later in the 1400s, Portuguese ships would begin to regularly arrive on the Ghana coast using the offshore Cape Verde Islands as a collection point for sub-Saharan goods. This opened an ocean channel for trade, especially in respect to human cargo destined initially for Europe and later the Western Hemisphere. Henry the Navigator, a Portuguese nobleman, recorded in his ship logs that on one of his first voyages in 1444 to presumably seek a sea route around the horn of Africa to the Far East he was able to exchange Moorish prisoners for African slaves. The western coast of Africa first visited by Henry would later be dubbed the *slave coast.*

On the eastern side of the continent, on the horn of Africa, the ancient city of Opone, situated on the Somali promontory (peninsula) jutting out into the Indian Ocean, was once a thriving port city. It served merchants from Phoenicia, Egypt, Greece, Persia, Yemen, Nabataea, and Azania as well as the Roman Empire. Its strategic positioning allowed it to serve as a rendezvous for cargo coming from the Far East as well as the south central interior of Africa. As such it was the prime entry point in the west for the spice trade (pepper, cinnamon, cloves, incense, etc.) coming from India, Indonesia, Malaysia, and the East Indies, and later silk from China. The city was a midway stopping point on the coastal route from the Mochan trading center of Azania to the Red Sea with caravans loaded with ivory and exotic animal skins.

Goods arriving in this ancient metropolis moved north to Yemen or Egypt and then into the Mediterranean, finding their way to southern European destinations. Although the most pronounced period of activity for Opone, today called Xaafun or Hafun, was from the first century BCE to the fifth century CE, archeological remnants indicated that the Mycenaean Kingdom of Greece traded in the region as far back as the 16th century BCE.

Early Arab Trading

Besides trade promoted by the Egyptian Empire, the Arab tribesmen of the Arabian peninsula were themselves carrying goods north to Syria in the summer and south to Yemen in the winter. Using goods from their home-ports to sell at destinations along the way, they returned with goods to both sell at home and reexport via their eastern ports across the Indian Ocean. The Meccans of this region often combined their commercial ventures in an ancient form of group-investment financing practiced long before the advent of Islam. Perhaps taking a cue from the earlier Assyrian agreement (naruqqum), these Arab merchants combined their fortunes with one or more of their colleagues and undertook the project of long-distance trade together and later divided the profit or loss among the partners according to a prearranged pattern. The rules governing such ventures were part of a well-established custom known as *musharaka*. Sometimes, the investing partners would employ an outside group of agents who, under contract, carried the goods and/or other mediums of exchange (money) to other trading groups. Upon return from the commercial expedition, they would offer an accounting to their principles and claim their share of the proceeds for such salaried service. This arrangement, called a *mudaraba*, is essentially an agreement between a financier and an entrepreneur; this forms the basis for one of the modern-day Islamic banking practices with the added introduction of an intermediary between these two such principles—the bank.

Such a modified form of mudaraba is used in conventional commercial banking in the form of profit-and-loss sharing investment accounts and financing deals. The presumable earned profit, based on the uncertain and unpredictable return on invested capital, replaces the concept of interest, a predetermined fixed return, which under Islamic law could be interpreted as usury, a forbidden practice. The principles of the Assyrian-based *naruqqum* agreement and the preagreed pattern inherent in the Meccan Arab *musharaka* arrangement are the forerunners of the modern-day venture capital partnerships while helping to construct the outline for the introduction of the public corporation centuries later. Capitalism with respect to the basic financing parameters may have been rooted in these Middle Eastern developed ancient forms of collaborative enterprise that enabled cross-territorial trade to be undertaken.

Petra: Jewel of the Nomadic Desert

To get a further feel for trade in the ancient Middle East and its effect on the people of the region, a profile of a historic settlement is helpful.

The uncovering of the ancient city of Petra in modern Jordan, built initially as a trading hub in the middle of the barren desert, is an excellent example of how trade can both construct and destroy even an advanced cosmopolitan center. Although the city is more than 2,000 years old, it was first discovered in 1812 by the Swiss traveler Jacob Burckhardt as it was hidden deep inside a mountain pass and guarded as a sacred holy place by desert tribes. Archaeologists at first wondered what allowed a nomadic Arabic tribe to achieve wealth, construct a major metropolis out of the harsh desert terrain, and exhibit a civilization whose language and technological virtuosity made it the most advanced society on earth at the time. The answer is its strategic geographical placement at the nexus of ancient trade routes, which connected the four corners of the ancient commercial compass. Over time, the merchants who plied their trade in the Petra region moved across routes also called the Frankincense Road or Incense Road and later the maritime trade route from South Arabia to India. Such land and sea commercial movements created the world-class capital of the Nabataean people, the city of Petra.

The legacy of this Nabataean society, the founders of Petra, includes their language as the basis for modern-day Arabic, while many of their other accomplishments have only recently come to light. Their construction projects in water conservation and transport (series of pipes, reservoirs, irrigation canals and dams) were the precursors of today's systems. The construction of a well-planned city with administrative-government-type structures along with residential and commercial areas, as well as farming and herding stations, was a prototype for the civilizations that followed. Libraries and places of learning flourished not only in the arts and literature but also in the sciences, which produced great strides in chemistry, whose formulas and compounds are still used today. The King's Highway, which passed through Petra, was traversed by the followers of Isis, Dushara, Jehovah, Jesus, and Mohammed with the message of such prophets being extended on the backs of their merchant followers.

An examination of the ruins indicates that it was a city that brought the greatest global artisans, architects, and knowledge carriers of the day to its gates. It was a truly international city, as its artifacts revealed that they have come from the Arabs, Greeks, Romans, India, and China over its 200-year life span.

So what attracted such engineering marvels to be erected, new inventions to emerge, great paintings and sculptures to be created, wondrous texts and writings to develop, and religious affiliations to congregate?

The simple conclusion is great affluence. But how was such wealth accumulated? As noted, it was due to the unique placement of the city at the nexus of Middle Eastern trade. The trade routes passing through and surrounding Petra were composed of caravans averaging 2,500 to 3,000 camels (the domestication of which came around 1000 BCE) stretching out over five miles. A single camel loaded with frankincense and myrrh (precious oil taken from trees) would yield an average profit in modern currency of more than $4,000, a virtual fortune in those days. Today, just before the entrance into the hidden city of Petra, stands the reminiscent camel caravan laden with trade goods and its merchant overseer carved into the mountainside thousands of years ago, a testament to the importance of the relationship in the building of the city.

Petra controlled this lucrative roadway, linking the exotic resources of distant lands with the prime consumers in the northern hemisphere. Merchants plying these trade routes not only made their homes in the Petra outpost but paid this dominant local controlling tribe a toll (forerunner of modern-day tariff-customs duty) to cross their territory. These payments could equal one-quarter of the merchandise value carried in the caravans. Such sums contributed to the city's wealth and power, which contributed to the construction of the metropolis and funded future trading endeavors. The money spent in the city by wealthy merchants created an economic boom that brought many immigrants to its gates.

While the imperial center of the Nabataean Empire was located in Petra the influence of this ancient tribe was widely felt across the northern Arabian region. The economic benefits that trade offered brought with it, to a large degree, social stability in an area fought with constant armed conflicts between the nomadic clans. Using their power to control the lucrative caravan routes, the Nabataeans entered into trade pacts with the various independent tribes giving each a share of the proceeds that cross-continental commerce produced. This financially viable wealth stream placated these often warring factions by unifying them toward a common purpose—keep the trade flowing.

The demise of Petra and the Nabataean Empire can be attributed to a number of circumstances. Technology in the form of more cost-efficient oceangoing vessels made overland transport from the East to the West obsolete. And, perhaps, as some archeologists surmise, a natural earthquake may have destroyed the city. But a certain historic event definitely contributed to the city's downfall. When Rome annexed its empire, it altered the trade routes in the area and chose to center its operations on the Mediterranean islands, which were much easier to control and administer. Petra became one of the first casualties of regional globalization trading changes, but its contribution to the growth of civilization is still evident in its ruins today. Throughout, history shifts in global economic dominance plague nations. Industrialized countries not only feared the loss of jobs to emerging nations but realized that other elements of their economic, social, and cultural strength could also evaporate. History tells us that great empires and even aspiring city-states are venerable to the relocation of the global commercial imperative.

The Phoenicians: The First Long-Distance Water Traders

Perhaps the earliest example of national trade as the complete if not sole driver of a domestic economy were the Phoenicians. As Steven Solomon recounts in his book, *Water: The Epic Struggle for Wealth, Power and Civilization*, throughout history, water was and still is "Earth's most potent agent of change"[13] and this natural resource has partnered with the exchange imperative throughout the history of mankind. The world's earliest empires in Mesopotamia, Egypt, and imperial China in the seventh century were constructed as hydraulic states, that is, land-oriented states that also used river irrigation and channels, as administered by a centralized authoritarian government, to grow and develop their respective civilizations.

However, it was foreign trade across open seas that empowered the growth of ancient societies, expanding their reign and influence beyond their borders. The ancient civilization of the Phoenicians was born in the northern end of the land of Canaan. They are considered the first large-scale maritime traders as their whole society was economically geared to a seagoing activity, a true export–import system. Not only did their trading empire encompass the entire Mediterranean, but they also ventured outside the Strait of Gibraltar in the west, sailing up to Atlantic, Scandinavia, and down along the western coast of Africa. Guided by the stars, these exploring entrepreneurs have even been said to have reached the coast of Brazil.[14]

The Phoenicians created commercial colonial outposts in the lands they touched; but unlike European explorers who came centuries later, they did not claim such territories as part of their political domain and put the inhabitants under their control. Instead, their colonialist policy was to establish trade stations along with merchandise marts and warehouses. Their sole interest was to export the native products they encountered and offer imports from foreign lands, an idea also practiced by the Chinese Star Fleet discussed in Gavin Menzies's book, as later presented. The breadth and reach of the Phoenician trading initiative allowed for the first inter-continental trading cartel stretching from Asia to the Middle East and into Europe. In 1200 BCE, this civilization held a virtual monopoly on the prized raw materials of the day, including tin, copper (to make bronze), and silver. They also exported cider from Lebanon to the pharaohs of Egypt, developed a highly valued textile dye referred to as Tyrian purple (named after their home port of Tyre), and discovered the technique of producing transparent glass. It is thought that the Hebrew word *kenaʾani*, or *Canaanite*, came to be associated with the meaning of merchant, per-haps making the Phoenicians the world's first global businesspeople, the real ancestors of our modern multinational enterprises (MNEs). The commercial prowess of these ancient people who dominated Mediter-ranean trade in the preclassical age gave the world the concept of inter-est-bearing loans, the idea of maritime insurance, and even an alphabet that today forms the basic communication system in the West. One of the chief trading partners of the Phoenicians was the Greeks, who used the Tyrian purple powder to color the garments of the elite and status-seek-ing members of their society. This specialized color designation is derived from the ancient Greek word *phoinikela*, meaning *purple*. Accompanying the cross-territorial merchant imperatives of the Phoenicians were some great physical structures that enabled societies that followed to reach new height. In the first century BCE, the port of Caesarea (Israel) was built by King Herod to honor the Roman emperor, Caesar. The construction of this docking facility, then the biggest in the world, was carried out on the ruins of a Phoenician port featuring the Stabo's Tower, perhaps the world's first functioning all-year and around-the-clock lighthouse. When finished, Caesarea was the daily home to more than 600 ships catering to global trade routes stretching from the Far East, through the Arabian peninsula, and on to Rome and Greece as well as other Mediterranean territories. Its sheer size and commercial importance dwarfed the areas other major port city of Alexandria built in 1900 BCE that serviced coastal commerce, including its own famous lighthouse, which is considered as one of the seven wonders of the ancient world.

Ferand Braudel remarked in *The Prospective of the World* that Phoenicia was an early example of a world economy (early globalization in the *known world*) surrounded by empires. Such a description might have been used to characterize events that later transpired such as the spice and silk trade out of the Far East; the exploits of European monarchs in the period of world exploration following Christopher Columbus; the United States after World War II as its international economic involvement materialized; Japan in 1960s with its aggressive export policy; China, today, as a new center for global manufacturing; and India as a worldwide service outsource center. Many of the site areas visited by the Phoenician still remain today (see Figure 3.2). Oea (Tripoli, Libya); Tingis (Tanger, Morocco); Olissipona (Lisbon, Portugal); Cadir (Cadiz, Spain); and

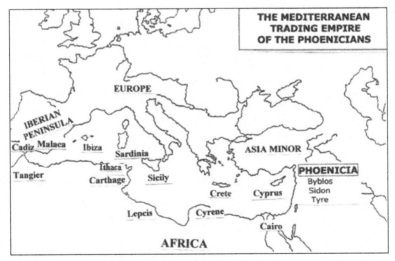

Figure 3.2 Phoenician trade empire

Sardinia and Sicily (in Italy), along with major cities in Algeria, Cyprus, and Crete were born out of the Phoenician trading imperative. Perhaps, the most famous descendants of the early Phoenicians were the Carthaginians on the Lebanese coast. Their North African empire rivaled the Romans for trade and political influence in the Mediterranean basin for years, resulting in a 100-year war between the two. These ancient Phoenician trading seaports not only knitted together the Mediterranean basin economically but also allowed for the parallel exchange of cultures and the interchange of new ideas from as far away as Arabia and Persia on the western steps of Asia.

The Early Greeks and Their Descendants

The Minoans sailed the Mediterranean Sea cultivating trading opportunities on the North African coast while also exploring Persia to join the valuable intercontinental commerce moving from the East and West. Their Athenian fleet dispersed the Persian navy in what history considered as the first major sea battle in 480 BCE. Part of the reason for the war was trading rights. The use of a governmental military to further the economic expansion of nations even then was not a new idea and was played again throughout history. The Minoans, the descendants of which would form ancient Greek society, began the rudiments of the written language—that is, pictographic and syllabic. But unlike the literary storytelling recording of events portrayed in the written expressions of their contemporaries (the Egyptians and their hieroglyphics), the Minoans employed such symbols "only to make inventories that kept account of their extensive commercial endeavors."[15]

Within their unique culture, the impetus for the written word was a commercial incentive, the recording of commercial transactions. It might be said that they were the first accountants. As noted earlier, the keeping of written records in any format is a prime ingredient for the development of civilization. The emergence of the written word based on a commercial necessity is a concept constantly replayed in other ancient civilizations (see Chapter 6). Years later, the descendants of the Minoans, the Greeks, would provide the world with the initial vestiges of today's modern shopping centers with the construction of the agora. They also developed the precursor of public commercial advertising as exemplified by a still-existing marble carving on a stone roadway in Ephesus, Turkey, announcing the existence of a house devoted to the world's oldest profession just up the street.

In antiquity, the Mycenaeans (the Greeks of the North) and the Hittites (forerunners of modern Turkey) controlled the rich trade route between the Far East and the West. Troy, a city-state, prospered as a natural strategic economic bridge between the two areas. The map (Figure 3.3) depicts the unique geographical position of Troy as it was situated on the Dardanelles (also known as Hellespont) between the land masses of Europe and Asia. It was also a port linkage between the waters of the Marmara Sea, which, via the Bospherous, led to the Black Sea in the north and the Aegean Sea in the south. Such positioning made it a

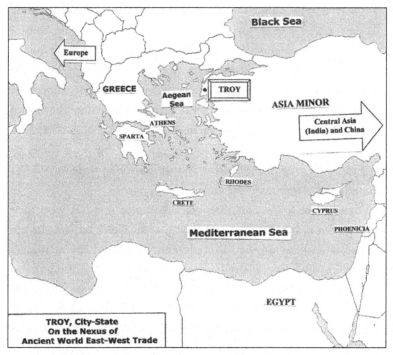

Figure 3.3 City of Troy: Straddling East–West trade movement

Note: TROY, city-state on the nexus of ancient world East–West trade central hub for intercontinental trade passages. Centuries later, Troy sat at the nexus where Xerxes the Persian king and then Alexander the Great would lead their armies in opposite directions. This ancient trade center was the regional predecessor of the great city of Constantinople (Istanbul, Turkey), the imperial capital of the Roman Empire in 671 BCE and later the Ottoman Kingdom.

While the romantic epic, as portrayed by Homer in the *Iliad*, speaks of the face that launched a thousand ships, the real historical impetus for this famous battle most probably was not Helen of Troy but the desire of the Greeks to consolidate their trading empire by securing this valuable passageway for themselves. Perhaps the mythical abduction of Helen followed by the siege of the city of Troy in Homer's work of fiction was based on Mycenaean's conflict (around 1193 to 83 BCE) with the Trojans, but in reality it is based on the desire of one group to acquire the riches of another. In this case, the war, like most wars, was collaterally not only about the acquiring of land resources and the enslavement of a society, but the prime objective was to gain control over the strategic geographical trade positioning of Troy as a conduit of trade between intercontinental regions. About 800 years later, historians have well documented the Peloponnesian War and cited that the war was based on the need of Athens and their Aegean allies to ensure the flow of foreign grain from Theodosia on the northeastern shore of the Black Sea through the Bospherous and into the Aegean Sea. This route passes by Troy and would support the contention that East–West trade was vital to the interests of all parties in the region.

Although not known for their colonial explorations, as were their European descendants in the late 1400s, ancient Greek settlements can be found in and around the Mediterranean. The island city of Rhodes in 292 BCE, like Troy, derived its wealth and prominence due to its attractive trade position as a hub in the eastern Mediterranean. Accessible by sea lanes to Asia Minor, the Middle East, and southern Europe, it acted as an interim shipping port and as a connection point for all these regions. Rhodes's rulers charged a 2 percent duty on the cargo of ships for port services, with grain transportation being the most lucrative freight. The Colossus of Rhodes, the massive bronze statue constructed across the harbor entrance, was a testament to the importance of ancient sea trade and a symbol that it was blessed by the gods. It was also a tribute to the local navy, which was praised for safeguarding merchant vessels from marauding pirates and thereby contributed to the protection of valued commercial operations that provided Rhodes with its economic strength. Only the famed dock structure of Alexandria, Egypt, and its enormous Pharos lighthouse built in 280 BCE rivaled the complexity and efficiency of the Rhodes facility. It is noteworthy that both the Colossus and Pharos structures are considered in the collection of the Seven (architectural) Wonders of the Ancient World, symbols of advanced civilizations that were also inspired by intercontinental trade and globalization.

The modern Spanish city of Ampurias was originally the Greek settlement of Emporion, which literally means *the trading station* (note the resemblance to the word *emporium*—that is, an important place of commerce, a center of trade, or a large store selling a variety of merchandise). Even though the Greeks did not establish a governmental colonial presence in Egypt, the Greek historian Herodotus recorded the trading settlement of Naukratis in the western Nile Delta where large quantities of imported Greek pottery have been found. Greek trading establishments have also been found in the city of Miletus, which today is modern Turkey.

The Greeks, being the first commercial global ambassadors, were also knowledgeable diplomats as they recognized that their national identities as traders sometimes worked against them. As such they employed foreign-born, free, noncitizen agent transients known as *xeno* (Greek root word meaning *stranger* or *foreigner*) to carry out long-distance trade. These straw men or intermediaries played an important role in their ancient economy while the principle of the foreign commercial agent relationship is still used today in world trade. Modern MNCs employ third-world nationals (those who are not citizens of the country where the company has its headquarters or host countries they are entering) in their organizations to bridge cultural and political differences in their commercial associations around the world. The Greeks also recognized the importance of cross-border or territorial trade in respect to construction of laws to ensure the safety of noncitizen traders in their harbors and markets. No matter the nationality of the merchant (the land from which he originated or was now from) he was given special noncitizen legal status (today's resident alien designation) and was safe of forfeiture of his persons and assets on grounds that he was a foreigner. The recognition of the beneficial value of alien residents, foreign nationals doing business in a country, and the specialized treatment afforded them was again repeated in the English Magna Carta signed many years later (see Chapter 9 and the reference to the Magna Carta). Many nationalities over the history of international trade were barred from ownership of land and other fixed assets in the domains they immigrated or traveled between but their knowledge of commercial affairs was nonetheless considered essential to the economy of their adopted countries. With such restrictions, many became merchants, agents of merchants, or money traders. The Jews of Europe as well as the Chinese and Indians outside their respective home countries found their services useful in foreign lands. In return for such a declared special trading standing, the Greek state charged duties on imports and exports on the exchange of goods moving across their borders, which in turn sanctified the process and contributed to improving the lives of all Greek citizens. The principle of an *in and out* tariff taxation is used in today's modern commercial transactions between nations with the revenue generated a prime resource for governments to finance their social agendas.

While early Greeks were well known for their extensive foreign trading activities, it was Alexander the Great who expanded the empire and created vast commercial linkages across distant regions. The extent of such venturing, more than 3,000 miles, is best illustrated in Figure 3.4.

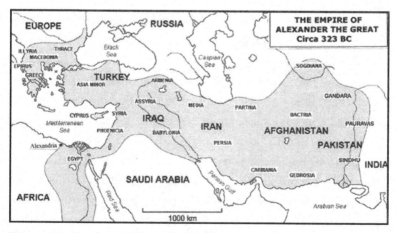

Figure 3.4 Empire of Alexander the Great

Perhaps the best example of this desire to make Greece the center of the global economy was the establishment of the ancient city of Alexandria founded in 332 BCE. From its inception, the city was intended to serve not only as a link between Egypt and Greece but also as a unifier of civilizations within the waters of the Mediterranean Sea as well as a conduit for commerce via the Nile River and overland routes across the Arabian peninsula that had already penetrated India and the Far East. Alexandria was designed to be a major international trade center in regard to not only the construction of the massive port but also the administration of activities surrounding the commercial imperative. According to a papyrus dated 258 BCE, a royal ordinance called a *prostagma* (a command document signed by the king stating an administrative declaration to be followed by all in the kingdom) was published that required all merchants entering the country to exchange their gold and silver for new Ptolemaic silver coins that were minted in the country. Other proclamations, beyond the control on foreign currency, specified regulations for commercial exchanges and acted to codify and establish a universal economic system for those within the empire. The influence and extent of international trading activities originating in Alexandria are best illustrated by another interesting papyrus found in the city during Roman rule in the second century. It detailed the private establishment of a commercial company for the importation of *aromata* (the Greek word for spices or herbs) from foreign incense-bearing lands. The legal document, technically a maritime loan contract, is noteworthy as the roles of the 12 parties to the agreement contain a blueprint for commercial arrangements structured across borders that one might find in use today. It consisted of a creditor, a banker, five debtors, and five guarantors while also setting out the varied national affiliations to which each belonged. The banker, through which the arrangement was managed, was Roman while the other parties came from Carthage, Messalia (Massalia), Elea, Thessalonica, and Macedonia (Greece) along with Nabataean merchants. The internationality of the consortium not only is a testament to the city's global reach and importance but also illustrates the gathering of players in early globalization activities. The Greeks' culture was born out of trade. Not only did they exchange products, but they also imparted their language, which became the international commercial communication standard as well as the conduit for knowledge transition (see Chapter 6).

Rome and Its Empire

While many internal and external factors contributed to the Roman Empire's rise and fall, one of the prime elements in the process was its ability to organize and sustain commerce throughout its colonial territories and its trading activities with foreign regions of the world (see Figure 3.5).

It should also be noted that the 100-year war with rival Carthage (originally founded by the Phoenicians) was fought to maintain North African trade control over grain, ivory, textiles, precious metals, and glass—all prized elements in ancient times and a source of great wealth for Rome itself. During the first century CE, a primitive European Union–type structure was initiated across the empire. A common currency, the silver denarius, was used across their federal provinces, while free trade, supported with local taxes eventually flowing to Rome, was initiated between them. Uniform civil and commercial rules were practiced across the empire while the state improved the overall infrastructure of roads and port along with administrative magistrates to enforce legal regulations. The military of the republic was used to ensure safe travel

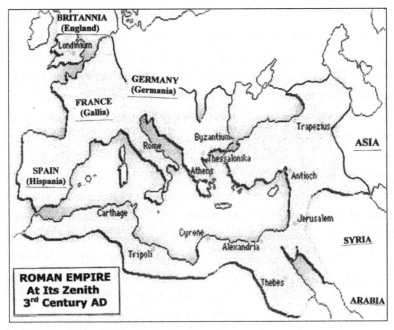

Figure 3.5 Roman Empire at its zenith

on the roadways, while its navy patrolled the sea-lanes looking to ward off pirates who attacked merchant vessels. Formal trade pacts were introduced with outlining recognized independent societies that stretched all the way to the Han dynasty in China.

Private companies called *publicani* were created and allowed to bid for state contracts to supply the army and construct public buildings. The Romans are even credited with the origination of the word *company*. Pronounced in Latin, the term links two words *con + pane* or *with bread*, a reference to a group of people who broke bread daily or ate together. During such ritual socialization, they held discussions on politics as well as the managing of their estate affairs harking back to the Greek idea of *oikonomia*, or economics. The actual etymology of the word *company* indicates that the term first appeared around 1150 CE in its written version *companio*, or companion, an applied extension of those with whom one shared meals.

It was later used to officially describe a body of soldiers broken up into a specific complement of men. While the use of the company concept as a collaborative group effort to further a common goal is attributable to the organization in military strategy and not withstanding that the root word denotes a gathering for a social collective purpose, the term had no direct business association until 1303 BCE when the word emerged to portray a group of craftsmen belonging to trade guilds. In more modern terminology, such commercial associations might be described as networking—that is, social gatherings with a purposeful or beneficial agenda for the connectors, the organization toward a common agenda. The idea of a company still carried the stigma of personal liability toward the individuals involved in the undertaking or venture as even Roman law recognized such legal responsibility. The Romans recognized this problem and came up with an economic method to depersonalize business—the notion of limited liability to separate an enterprise from its owners and managers. They created a de facto entity that possessed all the distinct features of a modern corporation including continuity, direct agency, limited liability, and entity shielding.

Romans used an existing nonperson, that is, a slave, as the fulcrum around which assets could be held and operations conducted as the owner of a slave was not responsible for his transactions. Since slaves, like modern corporations, could not be held individually liable, they were not citizens; any liabilities arising from their actions could only be satisfied out of the assets they held.[16] Hundreds of years later, this Roman-invented analogous device for limited liability using an indirect nonperson entity was codified under the privilege extended as a state-created entity, the birth of the corporation as granted by governmental charter.

This early Roman-inspired idea that a nonnatural person, a slave, can be recognized by law to have rights and responsibilities may have been the forerunner of the legal fiction used centuries later to give corporations equal protection under the law. In 1886, in the case of *Santa Clara County v. Southern Pacific Railroad Company* (118 U.S. 394), the U.S. Supreme Court decided that a private corporation is a person and entitled to the legal rights and protections the constitutions afford to any person. The doctrine of corporate personhood, which subsequently became a cornerstone of corporate law, was decided without argument. According to the official case record, Supreme Court Justice Morrison Remick Waite emphatically announced prior to hearing oral arguments that

> the court does not wish to hear argument on the question whether the provision (specifically Section 1) in the Fourteenth Amendment to the Constitution, which forbids a State to deny to any person within its jurisdiction the equal protection of the laws, applies to these corporations. We are all of opinion that it does.[17]

The ancient Romans, like their prior Greek philosophical writers, also commented on business associations, inserting them into a practical guide on establishing commercial relations, an ethical overtone. Such ideas are also found in early Egyptian writings and echoed later in religious teachings with respect to just and equitable treatments in business dealings. The following story by Pliny the Younger, an adviser to Emperor Trajan (98 to 117 CE) on matters of leadership and managerial or organizational structure, as well as his appointed governor of a region, recounts the need for insertion of a trusted mutual intermediary between buyer and seller. The lesson is to assure both parties that the transaction is fair and reasonable, a good principle for managers to emulate and one that also enhances future relationships:

> Tranquillas, my close associate, wishes to purchase a small property that your own friend is said to be trying to sell. I ask you to intervene so that he buys for a price that is fair, for thus he will look back on the deal with pleasure. Truly a purchase on bad terms is always disagreeable, especially for the reason that it seem to reproach the stupidity of the new owner.[18]

Danube Valley, the Lost World of Old Europe

Before the emergence of the most-often-written-about Western societies of Greece, Rome, and even in advance of the growth of the Mesopotamia region and its Middle Eastern cousins, the Egyptians of the Nile River basin, there developed in the twin geographical areas of the lower Danube Valley and the Balkan foots an Old European civilization. Relics of the period date this society as emerging earlier than 5000 BCE and lasting for more than 1,500 years. Although no distinctive name has yet been given to inhabitants, these early people lived in what are today Bulgaria, Moldova, and Romania. Researchers are not sure if this group can be classified as a civilization, but the artifacts found in the region indicate that the society did possess political, technological, and ideological advancements that would qualify it in such a recognized anthropological domain. One aspect of the society was its participation in long-distance trade, a factor in postulating that this group originated from perhaps Greece and Macedonia, and kept such exchange ties after arriving in the new land. In a catalog to accompany an exhibition of artifacts from the area titled "The Lost World of Old Europe: The Danube Valley, 5000–3500 BC," shown at the Institute for the Study of the Ancient World at New York University in December 2009, French anthropologist Michel Louis Seferiades concludes that the finding evidence of Spondylus shells from the Aegean Sea in the archeological dig is of special distinction.[19] This prized Aegean shell was imported as a special item of trade representing a valuable symbol of social status, recognition, and suggesting that the culture had links to a network of access routes and a social framework of elaborate exchange systems—including bartering, gift exchange, and reciprocity. Contributing to this cross-territorial trading consideration were the exchange networks, which also contained long-distance acquisitions of gold, copper, and shared patterns of ceramics from outlining colonies. Movements to the region of nonindigenous agricultural products and domesticated animals also suggest a pattern of cross-territorial trade that helped to sustain this quasi-civilization.

Carthaginians and Celts: Other Ancient Western Traders

As mentioned earlier, Romans and Carthaginians were at one time competitors for the dominance of the Mediterranean trade, with the monopoly of the region having to be settled by war. Unlike imperial Rome, which used its army to expand its commercial empire, the whole state of Carthage was geared toward establishing trade routes. Their commercial expeditions not only stretched across the entire Mediterranean Sea but also included the interior African landscape and the Atlantic seaboard of the continent. Some archeologists even contend that they reached the Caribbean, the shores of both eastern Mexico and South America, as well as Southeast Asia. Like their North African predecessors, the Phoenicians, the Carthaginians were known for their massive trading vessels, which were estimated to have carried more than 100 tons of goods—an enormous load requiring very unique shipbuilding inventions as well as port entry navigational skills. One of the commercial principles attributed to the Carthaginian trading prowess was their introduction of the auction process, an early open free-market-driven, bidding approach to business transactions. Built on the concept of self-regulating supply and demand, numerous buyers would compete to set the price of commodities. The same idea is also found in the writings of ancient Indian and Chinese social commentators (noted in Chapter 2); and much later, in 1776, with the concept of "invisible hand of the market," popularized by Adam Smith in his economic treatise, *The Wealth of Nations*.[21]

Another early trading group in the greater European sphere of influence were the Celts in the north. While they were primarily land traders, their prowess in the prized metalworking craft created interest in goods produced by such skills from adjacent territories. Unlike other trading societies of that day that relied mainly on exchanging natural resources not found in other lands, this was an early recognition in the ancient world of an intellectual proficiency creating a competitive commercial advantage via refined technological division of labor. This economic trade principle was repeated on a limited basis in other areas of the antique world, most notably in the Chinese specialty for silk-based woven fabric and porcelain pottery. Today, this conceptual orientation is referred to as global centers of excellence and is itself a prime driver of the globalization imperative. Because the Celts consisted of numerous nonunified tribal clans who mainly traded between themselves, there was no allegiance to a national ruling entity to establish a major trading center in their territory nor provide financial assistance from a liege lord to underwrite trading expeditions; no less a ruling body to establish rules governing the trading process itself. The Celts had to either travel great distances themselves on individual excursions or wait for the occasional merchant to come to their shores to deal with sparsely dispersed pockets of craftsmen. Both conditions severely limited their cross-territorial trading initiative. Sociologists have theorized that for a nation to prosper via the foreign trading imperative, a key requirement is the existence of some form of commercial unification system through a ruling entity that can impose universally enforced factors to stabilize and sustain the process of commercial dealings in a society. History seems to prove that when such national elements are in place, trade has a better chance of prospering both onshore and offshore. Instances of this principle in action are reflected in the social and political unification of the Mongol region under Genghis Khan, the Greek Empire under Alexander the Great, the Roman Empire, and other expanded territorial dynasties.

The Eastern World: India, China, and Japan

Indus Valley of India

Around 2250 BCE in the Indus region (India), a civilization emerged that some call the Harappan as its people were inhabitants of a city bearing such a name on a tributary. They were highly organized; and in their collective society, efforts resembled those in Egypt and Mesopotamia. Large granaries were erected, which allowed for the storage of surplus that could be exchanged for other imported commodities. A standardized system of weights and measurements was inaugurated, creating a uniformly acceptable necessary element that furthered and simplified the trading process. The importance of external exchange with neighboring territories was exemplified with the construction of a vast dockyard complex linked by a mile-long canal to the sea. This key infrastructure, along with warehouses, was constructed by the local administration. It provided an extended area to the suppliers to sell their products to merchants, who in turn placed them on ships going to the Persian Gulf to reach as far west as Mesopotamia while moving east by hugging the coastline to Southeast Asia and the legendary spice islands. The port structure dominated the landscape and was larger in scope and size than any temple or public edifice, attesting to the importance of the commercial trading imperative to this ancient civilization. The positive trade surplus achieved by their trade merchants gave rise to prosperous urban centers that were in turn linked to an extensive network of internal trade.

Literary records from that period paint a picture of abundance and splendor due to the maritime wealth of the cosmopolitan cities of South India. The *Silappathikaarum* (*The Ankle Bracelet*), a Tamil romance story roughly dated to the late second century CE with no specific author, provides a glimpse of the maritime wealth of the cosmopolitan cities of South India. The tale suggests that the markets offered a great variety of precious commodities prized in the ancient world. The prosperous port city of Puhar (Kaveripattanam) was said to be inhabited by ship owners described as having riches that were the envy of foreign kings. Puhar is portrayed as a city populated by entrepreneurial merchants and traders, where trade was well regulated. The city possessed a spacious forum for storing a bale of merchandise, with the inventories scrupulously marked indicating the quantity, weight, and name of the owner. It was so well organized for commercial activities that business streets were specifically earmarked for merchants who traded in items such as coral, sandalwood, jewelry, faultless pearls, pure gold, and precious gems. Skilled craftspeople brought their finished goods such as fine silks, woven fabrics, and luxurious ivory carvings.

All these products were destined for overseas markets to the East and to the West via the sea ports of southern India. Eastern commercial ventures conducted from the site may be the basis for Chinese influence on Indian society. Rice, a fundamental part of the Indian diet today and first grown in the Ganges Valley, was not a native-known agricultural asset of the area and conceivably it was imported from lands the merchant traders visited, most probably southeastern Asia and China. Excavated evidence indicates that specialized craftsmen utilized raw materials from across the subcontinent as well as other adjoining areas through an ancient trading network both to import resources and to export finished products. While much has been written of India's later participation in the spice trade that flowed west across Arabia, into the Mediterranean, and on to southern Europe, it should be noted that in the first century CE, regular maritime traffic connected India to the Malay Peninsula and other points in southeast Asia.

Although the courtly culture of the Mogul rulers of the Indian subcontinent is the most well known, a cosmopolitan outlook was not new to India. Several sources point to a thriving system of international trade that linked the ports of southern India with those of ancient Rome. The chronicles of the Greek historian Periplus reveal that Indian exports included a variety of spices, aromatics, quality textiles (muslins and cottons), ivory, and high-quality irons and gems, which were considered luxurious and in-demand items during those days.

While a good portion of Indo-Roman trade was reciprocal (Rome supplying exotic items such as cut gems, coral, wine, perfumes, papyrus, copper, tin, and lead ingots), the trade balance was considerably weighted in India's favor. The balance of payments had to be met in precious metals, either gold or silver coins, or other valuables like red coral (i.e., the hard currency of the ancient world). India was particularly renowned for its crafted ivory and fine muslins (referenced in Roman literature as "woven air"). According to Roman historical accounts, yearly purchases of Indian merchandise was in excess of 50 million sesterces.[21]

China: The Reluctant Trading Enigma

Genghis Khan in 1100 BCE not only united the Mongols but created an empire beyond the Chinese border, encompassing Korea and Japan in the east and stretching to Mesopotamia (modern-day Iraq and Syria) and into Russia, Poland, and Hungary. He instituted common laws and regulations over his domain, most notably the preservation of private property to enhance and protect the trading imperative. His decree, the Pax Mongolica, allowed for safe passage of merchants across his territory. This royal command was used by Niccolo and Maffeo Polo (Marco Polo's father and uncle, respectively), who met Kublai Khan, the successor to Genghis Khan, on their travels to distant lands in search of their commercial trading activities. These early khans recognized that for civilization to grow and prosper, unabated trade across their controlled territories was required. It was also a key consideration to ensure contentment of conquered people that they be allowed to continue their commercial interests with protection afforded by the new liege lord.

If the revelations as proposed by Menzies in his book *1421: The Year China Discovered America*[22] are to be universally accepted, thereby challenging Columbus's proclamation of original exploration, the portrayal of China as a masterful organizer of world commerce emerges. Their practice of harmonized trade indicates that globalization was a benefit, not a hindrance, to societal development. On March 8, 1421, during the Ming dynasty, a fleet of more than 3,750 vessels set sail to raise foreign tribute for the kingdom and to begin to unite the world in Confucian harmony, a religious connection to trade. The Chinese sought to entice financial homage in return for granting trading privileges with the homeland while also offering protection against enemies for those territories covered by their pacts. China, however, always gave its trading partners a greater value of goods—offering to trade silks and porcelain at discounted prices, often funded by soft loans—than was received from them. They allowed the societies they encountered to be woven into the global tapestry of trade and capitalized on the resources and skills of their native environments. The Chinese venture provided an opening to the rest of the world that such individual cultures could not achieve on their own.

A prime aspect of the Chinese initiative was that they did not go forth to create colonies nor construct the modern-day vestiges of subsidiary dominance and control but instead chose to organize the first global value chain through creation of strategic alliances. They, unlike the mercantilism principles practiced by Europe during the period of great exploration, did not rely on their strength and quasi-monopolistic trade methods but they recognized the principle of economic equity and the art of the fair commercial deal instead. It may be unfair and equally inaccurate to portray the Western colossus of business as the perpetrators and beneficiaries of globalization today when the idea was practiced close to 600 years ago by an Eastern dynasty.

The Star Fleet was commanded by Admiral Zheng. He had been taken prisoner in his childhood by the invading Chinese army. As a male captive he was castrated at the age of 13 as prelude to being placed in service to the royal house of Zhu Di. As a personal servant to the young prince a life friendship developed between them. When the royal was elevated to emperor his trusted youthful companion was made an admiral. Zheng, over a period of 30 years, lead numerous expeditions. The Star Fleet was his last as when remnants of the armada finally returned home, the emperor had been replaced. Advisers to the new imperial house felt that foreign contamination from such ventures would destroy China. As such, proclamations were issued to destroy all records of the voyage and a prohibition was issued for all future endeavors. Ocean trade was severely limited to prescribed coastal waters. Historians point to this event as the beginning of the Chinese reluctance to embrace the world, a position not reversed until modern times.

A number, but not all, of the propositions advanced by Menzies have been strongly challenged by other historical researchers. The idea that China dominated sea trade and therefore created subservient territories in the East and Southeast Asia acting as their protector and thereby making them economically dependent colonies, as opposed to favored trading partners, runs counter to charts made of the area. A series of maps ranging from the Song dynasty in 1136 through the Ming dynasty in 1624 would seemingly dismiss this contention. Firstly, non-imperial calligraphers who prepared these renderings do not show any of the Chinese kingdoms as the center of this world region but simply part of the Eastern area. Second, the charts depict shipping trade routes traversing Japan, Taiwan, China, the Philippines, Borneo, Vietnam, Thailand, Malaysia, Indonesia (Java and Sumatra), Myanmar, Goa in India, and beyond to the West with compass bearings from all points. This would indicate that the South China Sea and the waters it touched were free and open international trade waterways used by all coastal and trading nations during this period. The region was not ruled nor was it under the economic controlling influence of China. The individual kingdoms comprising it were neither commercially dependent on nor beholden to China acting as their trade master. These points do not however negate the great navigational exploits of the Star Fleet that perhaps took it around the world.

In his other book, *1434: The Year a Magnificent Chinese Fleet Sailed to Italy and Ignited the Renaissance*,[23] Menzies further raises the possibility of the extraordinary global influence of the Chinese as he postulates that their merchant fleet brought to Europe the seeds of intellectual expansion, new discoveries, and inventions that would change the Western world. They arrived, most appropriately in the Western hubs of world trade— Florence and Venice—to widen and expand global trade. Supposedly, during meetings with Pope Eugene IV, they shared their knowledge of world geography (perhaps the maps later used by Christopher Columbus and Ferdinand Magellan), astronomy, and mathematics for navigation, printing, architecture, steel manufacturing, military weaponry, and a host of other valuable insights and tools that enabled mankind to leap forward. While Menzies's contentions have been challenged, his hypothesis that Chinese-inspired knowledge and inventions did make their way to the West has merit. Such advanced information may have been carried by a series of intermediaries, merchants, and seamen who constantly moved between the two regions as opposed to his proposition that direct contact was made.

It is also interesting to note that in conjunction with the later ocean imperative in the Ming dynasty, the first Chinese emperor Ch'in Shih Huang Ti, in 238 BCE, over five centuries earlier (about the time of the building of the Roman Empire in the West) had also dispatched expeditions to China's eastern neighbors across central Asia; this was the real beginning of the East–West trade. The Qin dynasty is best remembered in the history of China as the period when the seven ancient kingdoms were unified and the empire was therefore created. It is also well known for the initial construction of the Great Wall across the north and western frontier and the 1974 discovery of the great emperor's underground pyramid-like tomb in Xian containing a massive army of Terracotta soldiers to protect and enforce his rule in the parallel or underworld. What is often overlooked is that in his plan to unify the kingdom, the emperor brought stability to his vast empire and three major projects were undertaken: (a) a common written system of communication was introduced so that commercial communication between the previous warring states could be undertaken; (b) units of measurement for weight and length were standardized across the land; and (c) a common currency, an acceptable medium of value exchange, was established. All these undertakings allowed for increased efficient trade across the land, the mainstay in holding the diverse population together and for its civilization to grow. As long as trade flowed, the empire could be maintained. The commercial venturing into Western lands was further enhanced by the Han emperor Wu-Ti (141 to 87 BCE) due to the extensive travels of explorer Chang Ch'ien, circa 132 BCE. It was during this period that the renowned Chinese export of woven material, silk garments, was first exchanged for glass and metal products from the West.

With the exception of the Mongolian period and its unification of the trading initiative across its vast empire in the 11th century BCE and the exploration of the world by great fleets in the 1400s, the Chinese never again approached the commercialization of the world. Given China's extensive shoreline and the major international trading port of Macao based in its own territory in the 1600s and established by the Portuguese, the impetus for reaching out never rematerialized. Why this technologically advanced ancient society—which gave the world paper for recording transactions, the printing press, gun powder to protect voyagers from their traders, the compass for ocean navigation, and the most worthy of seagoing vessels and trade goods like silk and porcelain desired by the world—failed to take due advantage of its comparative global resources is worthy of inspection. The answer may lie in a series of further introspections.

The Great Wall is the preeminent physical metaphor for the Chinese psyche, while the country's commercial relationships with the rest of the world provides the best representative example of the mindset at work. Societies construct walls to provide security for those behind them. But in return they do not allow those inside to venture out, be influenced by foreign contamination, and return to corrupt and disrupt the domestic harmony. China did not remain isolated as it created gates that were periodically opened and closed as various emperors ascended the throne. After the period of the great fleet that sailed from its base in China in 1421 on a commercial exploration around the world (perhaps visiting Italy in 1434),[24] the country strictly limited it merchants to foreign exposure via maritime trade for the next 133 years. During the voyages of the Star Fleet, as mentioned in Menzies's *1421*, the old emperor died and with him the vision he had for China engaging the world as well as leaving the empire in political and economic chaos. The new emperor was surrounded by advisers who warned him of the dangers of foreign influence and therefore potential contamination of Chinese society, which would threaten his rule during an unstable time. Upon the return of the remnants of the fleet in late 1423, he announced that such future ventures were frivolous. The great ships that made the journey were left to rot at their moorings and its was decreed that no vessels of their size and magnitude could ever be built again, only boats for coastal navigation—in between, short domestic harbor voyages would be allowed. All records of the fleets' new explorations were destroyed.

The precious maps, the trade alliance documents, and descriptions of the lands and the people they encountered were impounded by the state, not to be shared nor seen by others. All proof of their extraordinary feats was eliminated from public record. Given such considerations, Menzies' second book seems to contradict the factual events he recounts in the first. However, some historians believe that the maps and navigation techniques acquired by the Chinese in 1421 in their quest to circle the world were not entirely lost and that they were smuggled out of the country, falling into the hands of perhaps Indian or Arab merchants and later into those of European explorers' in the 16th century.

In 1567, the general prohibition was lifted due to the pressure of foreign demand for unique Chinese goods like porcelain and silk. But in 1628, the Chinese government again imposed earlier bans on long-distance maritime trade fearing the continued cultural, political, and religious influence of the Europeans.

Chinese law did not allow its own emperor-appointed state officials to travel outside of its borders nor could a diplomatic, no less a trade delegation, be dispatched without imperial decree. Even the lucrative and mutually profitable exchange (i.e., silk for silver) with its neighbor across the sea, Japan, was not on a direct basis. In the 1600s, both markets used middlemen, the Portuguese, to construct cross-border trade via the colony of Macao on the Chinese mainland and the Japanese port of Nagasaki. The size of China made the governess of its internal affairs the primary consideration of its rulers.

Sustaining the unification of the kingdom was a constant battle for emperors and their advisers at court. Interlopers both within and poised on the extensive land borders of the country were a continuing source of concern with massive resources via a large standing army devoted to protection of the central government.

The authorities viewed all foreigners as potential troublemakers and their influence as harmful to the harmony of the nation. Their anxiety produced rigid laws in regard to any exchanges with them. They branded such people with the generic derogatory term "ghost" (*gui*) to demonize their character and place them in a subhuman category. Chinese distrusted white men of European extraction, ranging from the Portuguese, called Macanese foreigners (*Aoyi*, due to their base of operations in Macao), to the feared "red hairs" (*hongmao*), or the Dutch. The Japanese, known as "Dwarf Pirates" (*wokou*), were most feared due to their prowess in combat as experienced during their frequent raids on Chinese coastal cities after a ban on maritime trade with them. The most obnoxious foreigners, however, were the black ghosts (*hiegui*), because the skin color of the African slaves and their North African Moorish neighbors was an abomination to the Chinese, as they were totally unlike anything they had ever known. Beyond discrimination of these foreign ghosts denoted by their physical ethnic traits, the Chinese were also scared of Jesuit priests, accusing them of infiltrating their society and using their Christian conversion activities as a destructive force bordering on cultural and political treason. Simply put, China wished to wall off its society from barbarians and such policy was the motivation for suspending its offshore trading activities.

Beyond these two prime considerations, Chinese cultural indoctrination made them very conservative people whose lives were controlled by tradition and historic custom. A portrayal of Chinese 17th-century geographers, as depicted in *Vermeer's Hat: The Seventeenth Century and the Dawn of the Global World*,[25] well demonstrates a desired limited vision of the world. In regard to recording new information in the form of world maps, as acquired through the visits of foreign traders, the preface to a book of that period offering new data indicated that it was designed to provide material for historians of another day and not for current mariners and merchants. The impetus to trade across territories was just not part of the Chinese ancient mindset. During the zenith of the age of discovery when European nations hammered to get into China, the Canton System (1760 to 1842) served as a means to control trade with the West within its own country as it limited the ports in which European traders could do business in China. The administration of the Canton system forbid any direct trading between European merchants and Chinese civilians. Instead, it required employees of the foreign trading companies to only trade with an association of Chinese merchants known as the *Cohong*. The reluctance of the Chinese government to entertain foreign trade transactions also meant that the movement of foreigners was restricted to specified venues in the approved harbors of the Cantons during the designated trading season.

It did, however, allow foreign traders to remain on Chinese soil on the island of Macao during the off-season, a mitigation of mainland restrictions. This policy eventually led to a concession allowing Macao to be administered by the Portuguese while maintaining the Chinese lawful integrity of the island for the Chinese citizens living there. Chinese trade policy continued to frustrate the Europeans, as did their merchants' acceptance of only silver bullion in transactions. However, the resentment was partially appeased when opium (grown in the English colonies of India) became an alternate medium of exchange. A balance or stalemate in the trading process remained intact until the opium wars, which established treaty ports in accordance with the Treaty of Nanjing, which were ruled not by Chinese law but rather the regulations of the specific country that controlled each port. The history of the country, as influenced by the imperialistic foreign trade requirements of the Europeans, has never been forgotten by its people. Even in the modern era, notwithstanding the years of communist influence on the economy, the Chinese tradition of not trusting foreigners seems to permeate their internal and offshore trade policies. Although China reached out to touch the far-away world during only two periods in its ancient history, it did develop trade with contiguous territories based on the simple principle of reciprocal needs. While the Silk Road, Spice Route, and King's Highway are all synonymous with famous cross-territorial trade passages in the ancient world, a little known pathway through some of the highest plateaus on earth, and perhaps the most difficult to transverse, best illustrates the fundamental impetus for the cross territorial exchange or barter process, the founding father of the modern commercial system; to fulfill an essential need that is not available locally. Although more of a path than an actual road, the Tea-Horse Road begins in the southwest China where its two provinces, Szechuan and Yunnan, join. It crosses the eastern foothills and deep canyons formed by several major river basins, then heads into Tibet and the Himalayas, finally reaching India. The journey is a dangerous one, requiring travelers to traverse through the snowy mountains and bad weather that is further punctuated almost year-round by deep gorges with steep cliffs. Even the ability to utilize the rivers is complicated by fast-flowing currents fed by mountain streams that periodically run off, causing traitorous conditions for the traveler. In spite of such terrains, the daily use of this route has been traced back to the Tang dynasty, 618 to 907, predating the afore-mentioned most notable trade route, the Silk Road that also runs east and west. The reason behind traders plying this dangerous route is the desire of two cultures, separated by almost impassable topography, to want an indigenous item that the other has. The explanation requires a contrast of the daily lives and needs of these two societies.

The main dietary staples of the Tibetan people consisted of butter, *tsampa* (roasted barley), beef, and lamb—all high in calories and very hard for the body to absorb—with little consumption of vegetables, especially at the high altitudes of the country. To assist in digestion of these foods and to offset the absence of vitamins found in vegetables, Tibetans like to drink *Pu-erh*, a post-fermented tea available in thick rectangular blocks or molded into flat squares or circle. Such tea was not consumed directly but mixed with yak butter, producing a rich salty beverage. The soil of Tibet did not allow for the growing of this healthy tea. Its cultivation was better suited to the neighboring region of the Yunnan province in China that produced Pu-erh tea in great surplus quantities, and hence was suitable for export. The movement of this valued commodity into Tibet would provide traders with excellent business and sustained profits, but as a barter system prevailed, merchants on both sides needed to find a valued resource to offset the purchase of Pu-erh tea to make any transactions feasible. The Chinese, it so happened, needed strong warhorses for their growing military campaigns. They were envious of the Tibetan mounted army, which was supplied by the superior horses reared on the plains of Central Asia and prized for their stamina and courage in battle.

Despite the contiguous land connections between Tibet and China, merchants carved a yearly usable path between the two countries for the purposes of trade for these two prized resources. Yunnan merchants traded their Pu-erh tea for potential military mounts, reselling them across China. Tibetan merchants in turn made good money by not only selling the tea domestically but also using it as a long-distance barter throughout Central Asia and into India. While the Tea-Horse Road allowed wealth to be transferred between the countries, in turn contributing to the economic development of each, it also provided a two-way cultural bridge that facilitated the introduction of Buddhism into China along with the exchange of ideas, customs, inventions, plus other tangible assets that both markets had within their respective domains. The desire for exotic and luxury goods stimulated many other regional and international trade routes, but this one is a bit more basic in application.

China's historic reluctance to enter into global trade may also be a function of geographical size and population. Its vast land mass covered varying climates and terrains that yielded an abundance of natural resources that made the empire virtually self-sufficient. Its great technological strides in all sciences early on eclipsed the European Renaissance. In contrast to the smaller European countries and city-states that needed to reach out beyond their borders in order to both survive and grow as well as their need to constantly protect themselves from geographically close in foreign aggression were not issues that plagued China. During the Qin dynasty, China was unified and did not fear an alien invasion force as it was simply too big.

While China is not normally associated with the application of commercial principles, the Zhou dynasty, circa 770 to 221 BCE, produced a set of *Lessons* for businessmen to be successful. They were written by Tao Zhu-Gong, also known as Fan U. Like his contemporary Sun Tuz the author of the great treatise, *The Art of War*, he was a military strategist who later got into politics but became one of the country's first millionaires via his trading activities. Relying on a combination of philosophical concepts and military disciplines his guidelines for business practitioners still remain an influential touchstone for Chinese managers today. His Lessons cover all aspects of running a commercial venture. They were originally *12 Lessons* to which another *12* were added. Over time, they have evolved into a consolidated list of 16.[26] They are:

1. In doing business, hard work is needed and laziness will destroy everything. Develop a sense of urgency.
2. In dealing with people, be polite and cordial. A bid attitude will destroy sales.
3. In negotiations, prices must be clearly stated and agree upon. Ambiguity will lead to argumenta and dispute.
4. In accounting, records must be properly kept, inspected, and monitored. Sloppiness and oversight will lead to cash-flow problems.
5. Display of goods must be well organized. Poor organization will lead to obsolescence and waste.
6. In granting credit to clients, be prudent. Carelessness will lead to defaulted payments.
7. In paying creditors, be on time. Delays will lead to loss of credibility.
8. In dealing with unexpected events, be agile and flexible. Negligence will lead to greater loss or lost opportunity.
9. In managing expenses, be economical and frugal. Extravagance will destroy wealth.
10. In conducting business (buying and selling), observe the right timing. Delay will lead to lost opportunity.
11. In selecting debtors, scrutinize them carefully. Carelessness will lead to uncollected debts.
12. In managing the business, good and bad must be clearly distinguished. Failing to do so will lead to confusion and chaos.
13. In selecting people, find those who are honest and upright. Using the wrong people will implicate the boss.
14. In purchasing, goods must be carefully examined. Careless buying will lead to a lower selling price.
15. In managing finance, one must possess good financial sense. Otherwise, it will lead to financial difficulty.
16. In decision making, be calm. Recklessness will lead to mistakes.

The esteemed author concluded his numerous points with a reference to opportunity, which he feels is only reserved for those who are prepared. This prime consideration remains as a common saying among modern Chinese businesspeople who often quote Zhu-Gong with the paraphrased direction:

> Opportunities will not wait for those who are not prepared since every opportunity has an expiry date. An opportunity that is out of date has no economic value.

Japan and Foreign Commercialization

Between Japan's southern Honshu Island and the Korean Peninsula, in the narrow strait, lies Tsushima Island. Such geography is the backdrop for the saying that "when a rooster crows at dawn in Pusan, one can hear it at Shimonoseki or vice versa."[27] It is not hard to conceive that a primitive land-hugging ocean vessel would have been used to bridge non-sanctioned trading groups from both nations. Similarly, merchants traveling down the elongated Malaysian land mass to Singapore and across the Straits of Singapore or Malacca to Indonesia and then east through the Java Sea would have access to the Pacific Island communities as well as Australia. Such journeys would entail less peril (in terms of blind water crossings); so presumably such paths were traveled by early traders. In spite of such geographical coastal navigation and proximity to southeast Asia, Japan experienced hundreds of years of self-imposed commercial isolation.

Early Japanese economy is well represented by the Kamakura period (1185 to 1333), which marked the Japanese *medieval* era, a nearly 700 year period in which the emperor, the court, and the traditional central government were left intact but were largely relegated to ceremonial functions. Power and control of the country were regulated under a localized or regional feudal system akin to medieval Europe. Both had land-based economies, vestiges of a previously centralized state, and a concentration of advanced military technologies in the hands of a specialized fighting class. Lords required the loyal services of vassals who were rewarded with fiefs of their own. The fief holders exercised local military rule and public power related to the holding of land around which the national economy was build. The imperial government did allow for the man-made island of Dejima in Nagasaki's harbor to remain open to foreign trade, but this was highly controlled. Initial foreign trade was primarily carried out by intermediary third parties, namely the Portuguese, whom the Japanese referred to as *Nanban*, or southern barbarians. While the domestic population was deeply desirous of Chinese goods such as silk and porcelain, their merchants were prohibited from direct contact with commercial agents of the emperor of China as retaliation for *Wokou* (Japanese pirates) on their shoreline. In the late 1500s, however, the demand for pure silver around the world rose dramatically and Japan found itself being dragged into the global economy. This was due to the precious metal becoming the first internationally accepted medium of cross-border exchange. At this period, the only other large-scale source of this valued ore was the Spanish colonies in South America. Japan held the Far Eastern monopoly while Spain at the other end of the world enjoyed theirs. While such a valuable medium of exchange helped the Spanish to expand their empire and economically dominate the trade of the world, in competition with the Portuguese, the Japanese held no such desire. They valued their isolation by severely limiting extraterritorial trade, both export and import. In fact, they chose to use an intermediary third party, Portuguese merchants, as their trading agents for the export of silver and their domestic desire for valued foreign commodities like Chinese silk. The journey across the Pacific for the Portuguese merchant vessels was filled with peril, not only from the unpredictable forces of nature but also from the pirates encouraged by nations not able to participate in the new universally accepted currency, mainly Dutch privateers. On the other side of the world, the same fate awaited Spanish ships in the Atlantic as they were besieged by English buccaneers.

The beginning of the Edo period (1603 to 1868) coincides with the last decades of the Nanban trade era, during which increased interaction with European powers, on the economic and cultural level, developed. It was during this time that Japan commissioned its first oceangoing Western-style warships—500-ton galleon-type ships—that eventually led to the construction of more than 350 designated Red Seal ships, three-masted and armed trade ships, for intra-Asian commerce. In spite of such outbound commercial advances, the country maintained a semi-isolated global trade position. The merchants involved in foreign trade as well as those in domestic commerce were considered below the elite ruling class, the warriors, educators, and craft artisans. Such positioning of those in commercial activities echoes many other societies around the world.

It was not until the advent of the *sogo shosha* (*general trading firm* or *trading house*) that Japan began its nation's formalized exposure to the global marketplace in 1868.[28] The detached nation island maintained its economic isolation, although periodic excursions were made to the Asian mainland, until extensive foreign trade was forced on it by Western countries in the intense pursuit of their mercantile policies.[29] The sogo shoshas, beginning with the Mitsui Trading Company and followed by Mitsubishi Shoji, were built on the same principle as employed by the early European sovereigns who bestowed charters on firms venturing into new lands controlled by the monarchs. In the case of Japan, the government (Meiji political leadership) dispensed such favors and promoted their development. This initiative, originally based on countering the influence and power of foreign firms in Japan, who controlled their export trade, was the forerunner of their future economic strength. It became the conduit on which the country opened its culture to alien Western concepts, allowing the nation to grow into a more tolerant and understanding society of differing values. It was in essence the bridge that transformed an island into a real global force. Between the two great Far Eastern powers today—that is, China and Japan—the other countries in the region also utilized trade as building blocks of their societies, borrowing and learning from them.

Korean Trade

Although often dubbed the "Hermit Kingdom," Korea enjoyed a rich trade history that included the export and import of products and technological advancements. The oldest artifacts found in Korea's national museums delineate the rapid expansion of trade between the peninsula and the outside world as early as the fifth century. From the ancient days of the Three Kingdoms, the country was conducting commercial arrangements with its neighbors as well as served as a conduit to others. This is perhaps best exemplified by the arrival of Buddhism in 372 CE from its origination in India as carried by merchants to their land. The Koran monk Hyecho, from the Silla Kingdom, wrote a travelogue called "*Wang ocheonchukguk jeon*" or "*Memoir of the pilgrimage to the five kingdoms of India.*" Hyecho's account of his travel on the Silk Road to ancient India is regarded as one of the best travel journals in the world, along with Marco Polo's "*The Travels of Marco Polo*" (also known as "*Il Milione*"), and Ibn Battuta's "*The Travels of Ibn Battuta*" (also known as "*Rihla*" or "*The Journey*"), both noted in the text, as well as Odoric of Pordenone's "*The Travels of Friar Odoric.*"

The mainstay of the internal economic exchange across ancient Korea, as exemplified by the records maintained during the Silla period, seems to have been either rice or textiles. The capital market was managed by *kwansi*, the state, and most of the high-level artisanship in the capital was concentrated in state-directed royal workshops. The imperial house was the biggest actor in these commercial transactions. For example, lots of paper for the sutra-copying at the state-run temples was annually required. *Mokkan* materials (inscribed wooden tablets) recorded these transactions with precise details. Private external trade started to flourish when central controls imposed by the imperial houses weakened in the late eighth to early ninth centuries.

While the Korean people were strongly influenced by Chinese trade goods and their inventions, the indigenous population adapted them and in many instances improved upon them, an initiative that in modern times is a mark of their savvy business accruement. For example, Chinese scholars had devised a rudimentary printing system using carved wooden blocks. But the adaptive Koreans took the invention to the next level creating the world's first movable-type metal in the 12th century. Although Japan started minting metallic coins in the late seventh century compared to Chinese production a millennium earlier, the Koreans were not far behind with their own brand of currency in the 10th century.

Mesoamerica: The New but Old World

Mexico and South America

Separated by massive seas from the development of trade as exhibited by natural land bridges between the Middle East, southern Europe, and the

Far East, the ancient societies of the Americas may have developed inter-continental trade routes of their own before their transoceanic commercial linkage was initiated by European explorers.

The old Mayan cities of modern-day Mexico, Guatemala, and Belize bartered up and down the jungle rivers of the region. Evidence shows that the Aztecs may have also traded with the Floridian Arawaks and other Caribbean-based Indians. Tlatelolco—the sister city of Tenochtitlan, which itself housed massive pyramids and was the center of the Aztec Empire—was home to thousands of vendors all contained in an orderly market adjacent to the main administrative buildings. The marketplace itself, attended by more than 60,000 customers daily, was supervised by government officials who regulated prices and sales. Exchange patrols, ready to punish violators, enforced legitimate weights and measures and collected transfer taxes. The government, recognizing the need for orderly trade throughout the realm, sponsored a hereditary caste of long-distance merchants called *Puchteca*, affording them royal status and proclaiming the god *Yaheateuetli* to watch over their valued activities.[30]

The Mayan civilization, close to the Mexican–Guatemalan border of today, mirrored the other great antiquated societies of the Aztecs to the east and the Incas in South America. The city of Calakmul housed about 50,000 people with their ruling influence stretching for 200 km. Their trading region, however, moved up and down Central America and even into the northern areas of South America. The city-state prospered around 800 BCE and it enabled the inhabitants to build some of the largest structures known in the Americas, including the largest pyramid in the world, La Danta. The Mayans prepared highly accurate calendars, sophisticated mathematics, and informative hieroglyphic writing, and the society was organized on a complex social and political order. What is most unique about these ancient people is that elaborate murals as unearthed by archeologists do not represent the activities of an elite class of rulers and priests.

They show elaborate market scenes of average people in their daily exchanges for the staples of life and also preparing or consuming products. Clearly shown are agricultural products like atole, tamales, and tobacco, as well as the sales of textiles and needles. The glyphs accompanying the murals describe the transactions taking place—a strong reference to the importance of the trading imperative in their lives. The Mayans engaged in long-distance area trade with a variety of the Mesoamerican societies, including groups in the central and even western gulf coast areas of what is now Mexico. They moved into the Caribbean islands and down into Colombia. Closer to their homeland, a concentrated lineal network was established that ran along the Boca Costa region in Guatemala, which connected Mexico with El Salvador.

On this path, large causeways were constructed for the movement of goods. Local farmers traveled to markets with their produce (a majority of which were cacao beans) using large baskets strapped to their backs and further supported by a forehead band. Inland waterways provided additional transport highways through canoes. Middlemen merchants ventured further, but as no horses nor pack animals or wheeled carts existed, they employed porters to carry their goods. While most trade was carried on by exchanging goods, a medium of equal value developed around the cacao bean, considered a luxury item. As a recognized currency in the region, one bean could buy one large tomato, three beans, and one poultry egg, while 100 could be exchanged for a rabbit or a hen, with 1,000 being paid for a slave, a fortune of war. Besides their accepted value in the exchange process, processed beans yielded chocolate, a then privileged drink for the elite such as the royalties, nobles, shamans, wealthy merchants, and artists. Cacao beans, while serving as a valued commodity and medium of exchange in the Aztec economic system, were also part of a transcontinental trade initiative between this ancient empire and the Pueblo people of the U.S. southwest. Recently, researchers have confirmed that this old American Indian tribe consumed a cacao-based beverage whose ingredient could only have been imported from a Mexican Mesoamerican source. Along with remnants of this widely ingested chocolate brew, macaws (colorful parrots), copper bells, and artisan objects indigenous to the Aztec-Mayan region have been found. Archaeologists surmise that, in return, the Pueblo Indians bartered turquoise.[31]

The cacao bean in this civilization was the equivalent of olive oil in the Mediterranean and salt in China and North Africa. It is also the forerunner of gold and silver in other parts of the world.

Long-distance trade yielded precious stones like jade and turquoise, as well as Spondylus shells used in jewelry, to which quetzal feathers were added as personal adornments for rich patrons. Raw and woven cotton; vanilla beans; and mined minerals like flint, pyrite, hematite, cinnabar, quartz, travertine, magnetite, and high-quality clays were commodities that all members of the Mayan culture used daily.

Beyond the widespread trading initiative, the commerce of the Mayan society exemplified an early form of a vertically integrated manufacturing system through the use of obsidian. This naturally occurring volcanic glass substance is renowned for its molecular thinness that can be used to produce sharp blades, and if highly polished, a mirror. Pre-Colombian Mesoamericans' use of obsidian was extensive and sophisticated, including carved and worked obsidian for tools and decorative objects. Mesoamericans also made a type of sword with obsidian blades mounted in a wooden body. The weapon, called a *macuahuitl*, was capable of inflicting terrible injuries, combining the sharp cutting edge of an obsidian blade with the ragged cut of a serrated weapon. Even today, this unique substance is used to make surgical scalpels. The production of consumable items from this material created an ancient industry structured on an elaborate and integrated foreign supply chain coupled with a separated and distant manufacturing process. The supply chain began with the collection of the raw material at the mines. From such regions it was transported by merchants—using a cadre of simple porters, usually slaves, who carried the ore on their backs—to the workshops or simple factories of skilled craftsmen. In order to make practical use of obsidian, it must be cut and shaped into smaller fragments that can be placed in tools, a tiresome precise activity. Overall, the production of obsidian was very labor intensive and required the commercial linkages of far-flung groups of entrepreneurs all working together as opposed to the simple exchange of one product for another. Around 700 CE, it is estimated that the sister city of Calakmul and a rival commercial center, Tikal, had close to 100 of these obsidian workshops.

Given the extensive commercial activities of merchants in the Mayan society, their contribution to its general welfare resulted in their status being elevated to the elite, as the commoners relied on their trading initiatives to provide for the importation of goods providing daily work and supply of basic substances. These dependencies entrusted merchants with substantial power and wealth, creating a rising middle class to offset the strength of the royalties, nobles, and priests while creating a societal link to the lower classes.

Such political and economic interplay enabled the ancient Mayan civilization to flourish as a culturally enriched society. When this trade pattern was disrupted, it contributed to their collapse. While the actual collapse of the Mayan society is still a matter of conjecture with theories of drought, epidemic, foreign invasion, or the revolt of peasants considered, the loss of their strategic intricate trading systems, especially those connected to the central Mexican civilization—the Teotihuacan—may have been a prime element in their eventual demise.

In the southern part of the Western Hemisphere, another great civilization developed, the Incas. This empire stretched the entire continent of South America (see Figure 3.6). An extensive network of

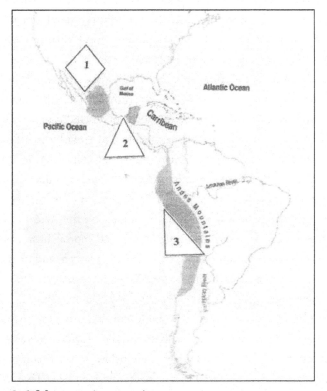

Figure 3.6 Mesoamerican empires

Note: 1. Aztec (ca. 1300 to 1531CE)
      2. Maya (ca. 200 to 900 CE)
      3. Inca (ca. 1200 to 1535 CE)

trade was facilitated by massive roadways that rivaled those constructed across Asia and during the Roman Empire for commercial travel (see Chapter 6). A tribute in the form of taxation of goods and services was paid to the royal house. It was said that the empire's feared tax collectors would know even if something as small as a sandal went missing from the inventory of merchants.[32] At the local level of agricultural products, cotton to potatoes, maize, and quinoa were bartered. Handcrafted goods in the form of clothes made from the sheerings of sheep, alpaca, and llama were valued commodities as was chichi or maize beer. Long-distance trade was administered and controlled by royal agents working with local or regional private merchants.

The Incas had no form of writing, and yet their system of numerical record keeping—multicolored string formations known as *quipus*— was incredibly accurate. Although the Inca Empire was constructed on military conquest, its maintenance and continuing development were built on a combination of economic and political alliances; all built around the commercial imperative dictated by the state.

A comparison of the commercial activities of the Aztecs and the Incas would seem to indicate that the Aztecs were more liberal in their economic systems and policies. Perhaps, due to a more open land geography and a more accessible land mass, Aztec merchants traded with distant groups and locally had a stronger open-market form of commercialism, while the Incas, secluded in the mountains, were closed to outside groups. However, the Incas built official roads to distant cities to connect their empire; such construction had been forbidden by the Aztec kings. In spite of not creating a state-sponsored brick and mortar infrastructure, the Aztecs developed a more sophisticated trading system and used cacao beans as a medium of exchange (a form of early currency). Aztec merchants were given more freedom and afforded a higher rank in society, while the Inca were not viewed as an important class. The merchant class in the Aztec Empire was a special subgroup called *Pochteca* (professional, long-distance traders). Although they were below nobles (mainly priests and warriors), they were placed above the common farmers. They formed their own guilds (the precursor to modern trade organizations and unions), had their own rituals, and acted like a secret society akin to the masons of medieval Europe. Their status even demanded that they live apart from other city dwellers.

There is no recorded evidence of nautical voyages by the Olmecs, predecessors to the Mayans in Mexico, nor the Aztecs. The trading expeditions of these civilizations were land based except for coastline travel. However, mythical tales do mention venturing out to sea. It is possible, however, that Caribbean tribes who did travel between islands may have visited the shores of the Aztec Empire but no chronicled trace has been left of such voyages. The inhabitants of these landmasses surrounded by water did maintain trading privileges with their island neighbors. They even went so far as to record barter transactions on a surface format called *amatl* meaning *bark paper* that they constructed from the inner bark of fig trees. Symbols were used to identify material objects exchanged along with a rudimentary counting system.

> While trade in this area remained rather geographically stagnant there is an example of the northern land spread of bartering by the people of Mesoamerica. The chemical appearance in the artifacts of the Pueblo people, those residing in what is now the United States southwest, of the consumption of chocolate would seem to confirm that some type of exchange took place between the regions. Researchers have established that a cacao based beverage was routinely partaken as part of their diet. It contained a base ingredient that could only have been imported from the Mesoamerican sources, as it was cultivated in prehistoric times from Mexico to Costa Rica by the Aztec and/or Maya civilizations. Also in evidence in the remnants of American indigenous tribes in the region were macaw (colorful parrots) remains, copper bells and decorative items whose origins were clearly Mesoamerican. Many archeologists feel that turquoise and other stone gems were the chief bartered items offered by southwest American Indians in exchange for such traded goods.[33]

With the coming of the Spanish conquistadors, Hernan Cortes entered the Aztec city of Tenochtitlan in 1497 and Francisco Pizarro invaded the Inca city of Awkaypata in 1521, each desirous of only accumulating gold treasure. They did not come as trading expeditions. Not only were such civilizations placed in a state of military occupation and slavery by these European invaders, but their extensive commercial infrastructure, the economic life backbone of these empires, was destroyed, and their societies vanished.

Without internal and regional trade, societies are doomed to extinction.[34] Today's MNEs, which are bent on dominating the emerging markets they enter and monopolizing the extraction of domestic raw materials or utilizing cheap labor, would be wise not to destroy the social and economic infrastructure they encounter but to work to strengthen such foundations.

Caribbean

The settlement of the numerous islands in the Caribbean has been traced back to the Arawak people of South America, who ventured into the sea waters initially looking for new people and places to barter with. Approximately 1,500 years ago, this native Indian group migrated northward from the southern western hemisphere continent to inhabit the Caribbean Sea basin. They scattered among the many islands over the next millennium moving from the southernmost isles chains like the Antilles to the larger masses north such as Jamaica, Puerto Rico, Cuba, and Hispaniola. Certain groups identified themselves as Lokono. Lucayan, Carib, and Ciboney along with the original Arawak but the majority called themselves *Taino*, which stood for the term "the good people" in their language dialect. While they all shared a common geographical heritage they maintained a continuing linkage via an extensive sea trading relationship based on the original initiative, the exchange desire. Large oceangoing canoes plied across the waters of the Caribbean moving goods around the region. Remnants of various plant, animal, and fish species not native to specific island masses indicate that a massive and interdependent trading union existed among the islands and atolls making up the Caribbean area. Some researchers believe that their sea-faring trading missions touched the shores of eastern Central America, Mexico, and possibly the southern U.S. state of Florida. But there are no native tales and no relics pertaining to such voyages to be found in the records maintained by these island natives nor in the archives of the Mayans or later Aztecs or even their predecessors the Olmecs.

Mid-Atlantic and North America

Artic archaeologists excavating ruins of the exploratory travels of perhaps the first cross-Atlantic travelers, the Vikings, have uncovered artifacts dating back to 900 CE.[35] These remnants demonstrated the trade value of exploring new territories. In what is now Iceland and Greenland, and even as far as Newfoundland, storehouses built by these Scandinavians contained caribou, otter and marten furs, walrus ivory, and bushes of soft bird down. These local materials were supplied by the indigenous Dorset hunting tribes. In the markets of Europe, they were prized luxuries. Among the artifacts were fragments of what has been called Viking *tally sticks*, notched wooden poles of various lengths to record trade transactions. Such similar record keeping, as found in other regions of the world, was indicative of the constant exchange routine as it enabled the parties to remember the values assigned in the bartered exchange process.

Further to the northeast, in what is now the United States of America, people along the Mississippi Valley Delta after 500 BCE used their domesticated agricultural experience to engage in long-distance trade across the continent. The most prosperous society of the time is the multitiered and earthen building of Cahokia Mounds, which is located just east of St. Louis, which housed around 20,000 people in 1200 CE. In the southwest, the Hohokam people (200 to 1500 CE) may have acted as the middlemen for commercial development between the California coast and the Rocky Mountains of Utah and Colorado while even stretching into the Great Plains of Central America. In Florida, ancient indigenous Indian tribes had trade relationships with the early Tainos (or the Arawaks), who inhabited the Caribbean Sea and bartered with other island dwellers along with native inhabitants of Central and South America.

While Christopher Columbus sought a western route to the Far East, the English established settlements on the east coast of North America with other European nations staking their claims in the New World.

While the Dutch made a major commercial center out of New Amsterdam (New York), the exploration of the continent's interior was still based on finding a faster and more efficient way to the riches of the East. Both from France, Jacques Cartier of France explored the mouth of the Saint Lawrence River and Jean Alfonse de Saintonge tracked the coast of Labrador in the 1540s in their attempt to find a western route to China. The Englishman George Weymouth's journey in the Arctic also mirrored such a desire, as evidenced by the fact that he carried with him a letter of introduction from his monarch Elizabeth I to the emperor of China cased in diplomatic wording of the day aimed at establishing mutual trading arrangements. A contemporary of Weymouth, Samuel Champlain was the leader of French mission of the Great Lakes region organized for the prime purpose of finding a northwest passage to the Pacific. Champlain's original commission for the journey at the behest of Henri IV in 1603 was based on traversing the New World to the countries of China and the East Indies. While Champlain did not succeed in meeting the continuing costs of such a venture, it was supplemented by his trading ventures with the indigenous native tribes, especially in respect to the lucrative fur trade—animal skins. Although the North American Indians had already established among themselves a medium of exchange known as wampum (made of shell beads); exchange between the European merchants and the native traders was still bartered goods. Traded goods originating in the marketplace of Paris in the 17th century valued at one livre could be exchanged for beaver pelts. These pelts, once brought back across the Atlantic, were worth more than 200 livres. Such a profit margin encouraged the various European commercial agents in the New World to build trade alliances with the unsuspecting tribes, fomenting wars between such rival groups in order to establish a regional monopoly for themselves.

Early Global Trade in Other Regions and Countries

Besides China and India, which make up half of the prime Brazil, Russia, India, and China (BRIC) countries, other markets are worthy of further inspection as their historic positioning in intercontinental trade events provides a background for dealing with them today. The BRIC acronym for the group composed of Brazil, Russia, India, and China was coined by Jim O'Neill in a 2001 Goldman Sachs paper entitled "Building Better Global Economic BRICs."[36] The ellipsis has come into widespread use as a symbol of the apparent shift in global economic power away from the developed The Group of 7 (G7) economies toward the developing world.

Russia

Reverting to its historic designation, after the demise of the Union of Soviet Socialist Republics (USSR) in December 1991, Russia has a rich past in the regional globalization of the world. Like many countries, early Russia grew out of a loose collection of cities that galvanized into an empire. This ancient land mass stretching from Eastern Europe to the Far East was more involved with trade routes lying to the north and south and then east and west. It was only through trade with Persia that spices from the orient, such as pepper, canella, ginger, and saffron, and other goods such as silk, goat skins, and dies from the Far East came into the Russian market. The northern route toward these lands did not allow for direct contact; so Russians had to also rely on the Silk Road for the prized exotic merchandise that followed from them. In the Middle Ages, the Volga Trade route ran to Scandinavia across Germany and the Netherlands using the Caspian Sea via the Volga River. Across the Black Sea, Mediterranean commercial associations moved from the Varangians to Greece. The Romans were said to have relied on Russian wheat production to supplement shipments from Egypt.

Even up through medieval times, it was specific cities in Russia that were recorded as worthy of business contact as opposed to people designated as Russian. The towns of Pskov and Novgorod were actively engaged as trading hubs for merchants plying Western Europe via north German towns. Scandinavian commercial records mention them as well as Kiev, Polotsk, Murom, and Rostove. It is noteworthy that the Vikings, notorious for plunder as opposed to trade relations, maintained normal business exchanges with Russian providers of craft goods; stone and metal workers, especially padlocks with complicated designed keys and icon painters. To the south, the Russians traded furs and leathers, notably sable, squirrel, marten, and beaver along with wax and honey. In return, they received Venetian glass along, Egyptian and damascene cloth, and Byzantine ornamental jewelry.

The early Slavs and other ethnic groups in Russia did not practice long-distance trade. However, the limited dealing they had with alien societies forced them to modify traditional clannish practices as influenced by religious tenets in the exchange process. Although Prince

Vladimir converted the East Slavs to Orthodox Christianity in 988, pre-Christian polytheism persisted for hundreds of years among the people, alongside Christian practices and beliefs. Historically, it was the arrival of Viking princes, who had been invited to rule over the various Slavic groups that brought about the first transition from tribal custom to the writing of what would later be called *Russkaia Pravda* (Russian law). It was the Vikings who introduced commercial laws, standards for weight and measure, and even uniform money as a recognized medium of exchange value to the ancient Russian people. The impact of Roman law on medieval Russia, given their contact with Byzantium, have led some to believe that Justinian's *Corpus Juris Civilis* (*Body of Civil Law*) may have had an impact on the Russian commercial legal tradition but no direct evidence exists. The Mongol invasion did little to alter internal business practices in Russia as these rulers were more like absentee landlords intent on just collecting rent, in this case taxes. It did however offer the opportunity for increased intercontinental trade under the principles of the Pax Mongolica. The Pax Mongolica was a time when Mongols brought peace, stability, economic growth, and the fusion of numerous cultures across and between their occupied territories. Mongolian rulers recognized the importance of trade for an empire to prosper and last. They kept their trade routes well protected so that merchants could safely move across their occupied territory. They even established a communication system, an ancient postal service, to link commercial parties so that long-distance trade could flourish pulling the Slavic majority into the global mix.

The people of the ancient Russian area did not contribute to globalization but they were certainly the unintended recipients of the more progressive commercialization its neighbors exhibited. Centuries later, after World War II, the expanded USSR benefited from the more extensive historic trading relationships its satellite nations inherited.

Brazil

Brazil, the largest country in South America, has been the subject of archaeological speculation as to ancient international trade contact across the Pacific and the Atlantic. Some researchers have proposed that Polynesian sea journeys made their way to the continent as evidenced by genetic sequences in the DNA of Botocudo Indians, a tribe of indigenous people living in eastern Brazil that is similar to these Pacific islanders. Other theories based on a time when the Atlantic Ocean was not as wide separating the east coast of South America with the west coast of Africa, with perhaps the legendary island kingdom of Atlantis in the middle, suggest that West African tribes or the Phoenicians along with expeditions from other kingdoms in the Levant journeyed there. This hypothesis is based on archaeological findings that place Phoenician relics consisting of shipyards and harbors built by them. Some base the idea on supposedly Phoenician inscriptions found in the Amazon, which reference the many kings of Sidon and Tyre, cities established by the Phoenicians from 887 to 856 BCE. Still others feel that expeditions from fabled Atlantis or perhaps the Vikings first established trade with the local natives whose ancestors crossed the Bering land bridge and eventually settled in the region. David Pratt[37] best sums up all these theories with a simple statement:

> It appears that voyages to the Americas have been taking place from all parts of the world for countless thousands of years. The predominant aim seems to have been trade and explorations or the establishment of local colonies, rather than large-scale military conquest and the subjugation and conversion of "inferior" races, as was the case with the European invasions in the 16th and 17th centuries.

Other stories abound that the Inca Empire, with primary trade routes situated on the west coast of South America from Peru up to Columbia, had made commercial expeditions over the Andes mountain range and along the Amazon River into Brazil (note preceding section on *Mesoamerica*). However, what is confirmed is that Brazil began its proven entry to globalization under the forced tutelage of European colonial rule. Following the dividing of the New World under the papal bull, *Inter Caetera* in 1493 (again noted in Chapter 8), the Portuguese claim to Brazil propelled the country into the global commercial arena. Following a nationalistic mercantile commercial policy Brazilian trade was strictly limited to their own citizens and registered ships. The prime exportable resource of this underdeveloped country was sugar and the Europeans could not get enough. Small farms became massive plantations and with the enlarged cultivated territory came the need for a massive labor force to harvest the prized sugarcane. This necessitated at first indigenous native slaves and then the massive importation from Africa as the local workers were highly susceptible to the diseases their European overlords infected them with (see Chapter 6 and the *Toxic Nature of International Trade*).

It wasn't until the 19th century that a shift to another worldwide desired commodity, coffee, replaced the sugar industry. So large was the demand for this new product that a wave of almost one million Europeans, mostly Italians, immigrated to the country. Both the forced slave migration in regard to sugar and the later voluntary immigration related to coffee comprised the two largest movements of populations the world had ever seen. Both were based on global trade.

The Dutch who had been the previous collateral carriers of Brazilian sugar and tobacco to Europe responded to smuggling but the economy of the country was in the hands of the Portuguese. Two centuries later, after the successful Portuguese revolt against Spain, the *Methuen Treaty* of 1703 was made with England, their ally in the war. Under the pact, British merchants were permitted to trade between Portugal and Brazil as long as the physical transaction touched both shores. Such required restriction was rarely abided by and British merchants made deeper inroads into Brazilian foreign trade. In the early 1800s when Napoléon invaded Portugal, a new treaty with the United Kingdom was reluctantly signed giving them carte blanch trading privileges with Brazil.

While there is no doubt that the ancient indigenous tribes in Brazil traded among themselves, it seems that all extraterritorial exposure to the world around them was initiated by the international trade initiative. This global commercial force had the effect of re-engineering the racial and social landscape of the country. As referenced earlier, the cultivation and subsequent harvesting of sugar for export created an economic need for an intensive low-cost labor force requiring the subrogation of the indigenous population and the import of slaves. The majority of African slaves shipped to the Western Hemisphere went to South America with the largest percentage ending up in Brazil. (See Chapter 6—*African Slave Trade*). Unlike other territories where the local natives and imported slaves were strictly separated from their masters, the immigrated Europeans engaged in mixed marriages with Indians and Africans to a degree not encountered elsewhere. As a result, a vast multiplicity of ethnic and cultural legacies is a notable feature of the current Brazilian population.

Connecting East and West: Initial Contact

In *Cathay and the Way Thither*, originally translated and edited by Sir Henry Yule and revised by Henri Cordier, the adventures of merchant explorers are recounted from Persia through India and onto China. This book, one of the first scholarly works to be published (Marco Polo's earlier adventure story is considered semifiction) on the intercourse between China and the Western societies, portrays a vivid picture of how people at both ends of the then known earth learned from each other as ideas were transferred.[38]

As Yule recounts, civilization developed on the back of intercontinental trade, hitching a ride on the engine of the commercial imperative. The spread of the Islamic religion to the East, a basic tenet of culture and a pillar on which civilized society was constructed, was enhanced by these multiregional commercial ventures. Arab merchants brought their faith with them, combining the commercial activity with their religious convictions. Today the populations in the Far East nations of Indonesia (87 percent) and Malaysia (53 percent), as well as large segments of the territories they crossed, Turkey (98.7 percent), Pakistan (97 percent), and even India (14 percent), bear the mark of such trade agents' inspiration homage to their religion. The exploration of the Western Hemisphere by Columbus and later Cortes and Pizarro intertwined their mercantile imperative with religious overtones, allowing for the blessing of the Catholic Church in their endeavors. The colonization of the territories discovered by them as well as other global expeditions based primarily on the commercialization of the region's resources carried a religious imprint that still exists to this day with such areas overwhelmingly bearing connotations of Catholicism. As presented earlier, one of the prime motivations for the Chinese imperial court to authorize the sailing of the Star Fleet to circumnavigate the globe was the desire to spread the works of Confucius.

Commercial caravans making their way across Arabian areas controlled by Bedouin brotherhoods were required to pay a tribute to those in control of their routes. Centuries later, as the American west was settled, wagon trains of settlers crossing Indian tribal lands also paid homage for safe conduct. One of the important initial acts of the United States after the war for independence and enacted by the first Continental Congress was the passage of an import tariff. Such an action not only proclaimed to the world their right as an independent nation to chart their own sovereign power over international trade but also helped to fund the fledgling federal government. The early trade routes connecting East and West also gave rise to two periods, which William Bernstein calls "the disease of trade."[39] While many are familiar with the Black Death that ravished Europe in the 14th century, a similar plague occurred earlier from 540 to 800 CE. Both pandemics have been traced to the then growing commercial exchanges occurring around the world.

As Bernstein recalls, the first act (the beginning of the Common Era) was due to infected fleas carried by black rats scampering over the mooring ropes of outbound trading ships anchored on India's western Malabar Coast. Traveling on the seasonal westbound monsoon winds, the disease that contaminated the cargo's vessels was carried across the Indian Ocean to southern Arabia and up the Red Sea maritime route to Alexandria, the Mesopotamia region, and Constantinople, reducing the power and prestige of the Byzantines and Persian Empires. The infection rate was so devastating that by 700 CE the population of Constantinople was cut in half. Since India acted as a geographical centralized trading hub between West and East, its merchant ships also engaged Chinese seaports. While quantifiable results of the plague in the East are hard to verify, it could be assumed that the Tang dynasty was deeply affected. Some reports of the era indicate that half of the province of Shandong died and that during a concurrent period to the Western devastation, the population of China decreased by 25 percent.[40]

The bubonic-type plague that returned in 13th century was not seaborne like before but was tied to the increased development of trade across the land route linking East and West, more commonly known as the Silk Road. While again attributed to originating from Central Asia, it was initially transmitted by the conquest of the Mongol armies marching across the continent westward. In the pathway created by the Mongol Empire came merchant traders who used the Pax Mongolica to move across the newly unified connecting regions of the Middle East, Asia Minor, and China; and from there, into the highly populated areas in Europe. At each caravansary, trading outposts created by these commercial agents, the disease spread among owners, workers, and guests and spread the progress of the outbreak by scattering survivors in all directions.

When the pandemic reached its peak in 1350, the European population is estimated to have decreased by 30 percent to 60 percent with the world population losing approximately 100 million inhabitants. According to Mongol and Ming census data between 1330 and 1430, the plague reduced the population of China, which lost 21 million people. The deaths, attributable to the illness, were caused not only by the disease but also by the destruction of economic life left in its wake. Trade, even between local towns, came to a standstill as each village tried to wall itself off from outside contamination. Agricultural workers and laborers in all trades were affected with the result that global production of necessities dropped severely and famine struck urban centers. Government revenue via taxation, tied to the exchange process, was depressed and normal administrative services were disrupted. Unable to understand how the sickness started, blame fell on anything foreign. Alien groups and religious minorities, especially Jews, in several areas were driven out or killed, being suspected as bearers of the plague. Cross-territorial movement came to a virtual standstill, and with it, international trade greatly diminished. Because of the devastation, the last vestiges of power and wealth previously centered in the Middle and Far East began to fade, ushering in a new era of European dominance on the historic trajectory of world trade. It is impossible to cover and relate the activities of all the societies involved in ancient trade in this limited chapter. Even local groups exchanging with each other were part of a far-reaching, interwoven network that covered a greater part of the earth, and each independent transaction eventually reached out to a greater circle of connected parties. The recent discovery and carbon dating of Arab-marketed silver coins have provided evidence that ancient global trade reached northern Germany 1,200 years ago. As these pieces of exchange originated in Northern Africa, Iran, Iraq, or Afghanistan and were made anywhere from 610 to 820, their discovery in the remains of a Slavic conclave, near a Viking settlement, is indicative of a century's old trading post between east and west.[41] Such findings seem to continuously support the contention that as archeological researchers dig deeper in the past of scattered tribal groups around the globe they will continue to find remnants and artifacts that support the simple fact that the world was much more connected by trade than first conceived.

It is outside the scope of this book to cover all examples of cross-territorial trade in the ancient world. The chapter materials are used however to illustrate the extensive networks and patterns of commercial exchanges that the pioneers of modern-day globalization constructed that traversed intercontinental areas and touched numerous early societies across and between vast geographical territories around the world.

CHAPTER 4

The Age of Exploration

The first threads in the tapestry of globalization began in ancient times as merchants began trading between their territorial regions and then expanded over intercontinental land routes. The extended navigation of the Mediterranean Sea basin further enhanced the process as ships moving along the Red Sea and then making their way by hugging the coast across the Arabian Sea to India opened up water venues to new territories. These initial commercial connections between the East and the West were dubbed the *Incense Road*, or the *Spice Route*, and then the *Silk Road*. These vestiges of international trade stretching from Europe to Asia operated from 100 BCE to around 1500 CE. The merchants who traveled in these early global trade routes exchanged not only goods but also knowledge—knowledge of different peoples and their cultures, sciences, and religions. The world grew up and civilization advanced as technologies in the fields of chemistry, astronomy, and mathematics were transferred from region to region. Even the more practical aspects of life—from paper making and printing to glass and ceramic production—were exchanged. Innovations in irrigation construction, architectural design, and navigation techniques—along with a multitude of new products and artistic use of native raw materials—found their way across territories, which enhanced the lives of these fledgling intergraded societies in the ancient world.

While it has been proven that people moved from one continent to another via adjacent land masses and coastal navigation, the first use of the world's two great oceans—the Atlantic and the Pacific—is open to historic interpretation as to which social group on the shores of either of these great water masses initiated first contact. John Blasford-Snell provides evidence that South Americans could have had trading contacts with Africa around 1000 BCE using reed boats to journey across the ocean.[1] This notion is exemplified by *Kon-Tiki*, the name of the raft used by Norwegian explorer and writer Thor Heyerdahl in his 1947 expedition across the Pacific Ocean from South America to the Polynesian islands. Historians have documented, to a degree, the Vikings' crossing of the Atlantic Ocean and the Chinese fleet's 1421 voyage around the world.

However, the golden age of world exploration, which was well recorded and evidenced beginning in the 15th century and lasting until the 17th century, is considered the next great step in the evolution of civilization and the second stage in globalization. It was ushered in by three motivational inspirations that converged into a singular initiative: (a) the desire to explore the world and to satisfy a natural curiosity as to what lies beyond one's borders—to reach out and touch others—as inspired by the Renaissance; (b) the drive to propagate religion and bring the world into the fold of European Christianity; and (c) the need to help cement the economic policy of mercantilism as embraced by the monarchs of the royal houses in Europe in the late 14th century. This last impetus for monopolistic commercialization of the world, whose real underlying intention was power and wealth, drove nations to seek out new lands and combine the aforementioned individual ideals into an imperialistic attitude—not only to colonize underdeveloped regions but also to literally carve up and control trading areas of the world. This era in commercial globalization was perhaps not only the most extensive but also the cruelest, as it robbed many indigenous populations of their sovereign rights and exploited their natural resources.

It should be noted, however, that early Chinese and European sea voyagers encountered some societies whose socioeconomic systems were deeply communal. In these systems, tribal sharing was a common practice, and the concept of individual property rights was an alien idea: People in the closed community simply took what they needed from one another with no offering of replacement in kind. Laurence Bergreen recounts the tale, as inscribed in the captain's log of Ferdinand Magellan's flagship, of the first visit by a group of natives on board Magellan's vessel.[2] He notes that, like thieves in the night, they scampered about picking up anything that intrigued them, expecting to take these things ashore with them. The recognition of personal property rights and the desire for individual wealth accumulation were alien concepts to highly collective societies whose isolated island social interaction never brought them into contact with other civilizations. Teaching such tribal inhabitants the concept of private ownership and hence respect for another's property became a fundamental cornerstone of the early process of barter practiced by other societies the Magellan fleet encountered. A similar experience is related by the Chinese fleet as they sailed around the world in 1421.[3] They also encountered previously remote groups whose geographical separation did not allow for contact with new resources; hence, these groups had not developed the notion of exchange of property. Barter may be one of the first practices of ancient peoples, but such an action might require a territorial proximity to a physically alien environment that offers resources they need or want to trade for. Barter, however, remains the *founding father* of the exchange process, the patriarch of today's globalization—that is, trade and commerce practiced on a worldwide basis.

Mercantilism

While the partnering of government and commercial trading is inherent in the history of mankind and continues today, this economic theory reached its zenith across the globe in the policies and actions of Western European countries from the early 16th to late 18th centuries and thereby affected the world as never before. The term *mercantilism* is defined as *economic nationalism*, the purpose being the building of a wealthy and powerful state by achieving a favorable balance of trade (exports minus imports) whose criteria are measured by the accumulation of gold and silver by a sovereign nation in constant competition with other nation-states. It is a form of protectionism that uses tariffs and subsidies to achieve its goals.[4] The mercantilist agenda emerging in Europe during the 15th century, and continuing throughout the rest of the world into perhaps the 19th century under neomercantilism, has been cited as the chief motivation for imperialism in the form of war and colonial expansion. Even before this extended period, the desire to dominate or monopolize commerce trade in a region or the global trade of specific commodities, such as incense or spices, is traceable to mercantilist principles. The development of the mercantile theory in the literature is perhaps best attributed to merchant Thomas Mun, whose 1664 posthumously published *England's Treasure by Foreign Trade*[5] was attacked by Adam Smith as the prime manifesto encouraging governments to follow this policy.[6] Smith, a free-market advocate, felt that such nationalistic policies stymied domestic growth and that free and open trade among nations provided a more beneficial economic outcome.

The mercantile classes, both domestic businesses and foreign merchants, prodded governments to enact regulatory policies that would protect their business interests against foreign competition, uniting the interests of the state and private parties. What makes this economic proposition different from the normal pairing of government and private commercial interests is that, during the mercantilism period, military conflict between states was more frequent and more extensive around the world than at any other time in history. A full-time state of global war was employed to support and sustain commercial objectives, with most entanglements situated on the world's oceans. The objectives of mercantilism on world trade were to strangle cross-border exchanges between nations and accumulate, via colonization, as many resources as possible to be placed under a singular national flag (i.e., control). Economic protectionism of the singular state from competing countries was the impetus and global commercial imperialism was the tool to achieve this mandate. Although the mercantile concept did not publicly emerge in the literature until the later 1600s, its basic tenets were embraced by Europe's royal houses although not announced as a national policy.

Setting the Stage

In ancient times, the vast riches of the East trickled into Western Europe via networks of connected overland routes. Merchandise on such paths changed hands many times before eventually reaching the final consumer. At each independent exchange, the price was increased. The transport costs were also high and the efficiencies low, as camel or horse caravans— each carrying a small load—were mostly used. Constantinople was geographically positioned on the crossroad of East and West in 1453. Controlled by the Muslim Turks, the valued cargos they permitted to pass through their territory created a virtual monopoly of trade and made them extremely wealthy. However, the Italian port cities, acting as middlemen on the next western stop after Constantinople, were satisfied with being part of the old trade route cartel. This prompted the monarchs of Portugal, Spain, England, and France to find a sea route to the East that would eliminate the stranglehold on imports from the Orient. They were prepared to outfit ships for sea captains sailing in search of the elusive ocean route that would bypass historic land passages and allow them direct access to eastern markets. With the kings' approval of the proposed enterprises and with the explorers' promise to defend the claims to discovered lands in the name of their liege lord and to share the rewards with the royal houses (the king of Spain received one-fifth of all gold and silver recovered on the voyages), the quest began. Governments' financial and political sponsorship of merchants was born and, with the blessing of the Catholic Church, the Western European exploration of the world was devised.

European Exploration: Behind the Push for World Trade Dominance

Notwithstanding the aforementioned global exploration of the great Chinese fleet in 1421 or the earlier legendary voyages across the Atlantic by the Phoenicians or perhaps the Vikings to the Western Hemisphere, the push for a route to the East from Europe to directly obtain the riches of China and southeast Asia was one of the prime motivations for the historic exploits of the European explorers who took to the sea. The desire to find a new, more direct, and more efficient route for the spice and silk trades, along with the quest for silver and gold, drove these courageous voyages. With the eastern Mediterranean and the land trade routes to the East being controlled by the Turkish Empire, it was inevitable that another route would be proposed to reach what the Venetian chronographer Marco Polo had proclaimed in his 1285 collaborative best-selling book *The Description of the World* (or simply known as *Travels*) as the golden land.

The publication of Polo's exploits was a door opener, a literary bridge connecting the East and West, and as such it was a demarcation line inviting the next stage in globalization. It described the mysterious wonders of foreign lands, from new products to alien cultural customs and sights. It was a book that changed the world. At the time of Marco Polo, the Silk Road from China to Rome was already a well-traveled merchant highway, as chronicled in the extensive essay *Cathay and the Way Thither, Being a Collection of Medieval Notices of China.*[7] Polo's widely distributed book began to transform previously exotic, opulent prized goods into more normal household commodities throughout Europe; the result was the development of the initial mass market concept. It also acted as a travel brochure, opening up a whole new culturally diverse world for the average European citizen. Marco Polo traveled with his father and uncle to the court of Kublai Khan, the successor to Genghis Khan; this merchant family used a document called the Pax Mongolica, a decree first introduced by Genghis that insured safe passage across the empire for traders. After uniting the world's largest geographical territory, stretching from China through Mesopotamia and into eastern Europe, the great ruler recognized the need to keep trade routes open and flourishing so that the economic prosperity of his subjects would continue. Besides instituting common laws, he preserved property rights, an important condition inherent in the trading process.

Upon Polo's return to Venice, around 1295, during his imprisonment in the rival nation-state of Genoa, he chronicled his journey with the assistance of the Italian romantic novelist Rustichello da Pisa, resulting in *The Description of the World* (originally published in French and titled *Le Devisement du monde*). The Venetians, so taken by the book's adventurous tales, which perhaps were enhanced by the creative imaginative efforts of Polo's collaborator, began to call him *Il Milione*, or *the Man of a Million Stories*. Like the mythical Persian queen Scheherazade, whose life was spared due to her ability to recite 1,001 nightly tales, thereby captivating her king, the book's detailed and colorful exploits made it a European best seller, as all levels of society were drawn to its amazing descriptions of a land filled with potential riches and wonderful sights. Not only was it valued as an adventure book, but it also served to educate a widening population on the unique and specialized goods the Far East produced. It was in essence a travel brochure coupled with a consumer-like introductory catalog to exotic new products that increased the appetite of the average shopper. It is said that even Christopher Columbus carried a copy on his first voyage to the Western Hemisphere to serve as an inspiration for his exploration. Some historians also note that the second Polo expedition was blessed by Pope Gregory X and that their merchant activities were intertwined with the church, a further reference to the partnering of religion with the commercial imperative as seen in later European explorations. However, the impetus for such a papal sanction may, as recounted in Laurence Bergreen's book,[8] have originated in reverse with Kublai Khan requesting the original introduction via the merchant intermediaries. Polo's book had the European population so excited that for the centuries that followed, the inspiration for travel to distant lands to seek fortune and fame was mutually shared by royal houses, commercial merchants, and even the church. It acted as a unifier of desire, resulting in the great explorers of the 17th century, and as a catalyst for increased globalization. While the human imperative to trade with distant territories for goods of unique and prized value is traceable to much earlier periods of time, the popularity and dissemination of Polo's account of his journey impacted the world like no other document before or after (with the possible exception of religious texts).

Francesco Balducci Pegolotti, a Florentine tradesman and contemporary of Marco Polo, authored one of the first managerial commercial references offering a practical guide for successfully transacting with intermediaries on the Silk Road. Called *Market Practices*, it contained information on exchange rates, customs regulations, and intercontinental shipping arrangements, as well as other tips for dealing with different cultures in the cross-territorial trading process. While it was the precursor for the numerous modern-day scholastic textbooks as well as trade and governmental publications on international business, it also served as a classical introduction to establishing relationships with alien societies—a cultural anthropological guide.

Another Early Explorer

While Marco Polo and other early European explorers of the world are routinely recorded in history books, perhaps due to a bit of Western literary bias, little if nothing is ever mentioned of Ibn Battuta (full name: Abu Abdullah Muhammad Ibn Battuta while also known as Sham ad-Din), one of the most remarkable travelers and chroniclers of the ancient world. Even geography books in Muslim countries, let alone those published in the West, tell of his remarkable journey covering over 75,000 miles, much more than Marco Polo. Battuta began his travels from Tangier in 1325 when he was just 20 years old, about 30 years after the recorded 1271 to 1295 excursions of the more famous Marco Polo. His initial goal was to go on a Hajj, a pilgrimage to Mecca as his Muslim faith required, but he continued on for 30 years. His exploits covered the equivalent of 44 modern-day countries. Under the insistence of Sultan Abu Inan of Morocco, who felt his story should be preserved for scholars, he dictated his accounts at the end of his life to Ibn Juzzay al-Kalbi. It is interesting to note that Marco Polo also did not write of his own exploits but also dictated them to another. The book is commonly titled *Rihla–My Travels*. But this designation describes its genre. The true title is *Tuhfat al-Nuzzar fi Ghara'ib al-Amsar wa-'Aja;ib al-Asfar*, which translates into *A Gift to Those Who Contemplate the Wonders of Cities and the Marvels of Traveling.*

Battuta's mainly traveled to areas of the Dar al-Islam or the Muslim World. He was traversing the land territories that Muslim traders had already ventured into and where they had established communities; so he benefited from their charity and hospitality, both tenets of the Islamic religion. He was also able to take advantage of the vast maritime activities of his fellow Muslim brethren who dominated 13th-century merchant shipping in the Red Sea, the Arabian Sea, the Indian Ocean, and even Chinese waters. The extent of the areas he visited is enormous. From the wide coastline of North Africa and even Granada he moved down the western side of the continent into the interior of the Mali Empire and its magnificent trading city Timbuktu. While traveling east he circumvented the Mamluk Empire from Cairo to Palestine and the Arabian cities of Medina and Mecca and then into the lower portion of Africa including Mogodishu, Mombasa, Kilwa, and Mozambique. His journey cross the Ilkhan Empire brought him to the Seljuks just shy of the Byzantine Empire and Constantinople and on to Baghdad. Venturing further east, he crossed Kabul and entered India, where he visited the Sultanate of Delhi where he was appointed an envoy. His official duties brought him to Calcutta, the Maldives Islands, Sri Lanka, Sumatra, and eventually the Chinese cities of Canton and Peking as well as others during the Yuan Dynasty, 50 years after Marco Polo. To get a better appreciation of the massive territories Battuta traveled across see Figure 4.1.

Figure 4.1 Travels of Ibn Battuta in the 14th century

The descriptions Battuta dictated of his accounts are very vivid and detailed. Unlike Polo, who took more time to comment on the authoritative and governmental aspects of his journey, Battuta devotes more pages to painting pictures of the landscape he saw. However, as a keen observer of local customs and traditions practiced by the people he met as they interacted with the environment around them, he offered great insights into how people lived their daily lives. He does therefore include references to their trading value system, noting what is most prized in their lands. While Polo's primary mission was to be a merchant, Battuta was more of an observational tourist. However, the profiles he offered, in conjunction with the Muslim business communities that served as his guides, provided a tacit consumer marketing survey as to the interconnected needs of people. His book deserves greater recognition for the contribution to garnering an understanding and appreciation of the ancient world. Just like Polo's book, they both provide an insight into the process of early globalization.

Exploring the World

Trans-regional exploration over land and via a confined body of water, the Mediterranean, was presented in Chapter 2 examining the beginning of recorded trade. However, the navigation of the world's oceans sailing from one continent to another, a truly global endeavor, has been harder to discern. The nautical timeline for humankind keeps getting pushed further and farther back in history as the inspection of seas and river beds yields the possibilities of earlier-than-thought cross-continental ocean venturing. Some researchers feel that the Phoenicians may have ventured into the Atlantic Ocean reaching the western coast of Africa with the Norsemen or Vikings touching Greenland, Iceland, and the northeastern shores of North America. Others consider the 1421 voyage of the Chinese Star fleet, as previously mentioned, as the first to navigate both the Pacific and Atlantic oceans reaching almost all the continents of the earth. Ancient maps detailing such marvelous adventures have not yet emerged to confirm such contentions.

The earliest recorded mapping of continents separated by oceans was drawn in 1513 by Piri Reis an admiral of the Turkish fleet that depicts the western coast of Africa and across a vast body of water (Atlantic Ocean) the eastern shore lines of South America as well as the ocean front land mass of Antarctica. The reference to a terrestrial body at the southern pole of the world is considered the most puzzling as, according to geological evidence, this could only have existed around 4000 BCE, the last period before ice covered the entire area. Admiral Reis's notes accompanying his cartographic illustration as drawn on a gazelle skin indicate that he compiled and copied the rendering from other sources dating back to the

Figure 4.2 Shorelines of land masses drawn by Admiral Reis in 1513 as superimposed on a modern-day map of the world

fourth century BCE. Supposedly, Reis used ancient renderings of land masses on both sides of the Atlantic Ocean as gleaned from illustrations contained in the Imperial Library of Constantinople; these might have been saved and then stolen following the destruction of the Library of Alexandria.

Some scholars have surmised that the venturing of the first European sailors in the 15th century to find a sea route to the East was not based on speculation. In fact, they already possessed references indicating that land masses did exist out and across the vast unknown ocean, perhaps those relied on by Admiral Reis. They further conclude that the only reason such illustrations survived was their value signaling lucrative trade routes used by ancient civilizations as clearly no sovereign kingdom claimed them as their own.

European Exploration

Chronologically, the age of European exploration of the oceans evolved as follows. It would seem natural that the first group of world explorers would emerge from Portugal, itself situated on the Atlantic Ocean. The first of the sea voyages of the age of discovery was that of Infante Dom Henrique (Prince Henry the Navigator), who sailed to the Madeiras and Azores while traveling south along the coast of Africa and reached the western bulge of the continent known then as Cabo de Nao in 1430. He was followed by Gil Eanes and Fernao Gomes, who reached the Guinea, Gold, and Ivory coasts. Years later, these ports would become staging areas for the slave trade. In 1486, Bartolomew Diaz rounded the Cape of Good Hope, continued north up the east African coast, and discovered a sea route to India. Numerous Portuguese sea voyages followed, many of them targeting the Brazilian coast, which was first discovered by the 1499 transatlantic voyage of Amerigo Vespucci of Spain, whose name evolved into terms denoting the North and South American continents. Various other Spanish explorers made their way to the New World in search of wealth. Ferdinand Magellan explored the coastal straits of Patagonia off the southern tip of South America and found himself in the Pacific Ocean, opening a new dangerous path to the Orient and in essence circumventing the globe. The actual attempt to militarily colonize or simply suppress the indigenous populations encountered by these early adventurers began with Hernando Cortez, who in 1521 conquered the Aztecs of Mexico and forced them to turn over their kingdoms' riches to the invaders. Twelve years later, Francisco Pizarro defeated the Inca Empire and in doing so claimed most of South America for Spain, the largest amount of territory taken by any nation during the age of discovery.

During the last 1400s, the English also sailed west looking for the illusive water gateway to the treasure-filled East. John Cabot, a citizen of Venice, Italy (born Giovanni Caboto in Genoa), set sail under the flag of England in 1497, reaching Belle Island on the northern coast of Newfoundland in North America. His second try was a disaster, as his four-ship fleet was lost at sea. Ten years later, his son Sebastian Cabot, born in Venice, supposedly also searched for a northwest passage to the East. The English did return, looking again for this magic water route in 1527 under Captain John Rut. But, like Cabot Sr., he only got as far as Newfoundland and Labrador.

The work of ocean discovery as noted earlier was initially undertaken by the sovereign commissioned agents of Portugal and Spain, and later joined by those flying the English and then French banners. It should be noted that not all other European nations participated. The Italian port cities were basically satisfied with their historic domination of the existing but constricting routes in the Mediterranean. The Scandinavian countries were far too removed from direct trade contact with the east, although, less than 200 years later, the Netherlands would create the Dutch West Indies Company and thereby explode on the global trading scene. Germany was split into too many small regional states, none of which could mount an expedition by itself or in conjunction with the others.

While the generally shared onus for European exploration was the desire to secure an alternative direct route to the riches of the East, thereby cutting out Middle Eastern intermediaries, the need to do so was made even more important by an event in 1453 that disrupted world trade. After the Ottoman Empire took control of Constantinople, it blocked European land access to the east, severely limiting commercial exchanges between the two sides of the world. Additionally, the Turkish kingdom similarly obstructed the southern trade routes across North Africa and the Red Sea. The necessity to find another way to make contact with eastern merchants and break the Ottoman land monopoly only served to intensify the magnificent quest of these brave explorers.

Christopher Columbus: The Prolific Explorer

Of all the early explorers the most prolific in terms of trips was Christopher Columbus. In the mid-1400s, while the Portuguese devoted all their efforts to going around the cape of Africa, the Spaniards, after science had established that the world was indeed round, were willing to hear a proposal to sail westward to reach the wealth of China. At the time, Venice, England, and Columbus's native land, Genoa, rebuffed his travel overtures. As he was willing to sell his services to the highest bidder, he continued to approach other royal thrones until Ferdinand and Isabella, the crowned heads of Castile, finally agreed to fund his expedition against the advice of their conservative counselors. This was a difficult time for the Spanish monarchy not only because they had just expelled the invading Moors but also because the loyal and commercially intelligent Jews had brought their nation into economic jeopardy. After 72 days at sea on his first voyage, his tiny armada of three small ships and 87 men reached an island in the Caribbean. His second journey discovered additional islands in the West Indies, while his third, in 1498, landed him on the coast of South America, presumably in the area of Guiana and Venezuela. During his fourth voyage, still searching for a western passage to the spice islands in the Pacific, he attempted to establish a settlement ostensibly to mine for gold.

The journal of Columbus, during his initial journey, reveals that while the mission was to secure gold, precious stones and pearls, and spices—"an infinite number of things that would be profitable"[9]—his thoughts also included strong references to control and dominate the native people not only under the rule of the Spanish monarchy but also under the protection of its Christian heritage from outsiders, a veiled reference to the political tenure of the times, as noted in the following excerpt:

> I say that if Christendom will find profit among these people, how much more will Spain, to whom the whole country should be

subject. Your Highnesses ought not to consent that any stranger should trade here, or put his foot in the country, except Catholic Christians, for this was the beginning and end of the undertaking; namely, the increase and glory of the Christian religion, and that no other should come to these parts who was not a good Christian.[10]

Columbus further advises the monarchy to build a city and fortress to convert the people as the new lands are acquired by Spain and all its riches should flow back home. The mercantile trading policy is recounted and it is further strengthened when joined by a religious determination. The blessing of the economic principle by the Catholic Church provided what was in essence a commercial venture with a spiritual undertaking and set the stage for a coming period with the righteous reward of forced colonization being rationalized.

The Commercial Imperative Continues

On the exploratory heels of Bartolomeu Dias rounding the Atlantic side of the Cape of Good Hope on the horn of Africa and Vasco de Gama retracing the route in 1497 but sailing further to east to India, the Far East was transformed via a closer partnership with Europe and the West. Ferdinand Magellan in 1519 set sail from Seville, Spain, and circumvented the world. Although other explorers and pioneers followed in their hallowed footsteps, the prime objective of each was a shared objective, the commercial globalization of the world for the benefit of the singular monarchs of major European nations.

Bergreen's documents explain that spices played an essential trading role in civilizations since antiquity and were the motivating force for early intercontinental trade and global exploration in the early 1400s.[11] Such exceedingly priceless merchandise was the forerunner of the search for other valuable materials and products that played an important role in the development of the globalization imperative. History tells us that other later prized resources—silk as well as gold and silver—drove the world's trading legacy. Like oil today, the quest in those days by Europeans for resources found in foreign lands drove the world's economy and influenced global politics; and again, like oil in modern times, the search for such rare commodities became inextricably intertwined with exploration, conquest, and imperialism—the drivers of both early and modern globalization.

Such considerations led to the period of mercantilism, the desire for national states to create ancient world empires by controlling the spice trade. Arab merchants traded spices across land routes from northern Arabia across Constantinople (Turkey), through Asia Minor, and finally to China. By concealing the origins of cinnamon, pepper, cloves, and nutmeg, such traders were able to gain a monopoly and control prices. Europeans came to believe that the spices came from Africa, when in fact they merely changed hands in the region. Such a middleman principle of value added at the intermediate level in the channels of distribution process is still with us today. Those who control the distribution stand to make more than those who actually make the items. Oil at its chief source is cheap but at the pump its inherent value increases manifold. The garment sewn by a two-dollar-a-day laborer in emerging nations translates to a high premium in the hands of the market distributor at the retail segment of the distribution channel.

Under the traditional trade system, spices, along with damasks (a prized reversible fabric of linen, silk, cotton, or wool, woven with patterns); diamonds; pearls; opiates (medicine containing opium and used for inducing sleep and relieving pain); plus other exotic goods reached Europe, the chief consuming environment, by slow, costly, and indirect routes over land and sea: from China and the Indian Ocean through the Middle East and Persian Gulf, arriving in Italy or the south of France, and then delivered overland to their final destinations. Along the way, they went through a multitude of hands, and at every juncture of the voyage, their prices increased manifold.

As noted earlier, the global spice trade underwent a political upheaval in 1453 when Constantinople fell to the Turks and the time-honored overland routes between Asia and Europe were severed. The prospect of finding and establishing a spice trade route opened up new opportunities for any European nation able to master the seas. If a direct ocean route could be found in the Spice Islands, the reward would be the control over the world's economy. The lure of such riches compelled monarch financiers—eager to extend their power and rule—to support explorers and hence launched the era of expedition. Such desires were assisted by the development of a new type of ship for the seas, a smaller, more maneuverable vessel distinguished by its triangular lateen sail. Until such time, ships were built like large floating boxes or galleys relying on oarsman or fixed sails for power. With the invention of the movable sail, coupled with construction of a more shallow draft hull, pilots could set a course close to the wind and permit the navigational concept of tack to be employed, allowing for the constant shifting of the track to take advantage of the wind from one direction and then from another—zigzagging against the wind to a fixed point. In Portugal, such pursuit attracted the best minds of the day, bringing together navigators, shipwrights or builders, astronomers, pilots, cosmographers, and cartographers. This ambitious exploration of the world resulted in the age of discovery and the next leap in globalization. The chief motivator then—commercialization of the globe through trade—instigated technological advances in much the same way that the desire to reach out and touch the world today has forced and nurtured communication improvements and other modern advances to bring the world close together.

Although scholars differ on the initial exploration of North America, noting the possible accounts of visits by the Vikings and the Chinese as previously mentioned, the opening of commercial undertakings with the continent is usually traced to the first celebrated 1492 voyage of Christopher Columbus. His second trip, laden with settlers, foretold the establishment of a true trading colony. While it is well accepted that mercantile-oriented European monarchs were desirous of accumulating wealth and power not via equalized exchange but through conquest and colonization of new territories, the specter of the religious influence helped to propel the process.

Potosi: The Colonial Spanish Bell

As the world grew up on the heels of the exploration begun by Christopher Columbus, the opening of the New World by European sovereigns led to a period of colonization aimed at extracting the riches of the Western Hemisphere. The Spanish, already the purveyors of newfound wealth due to their conquest of the Aztecs to the north and the Incas in the south, expanded their imperial influence across South America. Upon the discovery of silver-rich ore deposits in the mountain called Cerro Rico (*rich hill* or *mountain*), the City of Potosi was constructed in Bolivia in 1544. For the next 50 years, this area produced the most fabulous source of the precious metal silver the world had ever known and perhaps will ever know.

Collaterally, the city, perhaps the highest one in the world at 13,420 ft. (4,090 m), was one of the largest and wealthiest metropolises of its time. At its zenith, 200,000 people lived in the city, making it the most populous metropolis of its day, exceeding London, Paris, and Madrid. The mining of the silver ore made it the ancient world's biggest industrial complex. The process of extraction utilized a most sophisticated and intricate system of aqueducts and artificial lakes, as water was a key component in the extraction of the silver. Using the patio process of refinement, the raw silver ore was formed into an amalgam with mercury, washed, and then heated to burn off the mercury. This process, as well as the mining effort itself, was extremely labor intensive, as was the physical transport of the finalized ingots on the backs of human mules to the Atlantic and Pacific Oceans for export back to Europe and the Orient. Local indigenous Indians formed the bulk of the coerced workforce built on the *Incan Mita* institution of conscripted labor. Men from 18 to 50 years of age, taken by force from the 16 highland provinces, provided the mining camps with a virtual slave force for 17 weeks a year. Thousands perished, about one out of eight dying on the job due to the toxic mercury fumes in the refinement process, the foul air in the shafts as they toiled at depths of 700 ft. without proper ventilation, and the arduous journey to port facilities weighted down with loads normally meant for beasts of burden, not men. The necessity for such a large workforce was the eventual cause for the abduction and transportation of slaves from Africa to supplement the local work contingent. Records indicate that around 1608, approximately 2,000 slave workers per year were introduced into the mining operations and that a total of 30,000 were placed in human bondage during the Spanish colonial period. Portuguese traders acted as middlemen in the process, purchasing captured prisoners of war from other African tribes while also at times resorting to the outright kidnapping of native populations, aided and abetted by local Arab slave merchants.

Due to the export of silver and the construction of a mint that produced reals years later, the city was admired and valued. It was the prized jewel in the Spanish Empire, allowing for the accumulated wealth to be used not only to finance their consolidation of Western Hemisphere operations but also to travel around the world and solidify their influence in the Far East via the establishment of trading activities in the Philippines. The precious metal became the first universally accepted medium of exchange and its value was prized not only by all countries in cross-border trading but also internally in the everyday market activities of domestic citizens around the world. In some regions, silver was presented in bullion form, while in other areas it was minted into the coin of the realm such as the real or guilder. The base ore, however, remained as the symbol of material value and Potosi itself became synonymous with good fortune and the phrase *as rich as Potosi* made its way into the English language. For the first 50 years of the mining operation, Potosi was the most fabulous source of silver the world had ever known. It is estimated from records kept by local authorities that from 1556 to 1783 more than 45,000 tons of pure silver was taken from mountain veins of Cerro Rico. The architecture of the city was magnificent, as artists from around the world were recruited to build sumptuous structures featuring elaborate carved columns, lavishly sculptured gates, and Byzantine domes. More than 86 churches were erected in the city, a testament to the city's importance as the centerpiece of global social life, itself deeply influenced by the Catholic Church.

By the end of the 1700s, the mines were exhausted; competition from other New World sources had begun to grow and a drop in the worldwide price of sliver itself deeply affected Potosi's economy. Internal strife between the city's colonialist overlords and the native population caused further deterioration while a series of natural disasters from floods to earthquakes ravaged the land. Slowly, this once-magnificent city, prominent for being the world's supplier of silver, faded away. Although global trading expeditions had sparked the city's establishment, they were also responsible for its demise.

Such horrific treatment of native populations and perhaps the greatest wholesale abuse of global human rights occurred during the colonization of the Western Hemisphere by European powers. Tens of thousands of native Africans were sold into slavery and transported across the Atlantic. Placed in perpetual bondage, they labored alongside domesticated animals on plantations in the American south, the Caribbean islands, and Central America. In South America, as noted earlier, they supplemented indigenous populations in the mineral-extraction process with both groups considered savages, more like beasts of burden. As world trade was dramatically propelled forward, following the activities of 15th-century explorers, the business practices that emerged in underdeveloped countries were based on the deplorable commercial colonialism practices originally induced in them by the conquistadors. Many business ventures put aside respect for human dignity. Their treatment of the local citizens was overshadowed by the quest for new resources, which could bring wealth to foreign traders.

Obsessed with finding a northwest passage to the Pacific, commercial expeditions moved across the newly discovered North American eastern frontier only to encounter a local environment rich with animal hides whose value when imported back to Europe increased manifold. As noted earlier, those merchants involved in the process secured vast profits as trade goods, beaver and otter skins, valued at one livre when they left the New World were worth 200 livres when they arrived back in the fashion-conscious European capitals.[12] Area Indian tribes were pressed into service, first by the French and later the British and Dutch in the attainment of these precious commodities, with merchants of each nation looking to protect their valued monopoly. The tribes were manipulated and used like pawns, with wars between them instigated by these varying groups for dominance of the fur trade. They were supplied with guns and ammunition for the sole purpose of destroying competing hunters from other tribes. The Indians never equally participated in the extraordinary wealth inherent in their supply chain activities, a criticism often leveled at modern-day multinational corporations (MNCs) as they take advantage of the citizens of emerging nations of today. Certainly, the slaves on plantations in the North American south and those placed in mining operation in South America were deprived of not only an economic livelihood but also their lives.

Centuries later, the atrocities practiced by such business enterprises were still accruing. David Grann in *The Lost City of Z* recounts in vivid detail how genocide was used to control the native population used by the British-registered Peruvian Amazon Company in the extraction of rubber in the late 1800s. As verified by the 1904 UK government's Casement Report, public beheading was a common punishment, while rebellious Indians had gasoline poured on them and were set on fire, drowned, or fed alive to ravenous dogs.[13] They were castrated, physically mutilated, and starved to death. Company henchmen raped women and young girls while smashing their infants' heads to the ground—all to keep the precious rubber extract flowing back to Europe and the world. Such vile actions by Western companies—perhaps not to the degree practiced in Peru, but nevertheless still humanly despicable—have been historically accounted for in Africa, India, and the Far East, as the commercially engineered need to enrich themselves on the backs of the indigenous populations in search and extraction of local natural resources has always plagued business institutions in the expansion of their global operations. Reprehensible remnants of such policies are still noticeable today as some MNCs outsource to the sweatshops of modern underdeveloped countries and directly or indirectly partner with repressive governments to limit and suppress human rights. While the barbaric physical handling of people who came into contact with imported commercial activities is historically well documented, one should not overlook the unequal economic treatment of the indigenous population when it came to their rights to freely conduct business transactions not only between themselves but also with other cross-territorial parties.

Prior to the great age of discovery propelled by mercantile thinking, the idea of cross-border free trade first surfaced within one of civilizations hallowed documents, the Magna Carta. It is often cited as one of the first public instruments leading to an emancipated human existence and considered a catalyst for democratic principles when the English baron forced King John in 1215 to recognize their limited rights thereby curtailing to a degree his absolute sovereign control over all citizens in his domain. Beyond this social breakthrough, the document contains two chapters devoted to the recognition of cross-border trade as a necessary protected activity worthy of the sovereign's proclamation to be the law of the land. This hallowed declaration also echos similar concepts found in Pax Mongolica. It is also considered a fundamental announcement for the idealistic foundation of allowing the right of people to engage freely in cross-border trade found in the Declaration of Independence by the fledgling U.S. coalition of colonies in 1776 discussed in the following.

Chapters 41 and 42 of the Magna Carta allow for all merchants to safely and securely go out of England and come into England by land as well as water for the purpose of buying and selling. The term merchants included foreign traders and requested the same treatment for British merchant's traveling abroad, even during times of war. Such demonstrative language seemingly placed those involved in international commercial ventures in a specialized class and thereby recognized the importance of both domestic and cross-territorial exchange as valuable to the country and thereby the crown. The decree stressed the importance of the roots of globalization as a progressive complement to the development of civilization. But throughout the mercantile period, restrictions were placed on local colonial citizens that might conflict with or damage the exclusive trading rights granted to foreign merchants—that is, citizens of sovereign nations who control their countries. The commercial globalization of the world, which began in earnest during the age of discovery, would later lead to periods of colonization around the world and the formation of new countries. The accelerated process would also raise complicated questions as to the international trading rights of nations and the use of the high seas as the neutral transactional highways for a greater interconnected world.

Founding United States via Right-to-Trade Principles

The American Revolution was predicated on unjust trading principles. The famous Boston Tea Party of 1773 came to represent a contest between the British Parliament and the American colonies over international trade. As European developed a taste for tea in the 17th century, numerous competitors were in constant battle for the lucrative trade imports to England that originated in the East Indies. In 1698, the English Parliament gave the East Indian Company the sole right to import tea into the country but retained a tariff tax on the commodity. As tea became an equally popular drink in their colonies around the world, the government sought to also eliminate foreign competition in them by passing an act in 1721 requiring all colonists to only import their tea from England. Tea coming into the American colonies had to transit England, in effect extending the East Indian Company's territorial monopoly. Although the British government repealed the Townshend Acts—a series of burdensome monetary regulations concerning the colonies—it preserved the tea tax, partly as a symbol of the right to tax imports into their satellite territory and partly to aid the financially embarrassed East India Company. The tossing of tea from ships in the Boston harbor, then the largest importing location, became a symbolic rallying cry for the fledgling, but soon to be independent, nation. The colonists, taking their cue from the British Parliamentary elected representative system (which had the right to tax their own citizens), declared that they had a similar right, hence the slogan *No taxation without representation.*

Three years after the Boston Tea Party, the venerable Declaration of Independence in 1776 was issued by the American colonies. It set out the grievances on which this new nation was created. Beyond the document's famous rhetoric of proclaiming the fundamental rights of all men as endowed by their creator, it cited as the chief reasons the desire to be free and the right to *establish Commerce* as an independent state within itself despite continuing allegiance to the British Crown. In the Declaration the king was admonished *for cutting off trade with all parts of the world,* an economic imperative to declare independence and perhaps a reference to the lesson learned from England's desire to control global trade. The right to conduct international trade is commingled with the inherent unalienable legitimacy of all humanity to be free. Such proclamations continued the legacy of the Magna Carta along with an expanded veiled reference to the freedom-of-the-seas principle, with both documents recognizing the importance of international commerce as the inherent lifeblood of national prosperity and a universal right of sovereign countries.

Trade as a Right for an Independent India

Centuries later, international trade again played a large part in the Indian overthrow of British colonial control and that nation's subsequent independence. The British had controlled India since about the time of the American Revolution. Under British rule, the harvested raw cotton, a prime staple of the Indian economy and a chief employer of its masculine labor force, would be shipped to England where it was woven and spun into cloth using modern mill machines. In turn, the finished products were then shipped back to India, flooding the market with cheap cotton textiles. As part of their daily ritualized routine, women in India would traditionally spin cotton on their native loom, the *charkha* (a home spinning device), and they would gather village groups for the local process. This was a deeply rooted social and cultural phenomenon that was practiced throughout the country. Although a cottage industry, it was the backbone of most rural Indian economy and could not be replaced. Britain's cotton export–import policy crippled the village-based hand-spinning and cloth-weaving industry. Millions of Indians were thrown out of work and into poverty. Under Gandhi's pacifist-inspired resistance to British rule, he encouraged the men to spin (traditionally women's work) and weave their own cloth. The public wearing of homespun cloth called *khaddar* or *khadi*, meaning rough, became a symbol of the revolution. Even Gandhi himself would often spin in public. This economic-based revolution was one of the forces that eventually motivated the British to leave India. Indian men's refusal to harvest the cotton fields and the patriotic use of the khaddar widened the importation of British-made cloth and impacted English production and their economy. Even today, this historic resentment of colonial economic policy, which promoted free global trade, is remembered. The charkha remains as a symbol on some Indian money and is pictured on the flag of the Indian Congress Party.

Out of the vestiges of mercantile era policy enactment arose the independence of two nations. Their struggle was fueled by a desire for free international trade.

Trade as the Basis for a Religious Proclamation

While all religions recognized the socially induced need to barter and exchange in a rightful way and were thereby involved in commenting on the commercial process in their various doctrines (see Chapter 8), the Catholic Church may have had the greatest effect on international trade. The influence of the Catholic order on global trade reached its zenith with the publication of *Inter Caetera*, a papal bull issued by Pope Alexander VI on May 4, 1493. Following the great age of discovery and the first true commercialization of the globe, the bull divided the New World (i.e., the non-European foreign territories) between the Portuguese and the

Spanish, essentially settling the first global trade issue. The decree divided the two major oceans of the world through a meridian moving east and west, thereby conferring the lucrative trade in such lands via the routes such waters touched. Creating royal monopolies of trade yielded great wealth to these sovereign nations. From the East Indies, rare spices, prized silks, unique woods, and ivory, along with Chinese porcelain, fed the insatiable demand in Europe for exotic consumer products, while from the Americas flowed gold, silver, precious stones, furs, and eventually tobacco—the historic mainstays of material wealth. The massive traffic between Europe and the colonies not only created a new merchant class in society but also insured the continued funding of the state via the levy of the *quinto*, the monarchy's 20 percent tariff as goods transited the trading ports. It also helped solidify the power of the church as an architect of world economic affairs. The division was unequal due to Spanish influence in the Vatican (Alexander VI himself was of Spanish heritage), which precluded Portugal from trading in Asia. As a remedy to this injustice, the Treaty of Tordesillas was signed between the two nations in 1494 (see Figure 4.3). Known as the line of demarcation, it divided the

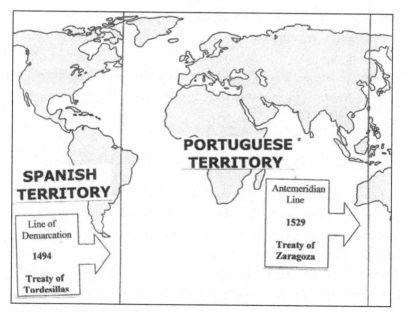

Figure 4.3 Treaties of Tordesillas (1494) and Zaragoza (1529): Division of the world

lands discovered initially by Christopher Columbus, who claimed them on behalf of Spain, while recognizing the already asserted Portuguese rights to the Cape Verde Islands off the west coast of Africa. It was a further ratification of the previously noted papal bull, the *Inter Caetera*. This declared division of territories did not, however, include lands on the other side of the globe (those touched by the Pacific and Indian Oceans). To settle state ownership in this part of the world, the Treaty of Zaragoza (Saragossa) was signed in 1529. It set an antemeridian line that effectively split the world into two hemispheres of national influence and control, limiting the military clashes of the two countries. These documents were precursors to international trade legacy agreements and the collateral creations of systems regulating and promoting global trade.

As the papal bull excluded other monarchs, both the British and Dutch (Protestant nations) were jealous rivals, with the leaders of both countries encouraging the raiding of Spanish galleons on the demarcated merchant transport lanes. In the late 1500s, English ships were especially active, attacking ships returning from the Western Hemisphere as Spain would not allow her majesty's commercial agents to trade with their American colonies. King Philip of Spain was well aware that Queen Elizabeth I supported such pirate adventures of her sea dogs, or privateers as they came to be called, while she gave her tacit approval to their rival gangs: the Huguenot corsairs and Dutch buccaneers. He called on the church once more for assistance. The pope, then Pius V, could not outwardly condemn such events. Instead, he issued a bull excommunicating Queen Elizabeth I for her supposed actions in extricating the Church of England from the mother Roman Catholic Church, while also accusing her of causing the persecution of its members in Britain. The declaration was in reality a backhanded punishment for the disruption of Spanish trade flowing back to Europe.

Argument for Global Free Trading Rights

By 1602, the exploration of the world with respect to navigating the waters of the Pacific and Indian Oceans to harvest the lucrative trading rights in the East Indies (the Far East including India, China, and the Spice Islands) was divided by papal donation between Spain and Portugal, as

noted earlier. The decree forbade all foreigners from navigating or entering such waters, reserving the territory for the designated nations only.
The Dutch West Indies Company retained Hugo Grotius, a young law-
yer, to argue their rights to sail the prohibited territory and trade with the
societies encountered. In 1604 to 1605, he wrote a dissertation, which in
effect was a legal brief to sustain the claims of his client. Titled *Freedom
of the Seas* (*Mare Liberum* in Latin), it is considered the first systematic
treatise on the law of nations and the seas and every country's right to
unencumbered trade. The document made a case that all nations being
equal have an equal right to the uninterrupted use of unappropriated
parts of the ocean for navigation in order to exercise the natural freedom
to engage in travel and cross-territorial exchange. The treatise linked the
inalienable right to trade with use of the nature's waterways as highways
on which the process was conducted and their intertwined duality was
declared a principle of international law. He specifically stated,

> No nation has "the right to prevent other nations which so desire,
> from selling to one another, from bartering with one another."
> Nature has given to all peoples a right of access to all other peoples.
> Commercial intercourse was a necessity to mankind… therefore
> the right belongs to all nations.[14]

These statements echoed to a degree the travel freedoms afforded
to merchants moving in and out of a singular nation, England, in the
earlier Magna Carta and laid the basis for the legal justification of a new
nation, the United States, to throw off the bonds of colonialist rule 172
years later. This little-known dissertation may have been the first publicly presented legally based document against mercantilist monopolistic
principles in advance of the academically based economic arguments that
later followed; and therefore a stimulator of globalization as we know it
today. Its basic tenets in the argued provisions remain a foundation for all
international legal disputes over trade.

It must be remembered that mercantilism was the dominant school of
thought from the late 15th century to the 18th century. Internationally,
mercantilism encouraged the many European wars of the period and
fueled European imperialism. Academic belief in mercantilism began to

fade in the late 18th century, as the arguments of Adam Smith and the other new classical economists such as David Ricardo, Thomas Malthus, and John Stuart Mill began to dominate people's thinking.

Out of the age of discovery and its accompanied provocateur—the commercialization of the world—great wealth was created. Although the period was fought with national imperialistic overtones fueled by mercantile economic policy that caused harm to the newly explored territories, it ushered in and became a platform for human creativity. The birth of the Renaissance—the reawakening of European intellect that produced new ideas—was founded in the trading city-states of Venice and Florence and collaterally linked to the indulgences of the wealthy patrons of the time whose financial empires were built on international trade. The Medici family—bankers and merchants—provided the capital that sustained both artistic and innovative thinkers like Leonardo da Vinci, Francesco di Giorgio, Taccola, Paolo Toscanelli, and Leon Battista Alberti to name a few. The use of finances generated from commerce to underwrite and foster the arts and sciences is an often overlooked beneficial by-product of this early capitalistic initiative. Besides the Renaissance in Europe, the previously described riches generated by the merchant trade in the Middle East and even sub-Saharan Africa helped create centers of learning and academic thought that also propelled civilization forward. Even today, outside of government-funded grant programs and charitable contributions of private patrons and their foundations, corporations, perhaps as part of a social responsibility factor, are one of the prime sponsors of artistic activities and academic research exploration in numerous sciences—a legacy perhaps inherited from the merchants of old.

Florence: The Italian Renaissance Gem

In the 14th century, the merchants of Florence grew rich from trade in wool and commercial finance, making it at that time the fifth largest city in Europe. The economic success of the city was attributable to the Medici family. Their banking enterprises were precursors for many of the principles used in modern banking systems; these innovations included the letter of credit, itself one of the chief instruments that allowed for the safe and secure flow of transnational transactions between distant, untrusting parties. The gold florin coin, picturing the Florentine lily on one side and John the Baptist on the other, became the valued common currency of the greater European community and was widely accepted in many foreign lands as well. Even though the city itself was landlocked on an unnavigable river, it nevertheless produced brilliant navigators who explored and mapped the New World across the Atlantic Ocean; one of these navigators, Amerigo Vespucci, lent his first name (Americus in Latin) as the christened designation for territories in the Western Hemisphere. When the country of Italy was finally united in 1871 from a collection of city-states, the new nation chose the Florentine dialect to be the official Italian dialect. This testament to Florence as a proud, influential leader in the history of the country is unique, as in 1871 only 2 percent of the population could actually converse in the Florentine vernacular. (Many historians believe that the choice over the majority parlances, Roman and Neapolitan, was more due to the desire to emulate the language of Dante, the major Italian poet and writer in the Middle Ages, and thus present a sophisticated and learned image to the world.)

Although primarily known for the golden age when the Medici family presided over the region and Lorenzo de Medici gathered poets, artists, philosophers, architects, and musicians while organizing all manner of cultural events, festivals, and tournaments, the city produced a merchant class whose activities in both the commercial and social arenas were felt throughout Europe. These local merchants organized themselves into craft guilds by 1250 and in that year proclaimed themselves the *primo popolo* (first people). This group used decorative shields to announce their professional skills. They resembled royal family crests and banners; and like the nobility, they were used to proclaim their status in society. They divided their commercial society into major, medium, and minor branches, sometimes naming them after the streets or districts where they conducted their business. This daring declaration by the nonnobility class was one of the first democratic chords struck in Europe. Although this episode lasted for only 10 years, the idea reverberated across the continent and showed the desire for social recognition that could be attributed to those achieving new economic power in a changing world. These Florentine merchants were papal bankers; they instituted the system of international letters of credit, a concept that originated from the activities of the Knights Templar, which is later depicted and helped create the gold florin—the international standard of currency then. With their economic strength and capital investment came a building boom. Public and private palaces and churches and basilicas were constructed, enlarged, or reconstructed, providing not only cultural enlightenment but also jobs for numerous trades. Sculptors such as Donatello and Ghiberti were commissioned to decorate them along with painters such as Giotto and Botticelli to paint the wall and ceilings in fresco. This renaissance of development, along with the desire to create a new group of citizens, the middle class, was merchant driven, as their intercontinental commercial activities provided riches and fueled their ambitious desires to be noticed as a new force in the world. While not succeeding in their endeavor to join the ranks of nobility and the landed gentry as equals, their strides certainly contributed to the growth of civilization and the recognition of the commercial endeavor as a recognizable source of wealth accumulation and social respect. Such principles still drive the world today.

Bruges: A European Trade Hub

Another European city that developed out of the early age of regional maritime trade exploration and its aftermath is examined by author James M. Murray.[15] He presents a most illuminating and detailed account of the medieval trading city of Bruges that reached the height of its prosperity due to the shift in trade from land to sea beginning in the 12th century. Again, we see a geographical placement as the impetus for the growth of civilization. But unlike Petra, this Flemish city had a dual advantage of being not only placed on the sea but surrounded by commercially exportable resources. A wool market, coupled with a fleece-weaving industry, located on the circuit of the famous Flemish cloth fairs enabled the city to grow. Buoyed by the accessible garment production centers in England and Scotland, the city's merchants prospered.

When the merchant fleet from the Italian port city of Genoa first docked at Bruges in 1277, it brought a link to the Mediterranean and in turn the lucrative Spice Route of the Far East. Bruges was founded as a Gallo-Roman settlement more than 2,000 years ago, about the time Petra began its rise to glory. Its name comes from the Old Norse *Bryggja* (landing stage), which became an appropriate moniker for the city's activities as its prominence as a trading hub grew. The city gave rise to international merchant traders of raw materials that soon attracted the entrepreneurial artisans of the day, turning such unprocessed goods into items sold in retail shops. As Murray recounts,[16] by organizing the movement of raw materials and goods, these merchant traders fueled economic specialization and speculation that drew populations into their geographical realm of influence. People in the Middle Ages moved to the city and a new era of civilization concentration began.

Even in Bruges, the use of Flemish hostellers to assist in the commercial process was well known. This group, with branches throughout Europe, provided a connected system of lodgings; warehouses; bookkeeping; and the administration of financial operations, credits, and payment services. These activities gave rise to the designation of certain places specifically known for financial transactions and were the precursors for the future stock exchanges of Antwerp and Amsterdam as well as other such facilities around the world. The city administration understood that the prosperity of its citizens depended largely on the welcoming of foreign merchants and the commercial leagues they created. They were keen to guard commercial privileges and to ensure trading regulations were respected, perhaps, the predecessor of democratic principles respecting a new class of citizens just below the privileged nobility and the propertied classes of the era that came to affect the social makeup of civilizations yet to come. Around 1500, the natural link between Bruges and the sea silted up and the great trading era ended with the port of Antwerp becoming its chief rival. While its maritime trade heritage still attracted tradesmen, the glory once bestowed on the city diminished, but the commerce lessons it taught the world still remain. Even as change descends on the commercial landscape of regions, it is wise not to discount their contributions to the business principles and the sustained effect of their legacy to civilization.

PART III

Building Blocks of Globalization

The first part of this book and its chapters offer the reader a philosophical, if not inherent, and biological argument of the ingrained human social need to engage in the exchange process, thereby laying the basis for the eventual evolution of the commercialization of this natural phenomenon. It portrays the commercial process as a collateral, if not supportive, element in the development of civilization on earth. Part II is broken up into the ancient trading world and the age of discovery that opened up the world to the enlarged commercial environment, a semi-chronological evolution of area-based civilizations and their trading exercises that contributed to the globalization phenomenon.

In this section, we take a look at globalization through the perspective of aligned business subjects to show how the building blocks, inherent in today's global commercial process, originated. The sale and marketing of ancient universal commodities such as olive oil, salt, incense, and spices provide an insight into the product-based principles of intercontinental trade while the desire for silk became the next key connecting component of East–West commercialism. As the world began to grow commercially, a number of complementary elements that supported and sustained the global business environment emerged while at the same time contributing to the development and growth of civilization. The advent of writing and language was fostered by the exchange process as an invention based on the need for keeping a record of transactions between commercial parties. An infrastructure of cross-territorial roadways became the chief conduit for the exchange of cultures as well as trade goods. Brick and mortar structures strengthened the process and became models for the design of cosmopolitan configurations and the socialization of people. The evolution of mediums of exchange, the advent of money, along with other commercial financial instruments, furthered the development of the global business imperative while contributing to the building of universal bridges of commonly accepted material values among people. A system of secular laws allowed for a platform of private commercially protected rights to be constructed that further enhanced the exchange process while also addressing the social need for regulated order of societies.

CHAPTER 5

The First Global Products

The recorded history of any era is often defined by the overwhelming events that occurred in it. If an economic inspectional criterion to investigate time periods is utilized, one could conclude that centuries have been, and still are, dominated by global trade centered on paramount commodities. That is categories of related goods, those universally appreciated by consumers to a similar degree, have been the drivers of integrated global commerce.

In the modern era, such trends are more easily identified. Future economic historians will most probably proclaim that technology, the computer age, was the building block of business in the 21st century. In the energy sector, oil was the chief commodity impacting the world in the 20th century. Agriculture-based products were prime components that stirred the economic growth of nations in the two prior centuries. The cultivation of cotton dominated the 19th century and ushered in the Industrial Revolution with the invention of the spinning jenny and power loom that in turn created cotton mills. The 18th century saw the development of large plantation systems using organized labor to harvest sugar and tobacco. Both these periods were stained by the need for large forced labor pools that begot human suffering as brought on by the required salve trade. The 15th through 17th centuries encompassed the age of exploration as nations strove to acquire gold and silver. The harboring of these precious metals due to their universally recognized medium of value did precede this period of human history and continues today.

However, in the ancient world, consumers shared similar material wants and needs, leading to the emergence of the first universal commodities. Most of these early common items like olive oil, wine, and salt were traded locally reaching their geographical zenith as they moved across neighboring regions. Others like incense and spices moved over contiguous intercontinental routes, further pushing out trade across the globe. Silk, perhaps the first global luxury product, fully united Europe and Asia and all regions in between. The commercial exchanges of these ancient consumer products acquired the roots of globalization and the principles applied in their international dealings helped form the platforms of conceptual business use today.

Ancient Commodities

Archaeologists exploring the seas and ports of ancient shipping lanes continuously uncover the cargos of merchant ships revealing the first cross-territorial commodities. The holds of most vessels contain a container known as *amphorae*. These curly shaped clay jars, holding about 18 gallons of liquid, indicate that they were routinely filled with olive oil and wine making such commodities the first transnational products shipped in bulk. The importance of these two cultivated materials was noted by Thucydides, a Greek historian writing in the fifth century BCE, who is quoted as saying that, "The peoples of the Mediterranean began to emerge from barbarism when they learnt to cultivate the olive and the wine."[1]

Olive Oil

For thousands of years, perhaps as far back as 37000 BCE, the inhabitants of the Mediterranean region have cultivated the olive tree and used its fruit in their daily lives. The stone mortars and presses used in the oil extraction process are part of the artifacts and archeological remains of numerous ancient societies, making this product the earliest commercial commodity in the world and qualifying it as one of the first globally marketed products.

This precious article of trade was used to light homes and for cooking and flavoring. When infused with flowers and grasses, olive produces medical ointments and cosmetics. Warriors ritually rubbed it all over their bodies while the leafy branches of the oil tree crowned the victorious. In ancient times, religious ceremonies decreed that drops of it should periodically anoint the bones of dead saints and martyrs through holes in their tombs. Clay jars of the valued substance have even been found in the tomb of Tutankhamen alongside his most prized possessions that symbolized his wealth and divine status. In the land of the Hebrews, King Solomon and King David placed such great importance on their cultivation of olives that empirical guards watched over the groves and warehouses to ensure the safety of the trees and their precious oil. Many citations about olive oil are contained in the Old Testament and other holy writings. After the great flood during Noah's time, a dove carried an olive leaf to Noah, suggesting that the waters had receded and that the land still existed. In mythical Greece, the olive was said to be a gift of Athena to the Athenians as a sign of her emblematic presence in the lives of moral men. In the sixth century BCE, Solon, the great Athenian legislator, drafted the first law protecting the olive tree, including prohibition of its uncontrolled felling, a crime punishable by death or exile.

Traditional historic inquiry places the origin of olive trees in ancient Iran and Turkistan, while some scholars believe that the trees grew in multiple locations as they seem to have appeared simultaneously in southern Anatolia (now Turkey), Palestine, and the Levant region (now Syria and Lebanon). Still others feel that its life-sustaining and ritual-like importance prompted its importation by adjacent cultures and introduced into other societies by merchant traders in agricultural products. The Minoans of Crete were among the first cultures to achieve prosperity based on the export trade of olive oil. Storage units with a capacity of 250,000 kg of huge *pithoi*-type construction have been found in the Minoan palace of Knossos. This large inventorying of the oil seems to attest to its commercial value as a trading good to be bartered and exchanged for other commodities in the neighboring lands and even distant ports in the Mediterranean Sea. Such a mammoth storage space would seem to have sustained its pivotal position as the driver of the agricultural economy of the region, as no other ancient product was awarded such revered capacity. Homer, the great poet of Greek literature, called it liquid gold, perhaps a precursor for the 20th-century term, black gold, as reference to the value of oil in the modern economic society.

The grinding wheels for oil extraction were the centerpiece of settlements throughout the entire Mediterranean basin and the Middle East, often placed at the gates of a town or city indicative of their importance in the daily economic lives of the inhabitants. Archeologists continue to uncover the stone pieces of ancient olive presses, often in the vicinity of wine presses. The importance of such instruments to extract the valued oil for early world communities cannot be overstated. They were the mechanical lifeblood of the people. Ancient settlements were constructed around the olive oil presses. The surrounding community of growers, buyers, and others gathered at the gates of towns, thus creating the first commercial trading markets. The commercial transport of olive oil provided the driving force for merchant journeys to both adjacent and faraway lands, providing the impetus for the construction of sea-going ships to haul the precious cargos. Those who traded in this first global commodity were beneficiaries of wealth and power. Most of us are familiar with the tradition of awarding an olive branch to winners at the ancient athletics games, like the Olympics. A lesser-known custom of these games is that the prize awarded to the champions of the most important events, such as the Panathenaea, was large amounts of olive oil contained in special amphorae and at times exceeding a total of five tons. Since the winners of these athletic contests were exempted from Athenian laws prohibiting normal citizens the right to export olive oil, they were likely to become instant millionaires, as trade merchants would flock them and offer to assist in disposing their prize overseas where it was highly valued. The import–export trade of olive oil was the backbone of the world's ancient economy, much like oil today. From 600 BCE, merchants from Phoenicia, Egypt, and the southern steppes of Russia (Scythians) were drawn to replenish their stocks of olive oil at the prosperous Greek colonial trading posts of the Black Sea (today Romania). Such trading importance for the word's then hottest commodity was the motivational force for the innovations applied to the construction of advanced ships built solely for the purpose of transporting olive oil from Greece to their trading ports around the Mediterranean. The necessity for technological advancements, like today, was driven by a commercial imperative in the ancient world.

The evolution of the modern concept of business marketing strategy based on (a) low cost, (b) differentiation, and (c) segmentation had its origin in the olive oil industry. Oil produced from groves near the ocean was considered inferior and sold in bulk at low prices while those varieties harvested from inland mountainsides were perceived as exhibiting superior characteristics and hence demand a higher price. The extracted oil had come from more than 700 cultivated varieties of olives, while the numerous varied filtering processes further added to differentiations in color (from mellow yellow to jade green) and in taste (peppery, sweet and buttery nutty, grassy, or even the flavor of green apples). Its consistency can appear in a clear version or cloudy with bits of fruit left in, which further denoted its marketing avenue as low cost or differentiated. The purest of oils were considered a luxury item and were targeted to a segmented group, the wealthy aristocrats who believed that it conferred strength and youth, a magical medical elixir for the body as opposed to a mere cooking ingredient or lamp fuel.

The value and quality of this prized commodity was often quoted with reference to the products geographically based quality, a precursor to today's marketing references to the "made-in" connotation. While Greek production was considered above others due to its initial development, other areas began to emerge vying for competitive consideration, chief among them Spain and later Italy. Romans during the spread of their empire did not immediately cultivate olive oil in Italy but relied on established producers in the distant lands, like those in Spain, they had conquered, thereby keeping the economies of such areas and the trade routes intact. After a time, however, olive oil cultivation was brought home. While olive oil was the first universal commodity due to its alignment in the necessary food chain and coincided with the ancient world's agricultural economic emphasis, it trade distribution was both domestic and regional. Other products also impacted the economies in these early times and their international trade movement was more intercontinental.

Wine

Similar to olive oil, as they were both ancient agriculturally based products that were systematically harvested and distributed across distances, is the production of wine. While there is a wide range of alcoholic beverages obtained by the fermentation of sweet liquids (vegetable juices, honey, milk), the most widely disseminated varieties are wine, beer, and cider. Wine is an alcoholic beverage produced by the fermentation of the juice of fruits, usually grapes, although other fruits like plum, banana, elderberry, or black currant can also be fermented to produce the generic product called wine. This specialized elixir is part of the folk law of almost every society on earth. The health benefits of wine are recorded in the literature of the most ancient civilizations to aid sleep, circulation, and digestion, while the communal aspects of consuming the liquid are said to aid relaxation, love making, and to help form all types of relationships. The beverage has been associated with religious practices of numerous spiritual groups beginning millennia ago. This fact makes it even more socially acceptable.

In ancient times, wine was used by idolaters in rituals and integrated into almost every holiday and religious service. Its use in a worship service is first recorded during the Sumerian Empire (modern-day Iraq) of 3000 BCE. An ancient goddess called *Gestin* whose name literally translates as wine, vine, grape, or all three, was chosen to represent the beverage's importance. Her name is also mentioned in the ancient Indus manuscript, the Rig Veda. Researchers reason that the first gods of wine were women, because the oldest deities were female agriculture goddesses of the earth and fertility. Centuries later, around 1500 BCE, there is a mention of another wine goddess, *Paget*, in the same part of the world, as associated with vineyards and wine production. Crossing the Levant the Egyptian wine goddess *Renen-utet* is found on hieroglyphic tablets as blessing the wine as early as 1300 BCE. *Dionysus*, the Greek wine god, appeared around 500 BCE while the Roman version *Bacchus* rose to eminence around 200 BCE as the Greek Empire was fading. The association of both deities with wine has survived. They continue to be revered by the beverage's enthusiastic supporters. Other wine god named *I-Ti* even emerged from China. While various pagan practices called for wine to be offered to the gods and consumed by worshippers on spiritual occasions its association with present-day religious orders continues.

Wine has always been an important aspect of the Jewish religion. There are laws governing the process of wine making, from their crushing to the sealing of the bottle. The Sabbath, a weekly observance, is highlighted by the Kiddush, a special prayer said over wine. The *Biblical Book of Genesis* first mentions the production of wine following the *Great*

Flood, when *Noah* drunkenly exposes himself to his sons. Even though Christianity has roots in Judaism, the main importance of wine in the faith comes from the use of the beverage in Jesus Christ's last supper, which was actually a Jewish Seder celebrating Passover. Wine represents a covenant with God through the blood of Jesus, represented by the beverage. Islam recognizes the influence of wine in society. The Koran states, "Satan seeks to stir up enmity and hatred among you by means of wine and gambling, and to keep you from remembrance of Allah and from your prayers. Will you not abstain from them?" (The Koran, Sura 5:91). However, wine is also recognized as a bringer of joy, but that its power of destruction is even greater and one must not overindulge in it. Later on in the Koran, Mohammad notes the joys of wine, and thus there is moderate disagreement over the correct interpretation of its place in Islamic religious principles.

The history of *wine* spans thousands of years and is closely intertwined with the history of civilization and trade. The earliest known possible evidence for the use of grapes as part of a wine recipe with fermented rice and honey was in China, about 9,000 years ago. More widespread evidence is found soon thereafter in the *Near East*. The *grapevine* and the *alcoholic beverage* produced from it were important to the economies of *Mesopotamia*, *Israel*, and *Egypt* while composing the essential aspects of *Phoenician*, *Greek*, and *Roman trade*. The origins of wine pre-dates *written records* so modern *archaeology* is still uncertain about the details of the first cultivation of wild *grapevines*. Unkempt grapes still grow in *Georgia*, the northern *Levant*, coastal and southeastern *Turkey*, northern *Iran*, and *Armenia*. The fermenting of strains of this wild *Vitis vinifera subsp. sylvestris* (the ancestor of the modern wine grape, *V. vinifera*) became easier following the development of *pottery* during the later *Neolithic period*, circa 11000 BCE. The earliest archaeological evidence of commercial wine production found has been at sites in *Georgia*, circa 6000 BCE and in Iran, circa 5000 BCE. Excavations of Iranian jars contained a form of *retsina*, using *turpentine pine resin* to more effectively seal and preserve the wine. Researchers have confirmed that wine production spread to other sites in *Greater Iran* and *Grecian Macedonia* by circa 4500 BCE, as all clay relics contain the remnants of crushed grapes.

Unique to this early global commodity was the fact that while it began as an exported product, grown in one place and shipped to another, it was perhaps the first produced item whose technology would be transferred abroad; a concept akin to the modern licensing or transferring of know-how. Viniculture, the science behind making grape wine, begot the flow of ideas as opposed to the traditional movement of products between and across territories. The Turkish *Uyghurs* were responsible for reintroducing advanced *viticulture* and the fermentation system to *China* from the *Tang dynasty* onward. The development of the wine industry around the Mediterranean can initially be traced to the transfer of winemaking skills by the Canaanites to the Egyptians of the Nile Delta. Wine making in Italy was devised with the help of the Greeks, not by chance but by design. Winemaking technology improved considerably during the time of the *Roman Empire as* many grape varieties and cultivation and production techniques were improved. Large commercial plantations emerged with added efficiencies. The design of the *wine press* advanced and *barrels* were developed for storing and shipping wine. Through these works, *the Romans were able to perfect wine production.* They improved the Greek process of extracting juice, classified which grapes grew in the best climate, discovered that tightly sealed containers improved the taste with age, were the first to use the noted wooden barrels, used corks, and may have been the first to use glass containers. The Romans were also known for adding fruits, honey, herbs, and spices to flavor their wine. They even used chalk to thin out the acidity. Water was even employed to dilute the heavy nature of the substance. Such new techniques soon spread across the empire. Later, the native Celts at Lattara in southern France needed the expertise and knowledge of the Etruscans to plant their own vineyards and begin making wine. With the fall of the Roman Empire, due to barbaric invasions, the essential factors for the production and distribution of wine collapsed. The only stable structure across the former empire was the Catholic Church, which preserved viticulture and wine making. In medieval Europe, wine was consumed only by the church and the noble classes but since it was necessary for the celebration of the Catholic Mass its continuing production was essential. The Benedictine monks were the largest producers of wine and owned vineyards in Champagne (Dom Perignon was a Benedictine monk), Burgundy and Bordeaux in France, and in the Rheingau and Franconia regions of Germany. These European areas began to eclipse the traditional wine regions of Greece and competed with Italy.

Wine production crossed the Atlantic as grape vines were first transported to Latin America by the Spanish conquistadores to provide the wine required for the celebration of the mass in the Catholic Church. They were initially planted in Spanish missions located in the colonies. Later, immigrants imported French, Italian, and German grape varieties as replacements for the native grapes eventually producing new assortments of wine with improvements in consistency and therefore quality whiling adding new body and aromas. In the Western Hemisphere, the remnants of this early adaptations gave rise to the wine regions in the United States (California), Argentina, and Chile.

As the new methods in cultivation of grapes were coupled with innovations to the fermentation process, improvements in storage and shipping along with alterations to consumer taste components began to appear in other territories and a shift from the original producing areas occurred.

Such ancient changes built around the wine industry gave rise to the creation of the product life cycle, a business principle widely in use in modern times. Wine began as an exported home-grown product whose production shifted to foreign locations where the process was improved beyond its original development; and eventually imported back to the originating market. In the contemporary world, electronic manufacturing moved from industrialized countries to developing countries where a similar metamorphosis took place. The buyer became the maker and eventually the seller back to the initial developer. History continues to repeat itself as the ancient lesson of winemaking impacts the modern business world. Also the ancient commercial principle that began as a transfer of knowledge, wine making was the onus if not the blueprint for today's global licensing and franchising models of foreign expansion and territorial entry.

Salt

Closely aligned to olive oil extraction and the cultivation of the earth for basic sustenance to sustain and improve life on earth was the early gathering of salt. Neolithic settlements were placed near salt springs as early man recognized its life-sustaining value. The mineral was prized for its health advantages, because when ingested periodically it helped the body retain water—a life-sustaining requirement. It was exalted for its ability to preserve animal flesh in the curing process along with fish and vegetables; when salted, the produce could travel beyond local boundaries and not spoil, thereby retaining its commercial value. Hence, it eliminated mankind's dependence on nature and the availability of seasonal food sources. Beyond its health benefits its ability to flavor food was another worthwhile attribute. It also acted as a mordant for fixing textile dyes as well as a principal component in the preparation of soaps and cleaning agents. In a spiritual context, salt was given as a blessing, as it was thought to drive out evil spirits, hence the old adage that throwing a pinch of salt over one's shoulder wards off evil. Religious texts attribute the mineral as forming one of the basic elements of life. In the Old Testament, the story of Lot's wife being turned to a pillar of salt is used to symbolize that once God removes the spirit or the soul due to an affront to his commands, the body is reduced to its basic physical component, salt. In the New Testament, Matthew 15:3 relates Jesus speaking to his disciples, telling them, "You are the salt of the earth," a reference to their valued importance in spreading his gospel and influencing the society of the day. Ancient documents record a central role for salt not only in the West but also in the East. More than 4,700 years ago, one of the earliest known treatises on pharmacology was published in China. Known as the Peng-Tzao Kan-Mu, a major portion of the text concentrated on the medical uses of salt in the treatment of and prevention of numerous bodily ailments. In many cultures around the world, there is a uniform tradition to offer bread and salt to welcome visitors.

While it is difficult to historically say for sure where the first salt harvest occurred, the Afar people, whose ancient tribes encompassed portions of Eritrea, Ethiopia, and Djibouti in the Middle East, harvested salt from the lowest and hottest region in Africa, Lake Assal in Djibouti.

Some historians feel that the gathering of this commodity precipitated the initial trading across regions on earth. The highly valued salty spheres tumbled naturally at the brine's edge in the extremely hot and dry conditions that enabled the tiny salt beads to grow into a size resembling a golf ball thereby taking this common commodity into the realm of today's designer-like arena of increased value. Afar salts, their signature product, were as prized as today's prestige brands, such as Rolls-Royce in the car industry and Louis Vuitton in leather goods.

In the ancient civilizations of West Africa, it was the key commodity that connected the northern and southern tribes. While the northern mines produced salt, the southern areas extracted gold from the hills. The old empire of Ghana, located between the regions, flourished due to its positioning on the prosperous merchant trade route that connected the two. The barter that took place was so highly valued that an ounce of salt for an ounce of gold was at one time the normal rate of exchange.[2] Ancient Ghana also derived power and wealth from its gold mines. Gold's true value was in the trading process and as a bartered exchange unit for salt. This African Kingdom on the southern edge of the Saharan trade routes became a prized commercial center where the Muslim merchants used their wealth to establish mosques and schools and the king drew on the talents of such scholars to administer his territory.

The accumulation of gold in the north, due to the selling of sub-Saharan salt, made its way across northern Africa, as Arab merchants operating in southern Moroccan towns bought the precious accumulated metal from the Berbers and transported them to the East. Early trade routes were constructed for the transport of salt around the world. Herodotus tells of a caravan route that united the salt oases of the Libyan desert as ancient traders carried this valuable staple from North Africa to southeastern Mediterranean ports and onto Europe. Caravans of up to as many as 40,000 camels moved across the 400-mile stretch. Hence, salt helped spark the trade process, which spanned an entire continent, contributing to the expansion of gold as a valued intermediary across the entire world.

During the era of the Roman Republic and their expanded territory, the price of salt was controlled. Such a monopoly over one of the prime economic resources of the period, a staple in the diet of its citizens, enabled the government to acquire funds to maintain the empire and its protracted war machine. Preceding precious extracted ores like gold and silver, salt at one time had been a medium of exchange. A possibly misguided word analogy is built around the use of salt in such a context. During the Roman era, soldiers were purportedly compensated with a *salarium argentum*, which means salt payment. Some linguistic scholars translate the term to mean they were given money, which in turn enabled them to buy salt, while others interpret the word to signify the receipt of a ration of salt. Whatever the exact interpretation, it is interesting to note that the conceivable origin of the English term *salary* originated with this practice, which signifies the use of salt as a value substitute for the legal tender of the realm.

Whatever one's take on the root of the word *salary*, the intrinsic value of salt in the ancient world is further appreciated by the fact that the Chinese also maintained a government monopoly on its production and that salt cakes bore the seal of the emperor, hence its acceptance as legal tender or money within the realm. Marco Polo's experiences with the commodity are well noted during his appointment by the khan as a collector of taxes on exchanges of the salt-water-extracted substance.[3] The movement of salt contributed greatly to our knowledge of the ancient highways of commerce. So important was the salt trade in world history that the routes in Europe, including Great Britain, and the Middle East over which this valued commodity moved were known as the *Salt Lines*. Some researchers have theorized that these early references to geographical positions on the earth's surface may have been the precursor of the later navigational coordinates, longitude and latitude.[4] On these series of long straight lines, the Alan Butler book describes the growth of towns and eventually cities built on perhaps a mysterious and spiritual influence that radiated from them as well as being the home base of some of the most influential families and men in ancient times. This fact helps to substantiate the related phenomena around the world wherein trade routes were the impetus for the construction of social centers and the furtherance of civilizations in such areas.

One of the oldest roads in Italy is Via Salaria (from the Latin word for salt), over which Roman salt from Ostia was carried into other parts of Italy. During the Middle Ages, the designation for networks of interconnecting routes was the term *salt roads*, in recognition of the prime commodity carried by merchants of the day as they crisscrossed Europe. It was an expensive resource not because of the extraction process but because of the high cost of carrying the heavy bulk goods by river, sea, and land, which required the coordination of numerous middlemen. The role of commercial agents in the maintenance and expansion across territories of a delivery network cannot be overstated. The commercial trading of this valued commodity and life-sustaining material enabled civilizations to grow and prosper. The mining of salt and the collateral need to establish commercial centers for its distribution were the bases for the formation of towns and cities like Munich and Salzburg; while the salt mines of Poland provided the wealth to establish a kingdom and later a state. Liverpool rose from a small English port to become the chief exporting channel because of the huge amount of salt dug out of the great Cheshire mines in the 1800s. While the mineral itself was the prime ingredient it was the merchant traders who provided the capital and intermediary steps that led to the growth of the civilizations placed around its core centers and surrounding areas.

Salt also played an important political role in India's successful independence movement to separate itself from the bonds of English colonial rule at a time when the British controlled most of the world's salt trade. Mahatma Gandhi's famous Salt March (known as the *Salt Satyagraha*) shook the British Empire in 1930. It was a nonviolent protest against England's salt tax and its monopolistic burden on the Indian people, which prevented them from harvesting local resources. It contributed to India's achievement of self-rule, which, on a global basis, underscored the need for free-trading principles via private enterprise. Today oil is the prime energy source and the number one commodity for the world, replacing the precious ancient dominance of olive oil and salt. Their combined legacy in the development of globalization and international business principles remains important.

Spices and Incense

The spice and incense trade is a generic reference used to describe the exchange for value by predominately Western consumers for the priced import of Eastern exotic plant extracts that stimulated the pallet and nasal senses resulting in a pleasant sensation that is difficult to articulate. The perceptions impacting the human body by these products completed with sight, sound, and touch for one's physical attraction.

The history of incenses and spices set the stage for the first real era of extensive international trade and was one of the forerunners of modern-day global integrated economics and the borderless world. Records of their East–West trading routes have existed since the beginning of recorded history. Some archaeologists date the cross-continental trading of spices to jars of cloves found in small ceramic vessels produced in Syria as evidence that trade with tropical Southeast Asia existed as far back as 1720 BCE. Babylonian and Assyrian clay tablets detail the existence of the incense trade in their regions but it was not until the Arab-Nabatean tribe (note that earlier they were profiled as founders of Petra) took interest and began to dominate the trade, which was previously controlled by Europeans, in the final trading links to the Mediterranean that originated in the East. The actual beginning of the cross-territorial spice trade is historically difficult to pinpoint. Archaeologists deciphering Egyptian hieroglyphic inscriptions during the period of the New Kingdom (Egyptian Empire) more than 3,600 years ago discovered references to the pharaoh's exchange relationships, including large cargoes of aromatic resins and other unique flavoring materials and scents. While a few of these exotic spices might have been produced in Africa, many of them, like cinnamon and cloves, could only have originated in the tropical climates of southern India and Indochina, leading researchers to conclude that the beginning of intercontinental trade is as old as recorded history. In medieval Chinese and Muslim texts, very specific details about these mysterious spice routes are recorded with directions and voyage lengths for each stop of the journey, which most scholars believed to have remained unchanged from the ones used centuries or thousands of years earlier.

The route—which consisted more of general directions through numerous integrated haphazard paths, then of a recognized singular roadway—linked the Mediterranean world with Eastern sources of incense and spices. The spice trade stretched from the Levant and Egypt south across the Arabian Peninsula through Persia, touching India, and onward to China and Southeast Asia. As early as the time of King Solomon (circa 967 BCE), the flow of trade was extensive, and it allowed his kingdom to profit through tax or tariff on such goods passing through his domain. It is estimated that more than 3,000 tons of incense moved along the trading trail a year, making the material the most widely exchanged commercial commodity in the world at that time.[5]

During its peak in the third century BCE until the second century CE, a span of nearly one-and-a half millennia, the existence of such valued items is a testament to their impact on the development of civilization on earth. The importance of the flow of international trade for incense and spices is perhaps best exemplified by the main character of the movie *Dune*, which was also based on Frank Herbert's science fiction epic of the same name, who proclaimed, "He who controls the spice, controls the universe."[6] The story in both the 1965 novel and the 1984 film versions depicts a time when spice is the lifeblood of the future fictional universe and it was essential that the spice must flow in order for all life to succeed. *Dune* tells the story of the fight for control over the desert planet Arrakis, the only source of the spice known as melange, the most important and valuable substance in the universe. The story explores the complex and multilayered interactions of politics, religion, ecology, technology, and human emotion as the forces of the empire confront each other for control of Arrakis and its unique spice.[7] Although it is difficult to exactly ascertain Herbert's motivations, there is no doubt that it was inspired, or at least influenced, by the historical importance of the aromatic and spice trade in antiquity, as the book closely mirrors real-world elements surrounding the spice trade and its prime principle: great demand on one side and highly controlled and funneled supply on the other. The value of ancient aromatic resins like myrrh and frankincense as prized riches was even mentioned in the biblical story of the hallowed gifts bestowed on the baby Jesus at birth when visited by the three kings. While the religious tale may be mythical, it is a fact that at various periods in mankind's history spices were as valuable as gold, silver, and rare gems.

Arab merchants dominated not only the trade of these rare residues from their lands but also the more lucrative spice trade during its emergence. In primeval Europe, as well as hundreds of years later, food was the chief concern of the people. Spices were used for preserving food, masking the appetite-killing stench of decay. It is also used in making poorly preserved food palatable. Heavily salted meat cured with pepper and cooked with a variety of spices was the only remedy to starvation. Those who traded in these heavily desired ingredients were the key players in the ancient commercial world. The Arab middlemen were able to weave a marketing fable to drive out early European traders from the spice trade, granting them a monopoly on the spices for centuries. They had them believe that all the spices they traded (cinnamon, pepper, cassia, cardamom, ginger, turmeric, nutmeg, mace, and a host of others) could be extracted only from their lands—a bit of mercantile guile. But, in fact, most spices merely transited Africa from India and Southeast Asia—the journeys to which required a multitude of intermediaries who initially transferred these valuable food seasonings by sea—making it finally to the eastern African continent and southern Arabia. The use of middlemen holding a monopolistic grasp on the channels of distribution in selected industries and the marketing practice of using a false or quasi-geographical sourcing or manufacturer identity to further induce consumer confidence in products are followed in the modern business world as well.

The historical importance of the spice and incense route cannot be overstated. The global trade it initiated supported civilizations, started wars, created huge wealth, and sustained nations. It was also a catalyst for cultural exchange between globally distant societies. As previously described, the European reliance on the spice trade prompted the great age of discovery and exploration by sea, as it was motivated by a commercially induced need to find a faster, more direct, and intermediary-free route to the East. The ocean voyages beginning with Christopher Columbus in 1492, followed by Vasco da Gama in 1498, and finally by Fernando Magellan's circumnavigation of the globe in 1582, were fueled by the desire to cut out the Middle Eastern middlemen and secure at wholesale prices the riches of the spice islands. The ventures of these explorers are best summed up in the chorus of their seafaring crew as they came ashore: "For Christ and spices!"[8] Out of the numerous commercial ventures undertaken by the merchants of the day as they traded spices and incense came the invention of many business principles and structures as noted in the earlier chapter on ancient trade. The legacy of these historic expeditions is found in today's conceptual practices and approaches.

Today the world trade in oil closely resembles the Arab spice monopoly in ancient times: It is dominated by the Organization of Petroleum Exporting Countries (OPEC, or the source) and the major multinational corporations (middlemen), which refine and distribute the product. In respect to geographical branding perceptions take the example of Haagen-Dazs, a premium ice cream made in New York. It was originally introduced with a lid containing a label depicting a map of Scandinavia with a bright red star in the middle, presumably giving the product an imported identity to differentiate it from domestic brands while adding a subliminal picture to the brand name. Arizona ice tea is produced in a suburb of New York and not the southwestern state. According to a rumor that has circulated in the wine industry, during a sluggish grape harvest in some of the vaunted French wine areas, the local wineries supposedly imported barrels from Sonoma, California, as substitutes for estate-grown vintages and used the word *bottled* on their labels as opposed to *produced*. Such a rumor was probably based on the fact that in 1976 a British wine merchant hosted a Parisian blind wine tasting, pitting France's renowned wines against the finest made in California. The American chardonnays and cabernet sauvignons were pronounced not simply equal but superior to the traditional French wines, with the judges easily confusing the two different varieties with each other. Many vintage brands that are historically identified by the consuming public with their historic home manufacturing source and thereby containing an inherent quality pedigree are in fact produced in countries around the world. The American-based IBM Corporation, one of the most respected names in the computer industry, for years had its central processing units made in the Far East but still relied on its respected U.S. affiliation. In fact, one of its prime manufacturers even bought the IBM laptop name rather than take the extended time and cost to build a trademark to rival this famed consumer line.

One of the keys to the aforementioned Arab monopoly on the spices trade in the Mediterranean was a secret, tantamount to a modern-day patent, about the monsoon winds across the Indian Ocean. The captains of early small boat crossings, moving both East and West, required a precise piloting of the shoreline with constant navigational stops. However, catching the seasonal and therefore predictable movement of strong winds, which in midyear reverse their direction, allowed vessels to sail more efficiently directly across the waters from the Indian coast to Egypt's Red Sea and the Arabian Peninsula. This led to making larger boats with wider sails, which could carry bigger cargoes and crisscross the ocean faster while also allowing for more scheduled trips. The Romans who used spices in every imaginable combination in their foods, wine, fragrance, and medicines, even anointing soldiers with perfumes before going into battle, were deeply resentful of the Arab stranglehold on the spice trade. With such pent-up demand and the fact that on average spices enjoyed a 100 times markup by the time they reached the Roman marketplace provided the motivation for an ill-fated invasion of Arabia in 24 BCE. This was not the first time in history that an economic provocation caused war and it would not be the last. Even after the Europeans discovered the monsoon secret via the discovery by the Greek merchant Hippalus in 40 CE, it took them some time before they could also uncover the real sources of the spices they valued so much and mount alternative routes to break the Muslim monopoly.

The rise of the Muslim world was propelled by their intermediary monopoly of the East–West spice trade into the European zone. By the ninth century, they began to make inroads into Asia and a massive trading relationship, the largest of the period, ensued. Such extensive commercial dealings allowed Islamic religious teachings to be introduced into the region, a condition that to this day still remains strong. The strength of the trading exercise allowed for magnificent cities along with centers of learning to be constructed in Muslim lands at a time when Europe began to sink into the Dark Ages. Notwithstanding the great eras of the previous Egyptian pharaohs and monarchs in the Middle East, it was a golden prosperous time for Arab communities and they reached the zenith of their cultural leadership in the world. The Venetians finally broke the trade curtain when they made a deal with the Arab merchants and received preferred, if not exclusive, distribution rights in Europe, a principle that global companies still use today to enter new markets. But it was not until the time of Chinggis Khaan, more commonly referred to as Genghis Khan, and his Mongol armies sweeping across Asia that the Muslim hold on the lucrative East–West trade began to evaporate. In their path westward, they destroyed the Islamic caliphate and caused the fall of Baghdad. As described in previous chapters on government influence, the unification under Genghis Khan, and his successors, of the continental landmass separating East and West reopened a more secure trade route, rejuvenating the old Silk Road, thereby joining the merchants of Europe directly with China and the territories in between. It was under a document of merchant protection offered by the Mongolian Empire that the literary tale of Marco Polo, traveling with his father and uncle from Venice, was based.

The economic and political grandeur of the Arab world, which produced some of mankind's greatest innovations in mathematics, astronomy, and chemistry that moved civilization forward, was based on their intermediary position in the spice trade. Perhaps, not until the fast-growing demand for oil energy after World War II did the Muslim region begin to recover its prominence and respect in the global community—a process that still continues to haunt what once was the world's greatest intercontinental trading culture. The spice trade changed the world, moving previous long-distance regional trade to the next level and paving the way for the modern era of globalization.

Silk

The emergence of silk, the mysterious fabric from the Orient, marked the beginning of the spread of the luxury market on a global plane and furthered the exchange process between the East and the West that first began with incense and spices. Silk is a natural fiber that can be woven into textiles. It is originally obtained from the cocoons of the larvae produced by the mulberry silkworm. The soft texture of the fabric on the body coupled with a high-absorbency characteristic makes it comfortable to wear in warm climates while its low conductivity enables warm air to lie close to the skin during cold weather. Such characteristics gave garments made from silk a unique and prized versatility, as silk could be woven into heavy brocade or light, delicate fabric providing comfort for all seasons and was therefore climate adaptable anywhere in the world. Its shimmering, almost glowing appearance attracted the eye of wealthy patrons in the ancient world although its use was first reserved for the emperors of China. Being one of the stronger fibers, silk is extremely durable. It was even used by the Chinese as undergarments in battle as its ability to reduce wounds from arrows was well documented.

The eye-pleasing beauty of silk is enhanced by the radiant shimmering glow due to light refraction off the triangular prism–like cellular structure of the fabric coupled with the soft feeling on one's body, which made the textile the most valuable desired product. Evidence of the initial weaving of the silkworm cocoon has been found to appear between 5000 and 3000 BCE in China. The earliest evidence that this rare fabric moved across continents is the finding of silk on the mummified remains in Egyptian burial ground dated in the 21st dynasty of the pharaohs around 1070 BCE.[9] The early Greeks used the term *Seres*, or *people of the silk*, when referring to the Eastern empire while even the Old Testament makes note of the garment, indicating that it was known in the Middle East as well. The intercontinental merchandising of this unique fabric is best traced to the first century CE, when commodity trade was established between China and the Roman Empire via the hands of commercial middlemen, the Parthians or Persians. The Romans initially encountered the magic fabric during their Eastern campaigns in the area of Syria where the legions fought Parthia, whose own army carried banners made of the brilliant material.

The cost of silk in China during the Han dynasty in the second century was priced at 100 times its original value once it reached Rome. During this period, it may have been the rarest commodity on earth. So important was the silk trade to China that the monopoly was defended by royal decree with the penalty of death for those attempting to export silkworms or their eggs. Silk, itself, was such a prized universal article that it also became a monetary intermediary standard for estimating the value of other goods, just as gold and silver pieces were used in some parts of the ancient world. The Silk Road was initially opened by the Chinese in the second century CE but reached its zenith two centuries later. The road out of Xi'an, the ancient capital of China and home at that time to a million people, took traders to Turfan, a thriving oasis city on the outskirts of the barren Taklimakan Desert in the northwest. Turfan's own marketplace offering sumptuous fruits and vegetables as well as other exotic products, and invigorated by the East–West commercial caravans whose drivers took refuge from their arduous journey across the desert, became an important center in Asia. From there, merchants ventured across the Pamir Mountains to Samarkand, an old trading station referred to as the city of merchants. The route then linked up with Antioch and the eastern Mediterranean coastline before moving on to Baghdad, a journey of more than 4,600 miles (more than 7,400 km and the equivalent of traveling across the United States and then halfway back again). Caravans of camels for the arid regions and yaks (the more sure-footed animals) would be used in mountains areas, each loaded with 140 kg (more than 300 lbs.) of merchandise. The groups that composed the caravan included trading partners, their guides, and caretakers for the beasts of burden. Consisting of 100 to 500 men, they banded together for protection from land pirates as well as for negotiating strength when encountering both royal tribute payments and demands of local tribal chieftains for a fee for crossing regions under their control. Such actions on the part of the civil authorities they came across created the principle still in practice today—the tariff or customs duty, the internationally recognized right of sovereign nations to tax goods transiting their territories. A similar practice had also evolved in the Middle East centuries before as again clans of warlords demanded a tool for safe passage through their desert domains. As Americans in the 1800s pushed west the same principle was used by the native Indians of the plains region. Often seen in movies, the act of settlers circling their wagon trains was not so much a protection device as a signal for the local tribe to approach and negotiate a settlement fee for crossing their lands.

In antiquity, the movement of silk as well as other early commodities like spices needed to travel great distances, across numerous territories while passing through countless intermediaries, each time at higher and higher values. The task was risky and difficult but extremely rewarding. The traders moving across alien territories not only exchanged goods but also music, language, numerals, medicines, religion, and philosophy from their own culture.

As noted earlier, Baghdad during the silk and spice trade periods was considered the Xi'an of the West and described by historians of the day as an elegant metropolis. Due to the wealth that accumulated in the city walls due to the merchandise transiting the Silk Road, the capital from such enterprises funded educational institutions that in turn contributed to the study and development in a variety of scientific fields, which not only advanced the knowledge of civilization but also produced the cornerstones of modern research in these areas. Baghdad at this time in history epitomized the Islamic golden age of discovery and invention, much like Florence during the Renaissance, which was further strengthened by the financial and trading activities of the Medici family. From this Syrian city, goods made their way first to Petra and then onto the southern Mediterranean ports and across the sea to Europe. Out of the merchant wealth rose a new religion, Islam, as the founder, Mohammed, was himself a trader (see Chapter 8). Centuries later, a southern seafaring collateral route in the Persian Gulf at Muscat in Oman would take merchant vessels across the Gulf of Oman to Karachi, then through the Arabian Sea, and onto the western coastline of India. More intrepid traders began to move down the Malabar Coast around the tip of India, to the island of Sri Lanka, and from there traverse the Indian Ocean to Malaysia and the spice islands. The *Business Week magazine*, in a 2009 article titled "Children of the Web," refers to today's global technology as equivalent to "the digital Silk Road," heralding back a reference to a transcontinental trade route tying East and West.

The modern market drivers of globalization can be simply expressed as the output imperative to exchange goods and services as determined by consumer needs and desires, a principle inherent in the histories of the aforementioned products. It is based on the simple principle to utilize one's locally available environmental resources and resident skill levels in order to acquire the harvested fruits of another area that inherently possess different bounties of the earth or has learned an ability that one does not have. In ancient times, not only was the market-trading motivator instrumental in enabling civilizations to grow and prosper, but the lack of something to sell, or offer in trade, held societies back and in some cases caused them to end.

Cotton

The historic domestication of cotton has been traced back to 4500 BCE. But its emergence on the world market is very complex and not known exactly. Several isolated civilizations around the world converted cotton into fabric inventing along the way combs, bows, spindles, and primitive looms to enhance the process. Some of the oldest cotton bolls were discovered in a cave in the Tehuacan Valley of Mexico and dated as being produced around 4000 BCE. Pre-Incan cotton fabric was used to wrap the remains in burial sites unearthed at Huaca Prieta iin Peru. The Indus Valley shows evidence in the ruins of Mohenjo-daro of spun cotton, circa 3000 BCE. Cotton has even been mentioned in Hindu hymns first recorded in 1500 BCE.

The transport of cotton fabrics across continents was first noticed by Herodotus, an ancient Greek historian. He describes imported Indian cotton as a wool exceeding in "beauty and goodness of sheep." When Alexander the Great invaded India in the fifth century BCE, his troops began wearing cotton garments as they found them to be more comfortable and more durable than their previous woolen ones. Such attributes of this unique foreign-encountered fabric was soon spread throughout the then Greek Empire. Strabo, a Greek historian, mentioned the vividness of Indian cotton fabrics in his chronicles while the Grecian writer Arrian recorded extensive Indian–Arab trade in cotton fabrics in 130 CE. The Egyptians grew and spun cotton as early as six CE gaining a reputation as makers of the world's finest fabric.

The global importance of cotton began its rise as European consumers desired better quality and greater choice in their cotton garments. Calico and chintz, types of imported cotton fabrics, became increasingly popular to the point that the East India Company was importing a quarter of a million pieces in Britain by 1664. By the 18th century, the demand for affordable, easily washable, and colorful fabrics among the poorer mass market made imported calicoes from India a threat to British manufacturing. In 1721, the Parliament passed the Calico Act banning calicoes for clothing or other domestic purposes. The use of governmental intervention to protect domestic industry, be it an outright ban or carrying an exceedingly high tariff, continues to remain as an effective tool in controlling international commerce. By 1774, the act was repealed as the invention of machines allowed for British manufactures to effectively compete with cheap imported Eastern-made fabrics. While advanced technology remains a buttress to low-cost labor centers around the world, the production of clothing in the Far East seemingly today replays history.

The cultivation of cotton and its effect on world trade contributed, as noted earlier, to other events. It brought about the horrific cross-Atlantic slave trade to feed the need for abundant low-cost labor in the Americas that itself was a factor in the U.S. Civil War. At the same time, cotton as a global commodity provided a stimulus for new inventions that eventually signaled the guiding impetus for the Industrial Revolution that changed the world. Harvard historian Sven Becket more deeply examines the role of cotton not just as a driver of global economics but how the financial system attached to it changed the world.[10] He reminds readers that, while the overwhelming bulk of raw cotton growth being at its height was attributed to lands in the U.S. south, merchants, bankers, and consumers in Europe were deeply involved in the process. Becket presents an interesting fact when he notes that, by 1850, more than two-thirds of American cotton was grown on land taken over by the U.S. government with a majority acquired from the Louisiana Purchase. The financing for the bond deal that almost doubled the size of the then young country was structured by Thomas Baring of Britain, at that time one of the world's leading cotton merchants. Becket also indicates how governmental intervention stretching from Demark to Russia, and in between, as well as back across the Atlantic to Mexico, was tied to the global cotton market. Regimes in all these areas began lending large sums to developing domestic clothing manufacturers in their respective countries in order to allow them to partake in the global demand for cotton products. The increased building of numerous physical infrastructures in Europe and elsewhere, comprising indigenous ports and roadways, were improved and newly constructed on account of the world cotton trade. Again, as earlier noted, the desire for cost efficiencies in cotton manufacturing begot the Industrial Revolution. Simply put, cotton was the fuel of the world's economic engine in the 19th century with ramifications that stretched into the next era and beyond. The colonization of India by Britain, partially begun in 1757, was to a degree based on controlling an offshore cotton resource and it lasted until 1947.

Gold and Silver

A discussion of ancient commodities, the first global products, would not be complete without a closing reference to the precious metals, gold and silver. While not specifically designated as commodities within the context of traded consumer goods, they are products as distinguished from services. Therefore, they are defined as commodities because they are material things with a use, advantage, and value. On the other hand, no historic economic time period with the possible consideration of the Age of Exploration, normally accepted as beginning in the late 15th century and lasting through the 17th century, can be directly associated with these rare ores. Tracing their exacting period influence on world trade is difficult as they have impacted eons. Throughout recorded history and even in modern times, these metallic objects have contributed to global commercial development due to their universal acceptance as a common medium of exchange. Their chosen role, first prescribed to them by traveling merchants and later in their use in coinage by the masses, to signify worth and thereby exchange value places them in a special category of commodities that cannot be tied to a singular or conjoined era.

Learning from the Marketing of Ancient Products

In the modern era, the ability of companies to expand into new territories has been helped and accelerated by the simple fact that world consumers have become, and are continuing to be, more homogeneous as to their material needs, a process first addressed in ancient times. Today, more than ever before, firms can approach new customers around the world on an equal strategic plane because they possess enlarged, universally shared desires. This translates into products and services that are uniform—that is, designed, engineered, manufactured, marketed, and sold through similar channels of distribution. However, the external design, size, shape, and color may need to be altered for local tastes so that the fundamental delivery of satisfaction remains intact. The world market is shrinking into a more and more harmonious unit. Such underlying basic motivational purchasing similarities not only make it easier to produce at vastly improved economies of scale but also enables firms to market—advertise and promote—using related stimuli around the world.

The basis for product universality, the marketing driver of globalization, originated with the first commercial commodities in ancient times. Even in ancient times, the movement of goods across vast stretches of land was practiced with some of the universal marketing themes used today.

To reach and induce both domestic and cross-territorial customers to patronize their goods, basic marketing principles were used via universal promotional themes that appeal across cultures and are rooted in ancient commercial activities.

Personal emotional attachments—like the need to protect and nurture the family or the desire for romance, which leads to procreation—are emotional nets that we are all caught in and respond to in a positive and universal manner. Olive oil and salt were initially marketed to insure the nutritional safety of the family as well as to promote health benefits. The use of olive oil in burial rituals, the anointing of the dead as they passed onto the underworld, showed respect for deceased family members. The mixing of olive oil with flower scents, an early perfume, was to attract the opposite sex into romantic activities.

Materialism is a timeless universal appeal as we all want to show that we have achieved some marginal measurement of success in life. It is symbolic of social status, whether it is evidenced in modern terms by the new sports car in the driveway, the expensive watch, a platinum credit card, or designer-labeled clothing. In ancient times, the same consumer desires laid the basis for the sale of precious metals like gold, silver, and bronze objects to adorn the body. The importation of exotic incenses and spices from foreign lands began with frankincense and myrrh, as well as pepper, which were found in the homes of wealthy patrons. Silk garments and porcelain-decorated serving pieces were material signs of prosperity.

Leisure time—simply being at rest, or enjoying some type of recreational or entertainment therapy in our daily work lives—permeates all cultures and societies. The creation of shopping outlets in ancient times (see Chapter 6) was as much a pleasant distraction from the labors of life as a stroll through the mega shopping centers in today's environment. The remnants of spectator events, as practiced in ancient societies from gladiator to other games of skill like the Greek Olympics, have been passed down to today's generation with a built-in commercial purpose. The Colosseum in Rome was next to the Trajan's Market (see Chapter 6), which featured six stories of merchant wares from around the world complementing the circus of imported actors and creatures from around the world. The Olympics was a gathering place for wealthy patrons to discuss associations and commercial partnerships, whereas today, it, like the FIFA (Federation Internationale de Football Association) World Cup, is a beacon for advertising beamed around the world. Festivals in ancient times had a commercially driven agenda as they do today.

Heroism—the placement of special status on others and the idea to emulate their achievements in one's rather mundane life—is found around the world. In ancient Greece, the divine gift of olive oil was promoted and people were advised to place it on their bodies to emulate the bodies of the Gods. Wine was promoted as the magic elixir of the Gods and as such enticed many area wineries to place the names of Gods and Goddesses on drinking cups. Heroism, as a marketing ploy, reached its universal zenith in 1992 when the makers of Gatorade, a nutritional athletic drink, advised the consuming public in their television commercials to "be like Mike," a reference to the basketball superstar Michael Jordon. The first use of this well-known personality to sell products began in 1986 with the launch of a new athletic shoe called the Air Jordan by the Nike company, which garnered the company a global consumer success. Many years ago, Coca-Cola, perhaps the world's best recognized trade name for a beverage, ran a television advertisement featuring a predominant American football player (Mean Joe Green, a lineman for the Pittsburgh Steelers) and his encounter with a young fan. The theme of hero worship and Coke being the magic elixir that brought them together was successfully replayed around the globe featuring the national sports stars of numerous countries replacing the U.S. player. The marketing principle, to copy prominent or famous people and the material objects they surrounded themselves with, provided the impetus for the wider commercialization of products in the ancient world. A purple dye to alter the color of bland garments in antiquity was first introduced to royalty and worn only by the nobility. Common citizens then begin to buy such colored clothes in order to show their wealth and status. Later, the wearing of silk clothing was promoted on the basis that these were initially only intended or reserved for emperors or kings and queens; hence, adorning oneself in them allowed one to feel admired by others and show off his or her own material well-being.

CHAPTER 6

Ancient Societal Infrastructures Originating in and Supporting Commercialism

Ancient cross-territorial trade, the prime root of globalization, effectively changed the world. The need to establish the first vestiges of communication within and between varying social groups was to assist in the bartered exchange process. The establishment of social mobility corridors was beholden to ancient trade passages. The initiative for developing faster and more efficient transportation inventions, from new forms of transportation to navigation tools, was the business imperative. The impetus for urban planning and the resultant architectural designing and construction of physical infrastructures was a response to the need for market centers. The increasing levels of civilized development around the world were built on the commercial imperative.

Trade: An Innovator of Communication

John A. Pierce, an American engineer in the field of radio communication, felt that communication was at the core of what makes us human and served as a vital asset to sustain life.[1] It is therefore a key element in the construction and maintenance of civilization on earth. The historic progression from savagery or barbarianism to a civilized society "included the development of agriculture, metallurgy, complex technology, centralized government, and writing."[2] The definition of the term *civilization* denotes "a relatively high level of cultural and technological development; specifically the stage of cultural development at which writing and the keeping of written records is attained."[3] Without communication—language in its oral and written format—the world would not have developed. It is the essential ingredient in the building of human civilization on earth. It is the way people express themselves—their needs and desires. It is the primary method for passing ideas, recording events, and practicing learning. Without it mankind would not progress. Improvements in language and the emergence of the written recorded word can be directly traced to the commercial imperative.

The requirement of language between people grew out of the process of exchange—the trading imperative. It was essential for man not only to offer one thing for another with his neighbor in order to simply survive but also to expand and improve life. The concept of barter furthered the need to communicate even when people lived in close proximity to each other. They traded with one another, as all of them were in pursuit of the same basic things. As such they had to have familiar words in order to accomplish such primary goals. As people explored territories beyond their normal living borders they encountered others in the trading imperative. The theory of *Sprachbund*, a convergence area for groups of people who ultimately end up sharing parts of a common language, was created. *Sprachbund* is German for *a shared linguistic area*. It is an ensemble of areal features—similarity in grammar, syntax, vocabulary and phonology—that results in common understandable messages passing between people. This principle of communication began in ancient times and was based on the need for different cultural groups to exchange their local resources with one another. While a universal language has never been forthcoming, one sees the same principle continuing today at a greater increasing degree and scale. Ask for a *Coke* today in almost any part of the world and the request is understood. The language of computers and electronics is becoming universal as is the recognition of international brand names. The trade factor is responsible for the increased phenomenon of Sprachbund as commercial globalization has allowed for common terms to be included in all languages around the world.

Up to the Middle Ages, the world was illiterate. The limited written word resided in the hands of the royal houses, their administrators and court-appointed artisans, and in many cases, the clergy. Recorded knowledge was used for imperial and religious purposes, something not learned by the common man. Its first extensive public use, however, was for the recording of commercial transactions between common folk. Historically, the merchants were the pioneers in bridging different languages. Out of necessity they created common trading terminologies, beginning with transcontinental material value assessment among and between varying cultural groups. They influenced the spread of shared linguistics and anthropology as they traveled the world in search of trade. It was the early traders who gave the world universal values of exchange, like gold and silver, so that a common appreciation of similar values could be developed. They created universal standards of measurement so that the exchange process could be unified and expanded thereby bringing people together.

In the beginning, instead of using the alphabet, symbols were grouped together to communicate the exchange of ideas, thoughts, and representations. The concept of a syllabary was created: a system of symbols that denote actual spoken syllables. The first use of printed or stamped images and drawings on the walls of caves tends to be identified with storytelling, detailing the exploits of the residents. In the Indus region (India) more than 4,500 years ago, bales of goods for shipment were wrapped with seals applied. These rudimentary identification signs allowed the receiver to recognize the geographical origin of the goods, presumably ascertaining their unique territorial source, which adds to their intrinsic value and reorder. These notations on exported goods, which authenticate them as produced in regions that consumers associate with high quality and superior workmanship, is still used today. The markings are considered the forerunners of trade marketing even though they originated as a geographical classification. Today, goods in their packing literature indicate their country of origin, the name of the manufacturer, and often include a demonstrative identifier like a trade name or trademark to further establish their uniqueness to the public. In India, these commercially induced inscriptions are indicative of an early form of literary or symbolic markings that bears resemblance to such use that is also found in the early Greek Minoan civilization. The Minoans may have also created the first vestiges of commercial product identification in Europe as did the Harappans of India in 2250 BCE. The Minoans used clay seals on individual products. Today, the museum of Heraklion in Crete contains a huge collection of seals carved out of clay, stone, or very fine hardwood that were used to mark merchandise "in a way that made it traceable to a particular point of origin."[4] Such mechanisms may have been the first accepted system used by merchants and consumers in the Mediterranean to differentiate competitive resource centers or producers of traded goods. Such markings used on bushels of goods by the Harappans and the Minoans were the forerunners of differentiation marketing strategy and branding—that is, the advertising information on the packaging and the *made-in* territorial designation.

Some archeologists examining the Minoan markings on clay seals placed on individual items discerned a reference, perhaps to the Greek deity Artemis, when phonetically pronouncing the symbols as *a-ra-tu-me*. Researchers have considered that such markings adorning the products with the name of the goddess of the wilderness connoted that the products possessed the goddess' characteristics: fertility, strength, and health—a kind of celebrity endorsement to trademark and identify goods in the modern commercial sense. No empirical nor accepted science has verified such a theory, but the idea is intriguing as the concept of using heroism as a marketing tool (as noted in the previous chapter) is used extensively today. Other Minoan clay tablets have also been found showing terms for commodities and transactions.[5] In the previous section on the development of ancient trade, Minoans' use of their symbolic writings as an accounting tool to record commercial transactions is referenced.

The early Greeks were great trans-territorial traders, and due to their vast commercial explorations, Koine Greek was the lingua franca or working language of business in the Mediterranean and the Near East for centuries. The word *Koine* itself means *common*, a suitable designation for a language that allows communication exchange for diverse people. No matter their spoken native vernacular language, educated literate people communicated internationally during the period from about 300 BCE to the close of ancient history around 500 CE using Greek. Translations from the originating languages of numerous cultures into classical Greek texts helped preserve learning while also assisting its expansion around the world. The New Testament, formed from various gospels composed by people living in Palestine who spoke Aramaic, was circulated throughout the world through Koine.

Basics of the language developed during the classical era and were spread abroad as ancient Greek merchant seamen carried it with them thereby forcing foreign parties desirous of forming business relationships with the foremost cross-border traders of the day to learn and accept it as the first language of international commerce. The language was expanded by the armies of Alexander the Great and his colonization of the then known world after the postclassical period and continued as the prime collective language through the time frame referred to as medieval Greek and the start of the Middle Ages. Koine not only became a common standard for commercial dealings in most of the Western world, even surviving the Roman period, but was also the prime learning language for knowledge expansion as well as the prime link in cross-cultural translations for important texts and documents. Koine shares a unique comparison with English in modern times. Both languages, due to the respective strength in specific historic time periods of their national economies and the global reach of their businesses, greatly influenced the rest of the world. They each became the second language of choice of international traders, which in turn impacted the domestic societies they came from. Many of the words and terms found in today's array of global languages have roots in Koine. The universal spread and use of Greek is primarily attributable to the extensive travels of global traders originating in the Greek region as in ancient times there was no nation called Greece, just a collection of kingdoms.

From the Greek word *embalo* we get the English word *emblem*, a stamp of authenticity to indicate the genuine article. Consumers rely on such markings in their buying decisions around the world today. Trademark designs such as the Nike swoosh, the Ralph Lauren polo player, and the IBM initials not only identify the products of these corporations as authentic but also act as advertising beacons on store shelves and packages themselves. They also inform the consumers of their social status. Global companies allot vast amounts of their expenditures to create and sustain product and service images, which are known by their corporate and individual trade names. The protection of these valuable assets has produced both national laws and supranational regulatory registrations for such proprietary rights. They are the subject of countless litigations and form part of worldwide trade administration. Both these ancient societies summarily drew from an exchange imperative to construct such designs and create an initial written communication vehicle from which a written language was constructed. The process itself also contributed to an advanced developmental stage of culture as writing in any message format, as noted earlier, is a prime criterion for progressive civilizations.

The ancient trading process was a key contributor to such consideration, as the earliest writing in the Mesopotamian and the Minoan societies were pictograms of memoranda, lists of goods or receipts as "their emphasis is economic."[6] The same attribution is found in Egypt and China, and is depicted in the Inca civilization. All these ancient societies used the wonderful new skill only to keep records,[7] of which most pertained to exchanges between individuals of traded goods.

The cuneiform markings of the Sumerians placed on clay tokens in 3000 BCE were characters representing numerals to quantify amounts and the names of such objects like sheep, amounts of grain, and reams of cloth, which are all daily traded commodities. The intent was to record possessions of people[8] and how they changed over time, representative of the bartered transactions between them. It also recounted the accumulation of wealth, which could be taxed by authorities. Essentially, the first Sumerian texts contained a clerical accounting system that included records of goods paid to the central government and agricultural rations given to workers. Only later did Sumerians progress beyond "logograms to phonetic writing," which included descriptive "prose narratives, such as propaganda and myths."[9]

The writing of the Sumerians predated Egyptian hieroglyphics by 250 years and replaced the Neanderthal pictographs found on cave walls in prehistoric times. As the Sumerians expanded trade with their neighbors around 2500 BCE, their written language found its way into other cultures. The Phoenicians in 1100 BCE adopted a phonetic (sound based) alphabet, a radical departure from pictographs and cuneiform scripts. They instructed their associates encountered on foreign trading missions in this new form of written communication and the legacy of such an introduction in the Mediterranean region was the foundation for modern-day Western languages. Recently, archaeologists have unearthed 4,000-year-old tablets representing some of the oldest and perhaps first written trade agreements in the area of Anatolia, Turkey. These cuneiform-script writings in the region occupied by Assyrian tradesmen contained recordings of transactions in tin and fabrics with businessmen in Mesopotamia.[10] The development of the written word owes its importance to recorded wealth creation and its distribution, both constructed on the first vestiges of organized commercial trade dealings and the earliest recorded heritage of modern globalization transactions. The Sumerian language, originating as a trading communication device, has survived for more than 6,000 years. So basic are its properties that it was included in the September 5, 1977, interstellar mission of the spacecraft on one of the Voyager Golden Records. This unique phonograph record contains sounds and images selected to portray the diversity of life and culture on earth. It is intended for any intelligent extraterrestrial life form, or for future humans, that may find it. The contents of the record were selected for NASA by a committee chaired by Carl Sagan of Cornell University. Of the 47 earthly languages recorded on the disk the first is Akkadian, which was spoken in Sumer about 6,000 years ago, and due to Sprachbund, is in essence the Sumerian text.

Today business to business and business to the final consumer take up a great portion of the communication that transpires around the world. Internet sites that help one navigate the knowledge network are endowed with commercial advertising while television programming abounds with commercials every few minutes. The exchange of information by companies, both internally and externally, via wireless technology, telephones, and computers competes with private messaging and is a key component in the establishment of international business. The ability of host countries to provide a comprehensive communication system is a key factor as multinational corporations decide on which markets to enter. Communication is the rail on which the exchange process moves and hence the need for advanced technologies to support trading practices was a natural outgrowth of the commercial imperative. From record keeping to transactional dialog to the modern age of information, gathering business has been both a motivator of and a prime beneficiary of advances in communication technology. In the modern era, trademarked goods in the language and pronunciations of one country are being transmitted identically around the world. Such universal sharing of language in both written and verbal communication has helped unite populations through the commercial imperative. More and more brand names with distinctive identification logos and accompanying symbols are recognizable by larger audiences of consumers around the world than ever before.

Early Roadways

The first roads created by humans, even back in the Stone Age, were for the cartage of goods that often moved over game trails used by hunters, such as the Natchez Trace used by Native American Indians in the southeastern United States. Improvements to these initial paths consisted of clearing trees and large stones along with the flattening and widening of the carved way to accommodate farm goods destined for local markets and then for the movement of larger commercial shipments of merchants. These early roadways—which in some civilizations like the extensive Incan Empire in South America and the Iroquois Confederations in North America, neither of which had the wheel—had massive interconnecting networks to mainly facilitate trade among other regions. The Incas of Peru traded up and down the Pacific coast of South America and may have been visited by the Polynesians of the South Pacific on mutual exchange trips. A large, diverse collection of crops, yielding vast amounts of products created by artisans from such raw materials, was transported by sure-footed llamas over sometimes torturous but well-established trade routes stretching from Argentina to Colombia and across the mountains to the tributaries of the Amazon and on to the Brazilian coast. On the four highways emanating out from the great plaza in Awkaypata were constructed state warehouses or way stations for trading. Even though Incas did not have knowledge of the wheel nor the use of horses (the Spanish conquistadors introduced them), networks of well-constructed roadways—the most extensive built in the Americas (many still existing today)—have been compared to and perhaps eclipsed those built by Rome. The Inca road system called Capaq Nan or Gran Ruta Inca has been estimated to have exceeded 40,000 km (24,855 miles). It consisted of two main arteries: one just adjacent to the western coast-line of South America running between Tumbes in Peru and Talca in Chile and another through the Andes highlands linking Quito in Ecuador and Mendoza in Argentina. Numerous additional routes lead across the empire with the most famous being the Inca Trail from Cuso to the ruins of Pachacuti, known as Machu Picchu. As the various routes were intended for foot traffic accompanied by caravans of sure-footed llamas as pack animals, the roadways were constructed of stone cobbles with the addition of rock steps or stairways to traverse mountainous paths.

Many were just dirt pathways with the ground padded down following the footprints of travels and hence only 1 to 4 m in width. To assure navigation through various terrains, bridges, culverts, tunnels, and retaining walls with elaborate drainage systems were constructed to assure safe travel during the rainy season. Placed 20 to 22 km along the more well-traveled commercial routes were a series of *tampu*, small clusters of buildings forming tiny villages that provided food and lodging for business travelers. Although not as extensive as the caravansary found along the Silk Road, they offered a respite for merchants, serving as a gathering place for the exchange of information and some trading activities. The Incas deeply upheld the need to keep these commercial passages well maintained as they were the lifeline of the empire.

Stone—crushed or whole—and other strong materials for street paving within crowded cosmopolitan settlements have been found in the cities of the Indus Valley Civilization on the Indian subcontinent of Harrapa and Mohenjo Daro. The Greeks used similar methods including marble fittings to accommodate the movement of citizens in their cities with the key objective of furthering the commercial exchange process between them. In the city of Ephesus in southern Turkey (founded in 281 BCE), the major street, Curetes, to this day supports tens of thousands of tourists each year, a testament to the excellence of the original stone composition. The Romans took the construction of highways to a new level. The phrase "all roads lead to Rome" is not so much a metaphorical reference to their early dominance of the world but to the recognized fact that their territorial colonies were constructed as commercial resource centers to serve the needs of and increase the wealth of the empire via the most extensive network of roadways the world has ever seen. With more than 180,000 miles created, and at the height of construction averaging more than 1 mile of new roadway every three days, such still-standing remnants like the Apian Way were the lifeblood of the state, allowing trade to flourish and the Roman Army to move around. In ancient Rome, farm roads were paved first on the way into towns in order to keep fresh produce clean on their way to metropolitan markets.

The Persian Royal Road—not to be confused with the King's Road out of Egypt that also had royal heritage—was enhanced by Darius the Great in the fifth century BC. Covering just more than 1,677 miles, it effectively linked Asia Minor with the eastern part of the continent. The roadway was initially constructed to facilitate efficient communication across the empire, a reported seven-day journey by rapid continuous horseback, an early version of the Western American Pony Express. The highway ran from Susa, the capital of the kingdom, to the southeast city of Persepolis near the Indian subcontinent, while moving east to Sardis on the Aegean coast of Lydia (modern Turkey) and down to Babylon in the south. (See Figure 6.1.) Centuries later, this vast road system would intersect with remnants of the aforementioned King's Road across northern Arabia and other local trade routes in India and China to form the cross-continental network commonly referred to as the Silk Road. (See Figure 6.2.)

In the Middle East, vast roadways were built specifically for the extensive Arab-led merchant trade. Perhaps, the most sophisticated systems were

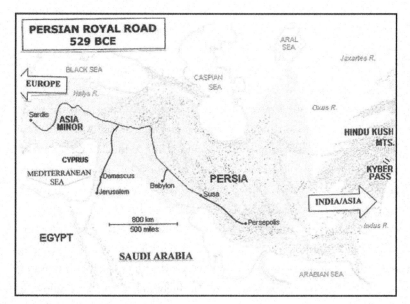

Figure 6.1 Persian royal road

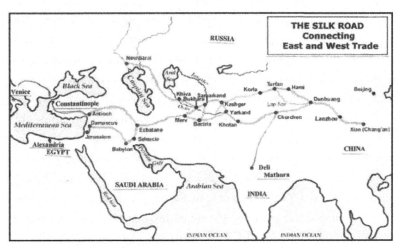

Figure 6.2 The Silk Road

found in Baghdad. Built under the insistence of the caliphate in the eighth century, they were paved with tar, which was derived from petroleum extracted from oil fields. The finished surface therefore resembles many of the modern streets and highways found around the world today.[11] All of these ancient road systems were the forerunners of a common national goal, the creation of an infrastructure to enable commercial development of their lands under their control and to encourage trade with neighboring regions. The echoes of the ancient roadways like the King's Road, the Royal Road, the Incense Road, the Silk Road, and even the little known Tea Horse Road invoke memories of the valiant merchant traders who used these commercial ancient highways to further social exchange connections, which contributed to the development of civilization and paved the way for modern globalization.

The Silk Road was a contemporary name given to describe a system of interconnected complex merchant routes that linked the East, China, and the Asian subcontinent with the West through the prime caravan city of Palmyra in Syria and from there to the Mediterranean (Europe, North Africa, etc.). The descriptive title bestowed on the trade route was due to one of the primary exotic goods that made its way westward on it, the prized exotic silk fabric. The German geographer Ferdinand von Richthofen coined the term in 1877 although its origin was centuries old in the making.

This early transcontinental caravan highway may have begun with the Han dynasty in 206 BCE, as the royal house reached out through appointed intermediaries to the steppe nomads in search of horses, glassware, gems, and other products from the West. This collective series of trade routes survived the demise of the great Han and Roman empires, reaching its zenith as the world's prime commercial corridor during the Byzantine and Tang kingdoms in the early Middle Ages. By the 11th century, this fabled land route connecting East and West, and later receiving the namesake of its most valued commodity that moved across it—silk—was in decline due to the intense competition from Indian Ocean merchant shipping and later during the age of discovery, as traders developed routes rounding southern Africa, connecting the Atlantic and Pacific.

The well-known terminology is still used today to describe a modern pathway, *a second wind for an ancient route*, by Chinese leaders. President Xi Jinping in 2013 made reference to it when he described governmental programs designed "to further communication and cooperation between China and the countries and regions along the (historical) route through trade, investment, cultural and currency exchanges." He called these initiatives the *Silk Road Economic Belt* and the *21st Century Maritime Silk Road.*[12]

Early Transportation Devices

Archaeologists consider that the initial step toward the development of man-made transportation devices began somewhere between 4000 and 3500 BCE with the invention of the wheel in either Mesopotamia or Asia. While the domestication of horses and oxen enabled and assisted early farmers to more efficiently till the soil for crop planting, the introduction of the wheel was followed by that of the cart and chariot—devices that made the transport of crops from one place to another less awkward and more labor economical—as increased quantities could travel over greater distances. Eventually, the four-wheeled cart took the burden of carrying products off the shoulders of the common man and increased the load capacity of beasts of burden. The chief beneficiary of this technological advancement was trade and exchange, as it paved the way for the establishment of centralized destinations for transactions—the marketplace.

It also allowed for the concept of competition to enter the commercial matrix, as previous individual agricultural locations needed to be visited and only singular concealed transactions could be completed.

While the wheel enabled man to overcome the cumbersome boundaries of land travel, his ability to also transit bodies of water was collaterally approached. Researchers tend to conclude that the first water transport vehicle was the dugout canoe used in rivers but the actual inventors are hard to pinpoint. This transport device also allowed for the movement of goods over natural water highways, again contributing to trade expansion over greater distances and with added economic efficiency although the power to move across water had to be supplied by man or with the manipulation of the river current. This engineering drawback led to the invention of the sail to harness the wind. The Egyptians are credited with inventing the sail, as living next to the Nile it was imperative that the navigation of the lifeblood of their civilization include such a technological advancement. The attaching of a cloth to the central pole of the vessel turned it into a self-propelled machine. Eventually, the addition of oars and rudders, then deck coverings in Greek and Roman times, provided better steerage as well as storage areas or shipboard towers to carry men and supplies. Such alterations in design developed into the medieval stern and forecastles as part of the ship's basic design. During the European Renaissance and the age of exploration, ocean-going ships gained tiers of rigging and rows of sails while also becoming sleeker, adding speed and agility to them and thereby making long-distance travel faster and safer. The progress in such water-travel vessels was collaterally aided by the advent of more precise map-making and open-water navigation tools based on astronomy. The Arab, Indian, and Chinese merchants, due to the lure of the spice trade across the Indian Ocean but originating in the so-called spice islands of southern Asia, studied the heavens for directional consideration, and it was the impetus of trade across continents that propelled the quest for such innovative and imaginative astronomical observation and knowledge to be developed. The Chinese invented the compass, although its initial motivation was as a land structure–building device based on the spiritual desire to construct homes facing north. About 70 years before Christopher Columbus sailed across the Atlantic Ocean to find a westward route to the riches of the Far East, the Chinese in 1421, under the command of Emperor Zhu Di's finest admirals, launched the largest fleet the world had ever seen. Called the Star Fleet, it consisted of 3,750 ships, the centerpiece of which were 250 enormous nine-masted treasure ships that were each estimated to be more than 500 ft. long. Columbus's ships—the Nina, Pinta, and Santa Maria—could, all together, fit on its deck. The mission of this armada was to sail the oceans of the world, chart them and their lands, while bringing the territories explored into the orbit of Chinese influence including Confucianism and the royal tribute system. Such a task was to be accomplished by extending trading privileges coupled with protection from enemy aggression.[13]

With the growth of trade via water-based routes and the advent of better-equipped larger cargo ships it was natural that the construction of ports would follow. Around 2250 BCE, in the Indus region of what is today India, a civilization emerged that some call the Harappan, in which people valued external exchange with neighboring territories, the import–export principle. This was exemplified by their construction of a vast dockyard complex linked to a mile-long canal to the sea, enabling area merchants to reach as far as Southeast Asia and the legendary spice islands through the Persian Gulf. The port dominated the landscape and was larger in scope and size than any temple or public edifice, attesting to the importance of the commercial trading imperative to this ancient civilization.

While Roman roads were vital in the maintenance of the empire, many of them were connected to ports, a growing source for the importation of valued commodities. Perhaps the most important stretch of highway was between Rome and the port city of Ostia at the mouth of the Tiber River, a distance of 15 miles. Grain to feed Rome was delivered from Egypt, the most important of the many foreign sources of supplies to the empire. Merchant ships also arrived from the North African city of Carthage as well as Hispania (Spain), Gaul (France), and even from as far as India and the Far East, all unloading their regional cargo, which in turn was placed on barges in transit to the capital city. Ostia was a major geographical player in the tactical downfall of Rome in 409 CE when it was captured by Alaric the Goth by starving the population of Rome into submission. The port city is also the starting place for the popular political rise of Julius Caesar, perhaps the most well-known Roman emperor.

During Caesar's early military career he was assigned the task of ridding the lucrative and necessary commercial sea lanes in the Mediterranean from the marauding pirates. As a commander of the Roman navy (much like the exploits of the later noted American Navy and the Barbary Coast pirates), his success in the campaign became the launching pad for his rise in the army ranks and eventually earned him fame and glory.

As the Roman Empire began to grow, it patterned many of its foreign territorial trading city centers on models developed in the home country. The Roman Empire's trading excursions far outstretched their military conquests and the parallel establishment of colonies under their rule. Italian-based merchants via overland trade routes through Anatolia and Persia made limited entries to the eastern lands while also trading with middlemen in the Kingdom of Axum (Ethiopian), which transacted directly with India. In the beginning of the Common Era, during the reign of Augustus Caesar, the conquest of Egypt opened up a southern water route to these lucrative trade regions. During the occupation of Egypt, the most important trading outpost was the port of Berenice (Berenki Troglodytica) on the Red Sea. Merchant ships from this strategic port sailed the Indian Ocean to the Malabar Coast of India. After nimble seagoing captains learned the secret of the mason winds, seasonally blowing both East and West, the journey was reduced to 45 days and allowed for a safer route than the old long and dangerous coastal path that was beset with traitorous offshore reefs that destroyed the hulls of cargo ships.

Archaeologists have uncovered precious parchments detailing not only the navigational directions but also information on exchange techniques— the secrets of getting the best deals from traders in the Far East. Perhaps, the most valuable cross-territorial freight of the day was incense and spices including pepper. The Roman amphora, the holding pottery jar, was the vessel of choice for these prized foreign-grown resources, and the capacity of small ships was up to 3.5 tons of these containers. The average shipment was valued at 7 million drachmas or $270 million at current exchange rates. Larger merchant ships had a 7-ton capacity and averaged 120 trips a year. Over five-and-a-half centuries, the cumulative value of the Roman–Egypt trade with India and the Far East is estimated at $10.5 trillion, a vast sum even by today's financial measurement and a testament to the globalization of the ancient world.

After unloading these resources at Berenice, they were moved inland via caravans some 200 miles from the Nile River and onward to the Mediterranean port of Alexandria, previously built by the Ptolemaic dynasty for commercial dispersal across Europe and one of the grand ports of ancient times. Roman garrisons were strategically built on the mountains surrounding Berenice and the overland route to the Nile to guard against attacks on the merchant convoys. Records maintained by the Roman overseers in the area indicated that duties for the movement of everyone and everything were extracted. People were taxed according to their vocation or skill. Prostitutes were charged a flat fee of $2,700 to enter the city of Berenice. Owners of donkeys and camels, the means of transport, were charged according to the animal's size while trade goods were taxed at 25 percent of their anticipated value. The profit to be made in the physical movement of just about anything in the region was so enormous that such a mandated additional expense was not prohibitive. The port city of Berenice consisted of a multitude of international nationalities with more than 11 different languages both spoken and written. Merchants who plied their trade in the region made enormous fortunes generating more income than the combined cities of New York and San Francisco do today. All this ceased after the fall of the Roman Empire in Egypt when Muslim armies overran their dominance of the Egyptian territory and the military protectorate of this lucrative trade route was lost. While this trading outpost proved to be a most beneficial wealth creator in the ancient world for Rome, the route to India and the Far East also allowed for the parallel exchange of cultures to take place, contributing to the growth of civilization, a valuable antecedent to the commercial process.

Social ideas moved with goods as merchants brought their customs, traditions, and beliefs with them. Mythical stories have circulated that have Jesus himself traveling on Roman merchant ships bringing the preaching of his gospel to these new lands while more tangent evidence suggests that the Apostle Thomas may have started a Christian mission in India using such commercial routes. In later centuries, the emergence of Islam in the Middle East also made its way on the trails of merchants traders to India and onward to Southeast Asia as represented today by Indonesia, the world's largest Muslim nation. In reverse, the teachings of Hinduism, Jainism, and Buddhism found their way into the Indian subcontinent through the use of similar commercial dealings.

The construction of roadways in antiquity, the emergence of ancient seaports as water routes emerged, railroads in the industrial era, and airports in modern times are all examples of physical infrastructure to support the exchange process and the maturing commercialization of the global environment. To allow for continued and expanded trade, both internally and beyond bordered territories, such technological advancements have always endeavored to further connect the world by shrinking the movement of goods into a more manageable system that is efficient, seamless, and cost efficient. The process continues today. Multinational companies are using their foreign direct investment funds in emerging nations not just to develop commercially valued enterprises but to contribute on a collateral basis to the improvement and modernization of the infrastructure. In Africa, Chinese quasi-governmental investors are marshalling their capital funds to primarily target the ore industry as well as other business projects with either outright contributions or soft loan arrangements to improve transportation infrastructure and communication facilities. Such technological advancements were necessary in the economies of the ancient world and they remain so today. From the building of new roadways and seaports to the refurbishment of dilapidated railroads, such developments propel a civilization forward and are a necessary component to further the global exchange process (they go hand in hand). Transportation, throughout history, has spurred territorial expansion and served as a precursor for modern globalization, as better transport devices allowed for more trade and a greater spread of people. Economic growth and the progression of civilization have always been dependent on increasing the capacity and rationality of transport.[14]

The Brick and Mortar of Ancient Trade

While roadways and advances in transportation played key roles in the globalization of trade in the ancient world, local store merchants serving the final link in the commercial chain, consumers, pressed authorities of ancient municipalities to provide better commercial infrastructures. Historically, town or village markets are naturally active around harvest time, when area residents gathered to exchange the fruits of their labors for those produced by others. The idea of a year-round marketplace that was a permanent part of a city infrastructure was introduced in antiquity and remains as a central planning tool for municipalities around the world today.

In the epic novel *Roma*, author Steven Saylor traces the founding of modern-day Rome on the banks of the Tiber in 1000 BCE to the dawn of the Common Era.[15] He begins the saga, woven across centuries of a common family heritage, by depicting the development of a geographical location due to the activities of two groups of ancient traders. One bares a precious cargo of salt and its transactional interaction with others is described as follows.

> *In return for salt, these people would give Lara's peoples dried meat, animal skins, cloth spun from wool, clay pots, needles and scraping tools carved form bone, and little toys made of wood . . . Their bartering done, Lara and her people would travel back down the river to the sea. The cycle would begin again.*

The route taken by these early salt merchants is then used by other natural resource gatherers as well as those who fashioned useful devices in this region of the Seven Hills. Out of these seasonal treks and scheduled meetings enterprising decedents of these original traders came upon the idea of a trading post. They permanently settled at this crossroad and set up a marketplace for the exchange of goods. By acting as middlemen and providing accommodations for travelers the settlers thrived. Sayor goes on to describe how this ancient trade hub grew.

> *The settlement by the Tiber continued to prosper and grow. The market by the river sawing a thriving traffic in salt, fish and livestock; these three commodities arrive separately, but after being treated with salt the preserved fish and meat could be transported great distances or traded for other goods that flowed in the busy market.*

As news spread of the facility devoted to product exchange it attracted a greater variety of merchandise as well as traders from distant lands. To provide for the growing population of residents and visitors, numerous other services where established to add in the exchange system. Travelers arrived by land and water at regular intervals with the array of the cargo they brought constantly growing. What began as a trading post soon grew into a hamlet, a village, a town, a city, and centuries latter an empire. This example would be repeated around the world as the transactional imperative provided the onus for clustering to not just exchange merchandise. With the practice came the cross-societal or cultural inter-change of news, stores, and in the end different ideas, all leading to the advancement of civilization.

The concept and type of business models have constantly evolved through commercial history. A very basic and popular model, since ancient times, has been the *shopkeeper model*, which involves establishing one's store in a location that is most likely to attract potential customers and make it easier to advertise the products or services being offered.

The Greek-inspired *agora* was the forerunner of the modern-day indoor shopping malls and centers. These retail centers, examples of which still exist today in places like Ephesus in Turkey, were founded for a second time by Androclus, the son of Codryus, king of Athens. The city, with a sheltered harbor, was described by the historian Aristo as being recognized by all the inhabitants of the region as the most important trading center of its time in Asia. Made up of colonnades that protected pedestrian walkways from wind and rain in the winter and from the sun in the summer, the architectural design originally supported an open-air market measuring 110 X 110 m. These outdoor stalls were converted into rows of permanently built shops of alternating or next-street entrances so that customers could come and go without store owners seeing which shop they came from. The fronts of the shops opened into vaulted store rooms at the back for a year-round protection of inventory. Signs were erected above the doorways with symbolic renderings of the merchandise available inside. Tourists visiting the site today still play a game of try-ing to identify the goods through the restored sign images archaeologists have placed on them. Perhaps, the most well known of the artifacts of Ephesus is a relief on the Marble Road depicting a left foot, a portrait of a woman, and a heart decorated with perforations, referencing the city's brothel. Such a graphic depiction is perhaps the ancient world's first outdoor advertisement, a precursor of American billboards that punctuated automobile roadways in the 1950s and the genesis of the commercial advertising industry today.

Shopping in ancient Rome was much like shopping in today's commercial environment. Rows of stores offering their wares could be found on the main streets of the city, which had specific areas devoted to specialized product categories. Like the Greek shops before them, elaborate signs adorned their entrances advertising to the strolling public the merchandise to be found within. Many were constructed using colorful inlaid mosaics while others were paintings. Besides the public signage, store owners were required to prominently display a government license, a document permanently sculpted in marble, to trade in particular categories. The idea of a license to service the pubic served a twofold objective. It allowed the government to keep an administrative handle on market trading activities and to collect a fee and thereby finance the municipality's treasury. In addition to the shops selling both everyday and luxury goods, there were food and drink stalls for the plebeians and slaves shopping for their masters, a forerunner of the food courts found in today's modern shopping malls. Most shop proprietors did not use employees to run their operations but instead purchased slaves. It was not uncommon for shops selling exotic imported merchandise to also utilize slaves from the foreign region that produced them, thereby creating an atmosphere that consumers found appealing and different, which is a concept today's retailers aim for—enhancing the shopping experience.

Beyond the commercial infrastructure of street shops, ancient Roman city planners introduced the concept of the forum or dedicated market and business center. Most noteworthy were the basilicas, not to be confused with large church buildings constructed during the later development and spread of the Christian faith. These commercial basilicas were several stories high and contained a variety of consumer services from business offices to lawyers and accountants along with rows of specialty shops. This mixed-use structure is still employed in modern commercial development projects.

Trajan's Market (in Latin, Mercatus Triani), the last great structure in the Roman Forum, is thought to be the world's oldest metropolitan shopping center. Constructed in 100 to 110 CE on a semicircular design, it sat opposite the Colosseum, positioned perhaps to attract spectators at the games. The entry to the vast marketplace was made in travertine surmounted by an arch. The ornately decorated interior hallways were made of delicately cut marble while the outside walls used bricks. It was roofed by a concrete vault raised on pier acting both as a covering and to allow air and light in the central space. The remarkable architecture of the building is considered a wonder of the ancient world as its splendor was not only to attract customers but also to proclaim to all citizens the symbolic embodiment of the grandeur of the Roman Empire.

This early tiered marketplace rising six stories high contained more than 150 shops and administrative offices, with medieval apartments on the top floor added later. Such mixed use of structure became a model of urban planning and the concept is still in use today. Shops on the ground level floor featured fresh produce of the day as well as taverns while those on the second floor were primarily devoted to olive oils and wines. The third level was for grocers' specialty shops along with exotic imported items such as rare incense, silk cloth, rare gems, ivory, and a host of foreign products collected from the far regions of the empire. Although the shops varied in sizes, most were rather small. Customers would most probably approach the shopkeeper at the door and make their purchases without entering the room itself. The chief reason for such a buying procedure is that the bulk of the premises was devoted to inventory warehousing as opposed to display selling. Patrons would rely on the expertise and recommendations of the shop merchant, a common practice in those days and still found in small traditional villages across the globe.

The remnants of the infrastructure still found in the Roman city of Pompeii are good examples of the commercialization of an ancient international port city. The explored ruins of the city reveals the use of a large banking facility for foreign specie trading as the international clientele of the city arrived with varying mediums of value (coinage, gold, and silver as well as precious stones from their respectful lands) all requiring the services of local money exchangers that made a market in such transactions; the forerunner of today's global currency arbitrators.

Vast markets or bazaars for all varieties of exotic imported goods, erected and maintained by the municipality government, dotted the landscape.

Such an action served a dual purpose: (a) it provided a protected commercial environment for the stimulation of business and (b) allowed for direct oversight to insure proper payment of a transaction levy, the precursor of the municipal sales tax. The city's main entertainment attractions were its 80 wine bars and 28 houses of prostitution, many based on interlocking ownership, an early use of the franchise concept. These establishments were often connected by adjacent alleyways, a kind of a cross-product marketing promotional program that many companies use today. Even the brothels contributed to the growth of the commercial advertising process using, like the Greeks before them, signs of their services in the form of phallic engraved street carvings directing potential clients to their premises. In these establishments, they catered to the foreign visitor via the use of menu-like murals on the walls to get around the numerous language differences—customers only needed to point to receive the services they desired. Today internationally directed products also use diagrams and illustrations to explain their product benefits and instructional use. Specialty craftsmen such as bakeries provided the impetus for modern-day marketing concepts. Their individual breads were branded with a hot iron featuring a symbol to identify the specific establishment that prepared it. While slaves did the majority of sustenance shopping, such commercial markings enabled their wealthy patrons to distinguish which ones they enjoyed at the dining table, instructing these illiterate servants to return to such shops in the future to assure continuing supply of the specific breads they liked. The use of the trademark or brand name on everyday consumer goods was established ahead of today's use of distinguishing packing. This idea was a commercialized progression from the seals placed on large amounts of commodities to distinguish the lands and providers from which they originated. The merchant shops in the city were constructed using the agora template but with a unique addition. They were originally built as two-story units but later ranged up to seven. Called *insula* the design introduced the concept of mixed use space—commercial and residential. The ground or street level housed *tabernae*, commercial shops and assorted business service establishments. The second floor served as apartment living quarters for the shop owners and their families. Such arrangement was initially devised, not just for convenient accessibility, but to afford proprietors of the businesses below the ability for onsite round the clock protection of their investments by living just above them.

This multipurpose housing unit, combining a commercial and residential venue, became the prototype for architectural city planning and was repeated for thousands of years across cities in western Europe. It later found its way in the late 1800s and early 1900s to the cities of New York, Boston, Philadelphia, and Chicago when European immigrants came to the United States. Even today, builders continue to construct intercity combinations featuring commercial establishments on the lower levels and an enlarged series of apartments and condominiums on the upper floors.

In the modern commercial world, the emergence of similar retailing venues across borders, as well as the Internet, has created duplicate patterns of channels of trade where products are purchased through. From the American grocery Walmart to the French retailer Carrefour to the United Kingdom's Tesco, these traditional brick-and-mortar retail chains have expanded their uniform merchandising platforms throughout the world. Franchises like McDonald's and Kentucky Fried Chicken use similar business models and service systems to attract customers in different markets with little adjustments for local tastes in respect to menu items.

Beyond the creation of the exchange imperative, localized market and the subsequent construction of centralized grouped shopping areas to accommodate larger commercial requirements, the brick and mortar development, as occasioned by the trading initiative, had two other elements in antiquity. Storage facilities for grain and other required commodities were erected. They were first used to insure against famine due to natural disasters, then as collection points for governmental decreed taxation. They were later built at port cities to act as domestic surplus warehouses containing goods for export in support of the foreign trade activities of kingdoms and merchants. Such massive edifices were the first publicly constructed infrastructures along with roadways designed to bolster and sustain cross-border trade.

The other major facility that directly owed its development to intercontinental commerce was the caravansary. The word originated in Persia and is a formation of the terms *karvan* (caravan) and *sara* (a palace or building) with sheltering fortifications. These were initially roadside inns where merchant traders could rest and recover from their argent daily journeys but they also serviced pilgrims and other travelers. Thousands of these facilities were built along the Silk Road and in cities to support the movement of commerce across the interconnecting networks of roadways moving from across Asia, North Africa, and the Middle East as well as Southeastern Europe. In his *Guidebook to the Silk Road*, written prior to the Black Plague of 1348, Baladucci Pegolotti, an Italian merchant, observed that the journey from Khanbalik (Beijing) to the Black Sea could take 300 days but advised his fellow travelers that the roadway was perfectly safe, whether by day or night, according to what the merchants said who used it. A contributing reason for the safe passage was the ability to spend nights in a caravansary. These commercial fortifications also became conduits for the flow of information and learning, furthering the flow of multicultural exchanges, a by-product of cross-territorial commerce.

Many of them, built by Seljuk sultans and grandees to encourage and protect intercontinental traders, have retained their original physical properties, such as the walled conclave built on the Mediterranean Sea coast in Acre, Israel. Some like the Kiirkcii Han, the oldest caravansary in Istanbul, still function as a shopping arcade. The traditional caravansary was built like a box, a walled fortress with a single gate opening that allowed caravans of work animals laden with merchandise to enter and leave. An open interior courtyard was surrounded by gated chambers rented for individual merchants to board their animals, drivers, servants, and off-loaded commercial products. Some were of two-story construction with apartments on the top to allow traders to find respite from the road. The bottom storage bay was also used as a makeshift store allowing merchants to display and trade merchandise. Fresh water, food, and other amenities were provided at a price along with money exchange and translation services to assist in exchange transactions with fellow travelers. Libraries offering both entertainment and educational value and even elaborate baths to allow for the travelers to rejuvenate and relax as well as perform ritual cleansing were placed in such facilities. It was at such establishments that news from distant lands was dispensed along with stories, ideas, and religious teachings. It was perhaps the first true multicultural cosmopolitan structure built on a commercial imperative. The caravansary system survived numerous political, military, religious, and economic calamities with many becoming the forerunners of villages, towns, and even cities that grew up around them. Palmyra in Syria was originally founded by a series of caravansaries as were other metropolis along the extended cross-continental trade routes.

Toxic Nature of International Trade

The natural progression of the ancient exchange process evolving into a worldwide commercial system is not perfect. Like all secular human-developed schemes, it is flawed. Notwithstanding the legal constraints imposed on global business institutions both nationally and internationally, the questionable ethical actions of organizations involved in cross-border trade are full of direct immoral injustices as well as indirect culpability. Benjamin Franklin, an admired American statesmen and inventor, has been credited with saying "No nation was ever ruined by trade." However, upon closer examination as to what the exchange process over history may have caused could bring one to argue the point. The effect of the trading initiative on society has brought some rather dramatic damaging social events to unfold.

War

Armed conflict between groups of people is rarely encountered on ideological grounds, although religious wars could be labeled as emanating from strong spiritually inspired philosophical differences. Or as the pseudopigraphica attributed to Napoleon but heard in the comedy routines of satirizer George Carlin describing the event, "Basically people killing people over who has the better imaginary friend." Nonetheless, holy wars or the hijacked term *Jihad* did and does account for armed or military struggles between societies. Outside of this consideration, the basic provocation was to gain the resources of a neighboring or regional group. With the advent of international trade however the ability to control the movement of resources as opposed to the outright indigenous ownership of the lands they came from ignited imperial conflict between rival realms to exercise control over trade routes. No longer did countries need to invade the domains where precious materials or manufactured products originated as the real value in them was not tied to the homeland but the selling price they garnered during the cross-regional exchange process.

Spices that sold for the modern-day equivalent of a dollar a bushel when first harvested could demand 100 times that amount in the distant markets that prized them. Riches were to be made by the intermediaries and not the originators. Land routes over which caravans passed or the sea lanes used by merchant ships became targets of war.

As noted in Chapter 3, the Trojan War, the true imperative for attacking the city of Troy, was to gain control over its lucrative strategic geographical positioning in East–West trade. It was not the fabled love affair portrayed in Greek mythology when Paris of Troy took Helen from her husband Menelaus, King of Sparta, that sparked the war. The centuries later Punic Wars, circa 146 BCE, between the Romans and Carthaginians, were waged for control of Mediterranean commerce. Carthage controlled trade not only on the North African coastline but had profitable outposts in southern Spain and Sicily. In 533 AD, hostilities again erupted concerning the lucrative trade ports in the Mediterranean. The Romans at the Battle of Tricamarum defeated the Vandals, a Germanic people who had built a fledgling but expanding maritime domian around the vestiges of the old Carthaginian commercial empire that threatened the sea trade monopoly the Romans historically enjoyed across the Mediterranean. In 1148 AD, under the banner known as the Norman Conquest European, rulers pushed back at Muslim control of the Mediterranean coastline. The army of Roger II, Norman King of Sicily, captured Mahdia, a valued trading point for the transient rich resources of Africa and a terminus for the gold caravans moving across the sub-Sahara as well as the port of Tripoli.

In the 17th century Western Hemisphere, the riches of the new world primarily controlled by Spain gave rise to a group of French, Dutch, and English seamen who turned to piracy against Spanish shipping. They used a small craft to attack galleons transiting the Windward Passage to Europe. Eventually, they became so strong and bold to attack Spanish colonial cities in South America. They were known by the collective name *buccaneers* after a book by Alexandre Exquemelin chronicling their exploits was translated into English. The English crown, at war with both Spain and France, recognized the importance of their disruptive economic activities and issued letters of marque legalizing their operations in return for a share of their profits. Supposedly, Royal Navy officers were placed among the buccaneers to assist in their efforts to disrupt and destroy the valued trading lanes used by their enemy. The emergence of pirates in 1804 became a threat to cross-Atlantic trade. Barbary corsairs raided ships in the Mediterranean to extract ransom and tributes. A consortium of European countries and, added by a fledgling naval power, the United States, bombarded and invaded Tripoli effectively destroying the protected safe haven of the pirates. Armed conflicts were a direct outgrowth of international trade during the periods of early globalization.

Besides the making of war as a violent method to acquire the resources of another territory or attacking trade routes between regions, other obstacles to the free exchange between nations have also led to military confrontation. High tariffs erected by countries along with other restrictive programs to hamper or limit the movement of products, and sometimes services, have encumbered free trade. These barriers have been identified as contributing to the slowdown of globalization while also causing world economic depression resulting in two world wars. "Trade is one of the few areas on which mainstream economists firmly agree. More is better."[16] One might conclude that the freer unconditional trade between nations exists, the greater the possibility for economic prosperity and perhaps the less chance for warfare. The simple principle that if one trades for the things he or she needs and wants with others then there is no need to force him or her to give them up would seem to make sense. However, this statement too easily forgoes the fact that any exchange has to be amenable to both parties or the concept falls apart. If there is value inequality or one party attempts to gain a competitive advantage in the process, the transaction imperative as an inhibiter of cross-territorial armed conflict does not work. In the end, global trade can cut both ways; it can deter war or it can trigger it.

Disease

The most devastating pandemic in the course of human history was the Black Death. It overwhelmed populations stretching from the Far East to Europe. Researchers have estimated that it took the lives of anywhere from 75 to 200 million people in a period of 15 years, from 1338 to 1353. Numerous theories have been promulgated as to the precise etiology of the disease. However, scientists in recent years using DNA analysis have identified the key pathogen, a bacterium they called *Yersinia pestis*, which was the root *epidemiological* cause of the many forms the plague took. Medical researchers have surmised that given the generic makeup of the bacteria and the historical accounts of its chronological movement across distances, it is most likely that it originated in the arid plains of central Asia and then spread out across the earth. It is the movement of the disease that has led many to surmise that it was carried by commercial travelers from this initial incubation sector. This was because the main route that crossed this disease-infested territory was the Silk Road, the intercontinental land-based trade passage between the Far East and the outlining eastern borders of Europe. The disease reportedly reached the Crimea region in 1343. Other pandemic theories also trace its spread to the transcontinental ocean crossings of merchant vessels attributing the carriers to Oriental rat fleas attached to black rats that infested ships that regularly transited the Mediterranean harbors of Southern Europe. While the disease contributed to a high death toll in China, possibly 25 million, it supposedly was responsible for killing 30 to 50 percent of the 14th-century European population.

Beyond the terrible loss of human life, the Black plague also deeply affected the very culprit that may have spread it. Not only was trade between Europe and the Far East damaged but the uneducated scared people of Europe began to suspect that strangers and even known merchant travelers who plied their wares across the villages and cities were responsible. Commercial traffic came to a standstill. The economic upheaval produced social unrest and contributed to the dark ages. While not an intentional act, the activities of global commerce predicated the events that devastated major populations around the world.

Questionable Ethical Practices

The ethical practices of multinational companies in the modern era of globalization garnered increased public attention beginning in the 1990s. The picture of a 12-year-old Pakistani child stitching Nike soccer balls and working the whole day for $0.90 released by *Life* magazine was a shocking example of depressed labor conditions in underdeveloped countries.[17] Fostered by the unscrupulous associations of firms in their global supply chain associations, the term *sweat shop* has become a universal sign of unethical conduct. The destruction of the Amazon rain forest as well as the harmful effects of other resource extraction industries on land and water around the world has called into question global commercial development. Environmental disasters like the 1989 *Exxon Valdez* tanker spill off the coast of Alaska to the 2010 oil rig leak in the Gulf of Mexico threatening the southeastern shorelines of the United States only serve to highlight the perhaps unscrupulous nature of business enterprises. The global financial crisis of 2009 is also a blot on the tarnished reputation of globalization, but its most offensive action was the international commercialization of the slave trade.

The dangerous attraction to trade is well expressed in a segment from the fictional memoir by Lalla Lalami regarding a Moroccan slave during the European age of exploration.[18] The father of the protagonist advises him not to become a merchant with the warning that "trade would open the door to greed ... an inconsiderate guest." The ominous prediction comes true and the son reflectively lament's, "I fell for the magic of numbers and the allure of profit. I was preoccupied only with the price of things and neglected their value. He goes on to account that "it no longer mattered to me what it was I sold, whether glass or gain, wax or weapons; even I am ashamed to say ... slaves." Ironically, he becomes a slave to the Castilians and journeys to the New World to plant the Spanish flag. The fictional period in which the hero of the novel is placed predates by a decade the largest forced migration of people the world would ever see as slavery becomes a driving global commercial venture.

Slavery

Historically, however, the commercialization of the world was always beset with incidents of immoral turpitude on which the phrase "behind every great fortune lies a great crime," as uttered by Honore de Balzac, may be based.[19] With the exception of murder, slavery could be considered the most morally wicked action one person can do to another. But the practice of assigning property rights to a person and allowing them to be treated as chattel, and thereby exchangeable like a common commodity, is embedded in human history. The Bible, both the Old and New

Testaments, recognizes the treatment of slaves. It specifically comments on their physical management including; how hard you can work, no less beat, them and even when the owner can have sex with female slaves. While interpretive translations of such revered social religious guidelines use words like *servant*, *bondservant*, or *manservant* to mask or mitigate the concept of slavery, the ability to buy and sell them is approached with the same conditions of livestock and other valued products of the day. According to Leviticus 25:44—46 in the New Living Translation (NLT) edition advises that "you may treat your slaves as property, passing them on to your children as a permanent inheritance." Ephesians 6:5—8 (NLT) admonishes, "Slaves, obey your earthly masters with deep respect and fear. Serve them sincerely as you would serve Christ." The Bible in Exodus 7–11 and 13:14 does however depict how God feels about racial slavery, noting the plagues he poured down on Egypt to release the Hebrew slaves. Both the Old and New Testaments condemn the practice of man stealing with the penalty written under the Mosaic law: "Anyone who kidnaps another and either sells him or still has him when he is caught must be put to death."[20] A similar consideration is directed at slave traders, as they are portrayed as "ungodly and sinful."[21]

African Slave Trade

The idea of man stealing originated in Africa and is directly attributable to the commercial exploits of slave hunters who rounded up or sometimes traded for them with tribes who had acquired slaves during tribal warfare. The Portuguese began dealing for black slaves in the 15th century, purchasing them initially from Islamic traders who had established inland trading routes to the sub-Saharan region. Along with prized products like gold, ivory, salt, and other spices, the interior of Africa also provided for the opportunity to deal in human commodities. It was not until the 19th century that the international wholesale trade in slaves reached its zenith as occasioned by the need in the New World, the Western Hemisphere, to work on plantations and farms, and later silver mining operations. Slaves from the continent's interior were forced to march hundreds of miles to the east coast to be resold and placed onto ships owned by Spanish, English, Dutch, and French slave merchants. Many perished on the land route with loss estimates of up to 40 percent, from the point of capture to arrival at these slave trading forts.[22] With a figure of approximately 11,128,000 slaves delivered to the New World during the Atlantic slave trade,[23] the number of captured African slaves (using a 40 percent casualty rate en route) would be as much as 23.5 million. This does not include those killed in the process of capture or who died during the sea voyage to the Americas,; so the number of those caught in the international slavery trade may have been even higher. The dispersal of slaves shows the vast majority going to the West Indies (4.5 million) and Central and South America (5.7 million). Only 500,000 or 4.5 percent of the total were delivered to British North America. It should also be noted that about 300,000 went to Europe.[24] This massive shift in the population of the world, the wanton killing of human beings and the deplorable conditions of those who survived, is unmatched in history and attributable to globalization. The immoral stain of the international African slavery trade continues to plague the global commercial imperative, an atrocity that should always be remembered so that it is never repeated.

Slavery in the Classical World

The ownership and trade of slaves were a common business venture in all parts of the ancient world. The population of the Greek city of Athens in 313 BCE consisted of 84,000 citizens, 35,000 resident aliens, and more than 400,000 slaves.[25] A portrait of the Roman Empire at the end of the republic period around the third century BCE indicates that it was a slave-based economic society. Estimates indicate that the slave population just within Italy was 2 million, which would yield a 1:3 ratio of slaves to free citizens.[26] Slavery for Romans, and as with the Greeks before them, was a matter of citizenship with neither religion nor race factored into the determination. The qualification for slavery was being born outside the state, assuming that the birth was not attributable to a domestic slave, whose offsprings were automatically slaves. Upon capture, such individuals—considered barbarians, as they were not citizens—were considered booty, just like other possessions or property acquired by the victor in war. Prisoners provided the greatest resource and legitimate slave traders would often contract with military units for a set quantity at agreed-upon prices, extending their supply chain to distant lands. Many campaigns were paid for by the selling off of slaves, the spoils of war. It was possible for such potential slaves to buy their way to freedom. There was however no class distinction as the rich and poor were subject to slavery. Many of those captured were well educated and possessed skills and knowledge, which only contributed to their value when sold to new owners, thus fetching a much higher price on the auction block. Even slaves had discernable marketing differentiations. Slaves were promoted just like products for their unique attributes with their birth origins acting like a geographical trademark denoting that they came with built-in skills found only in their specific birth land.

As abhorrent as the commercial slavery trade was it was also one of the primary contributors to the dispersal of knowledge in the ancient world as the slaves brought new ideas and techniques, even new inventions, to their master's abodes. They were not just beasts of burden: Many slaves became governesses and tutors to the children of their masters while others were secretaries or scribes in the household and business interests of the family. They imparted wisdom and information from around the world to the households they served in.

The business of slavery also came with caveats, just like those attached to all commercial transactions. Reputable dealers in slaves had a duty to provide buyers with a certification of the slave's good health and criminal record. It was also their responsibility to attest that the sold slaves were in appropriate physical or intellectual condition for the buyers' requirements and were not runaways—someone else's property. Such conditional elements in the transaction were the beginning of product or service warranties—that is, items sold should be suitable for the purpose for which they were intended, a basic tenet found in today's Uniform Commercial Code. In Roman society, aediles—one of the board of magistrates in charge of public buildings, streets, markets, games, and other administrative duties—were appointed to oversee slave market transactions. Like special masters in law, they acted in a semi-judicial manner to settle disputes between parties and to generally oversee that the sellers at slave auctions presented all the required certifications to the buyers and that the process was dispute free. The concept of business rental was introduced as collateral to the sale of slaves. The option of renting was available to those who wanted their services for a limited period of time (to assist with a harvest or to cover for an unwell slave). The public display of material wealth illustrated the social standing of Roman society just as it does today. The ownership of slaves was the most common way for a man to display his status and power with the elite maintaining a large cadre of slaves at their residences. It is considered a matter of reputation that Lucius Pedanius Secundus, a Roman politician in the 1st century CE under Emperor Claudius, kept more than 400 slaves in his personal household. He was eventually killed by his slaves. Most slaves were utilized as field workers on the latifundia (large Italian commercial estates), which caused unemployment within the free Roman community and later contributed to the institution of land reform laws in the empire.

The economic value of slaves in the ancient world is well exemplified by the high percentages they occupied in the populations of Greece and Rome. The enormous transfer of slaves from Africa to initially promote and then sustain the economic growth of the New World is also a testament to their commercial importance that also impacted other economic segments along with additional areas of the world. In the later 18th century, cotton was the most important universal raw material commodity. Slavery was the manual instrument that drove the global supply chain but such abhorrent practice also ushered in the Industrial Revolution. As noted earlier, the invention of the spinning jenny or steam-operated loom to increase the speed and efficiency of weaving raw cotton, as picked by slaves, into clothes eventually changed the world.

However, to quantify the impact of slavery, consider that in the mid-1800s the slaves in the United States were the single largest financial asset, worth more than $3.5 billion in 1860 dollars—larger than the combined value of the country's rail-roads, banks, factories, and ships.[27] The American slave industry provided the financial fuel that drove the nation's emerging capital markets while also having an international economic effect. The accumulated wealth based on cotton cultivation flowed not only into the hands of southern American plantation owners but also into the coffers of northern merchants and across the Atlantic to British bankers and manufacturers as well as European commercial interests. In the 1830s, slavery also provided for the further development of a fairly new financial instrument, the issuance of bonds with slaves as collateral. It allowed planters to borrow enormous amounts of money to acquire new lands, which in turn only cemented and extended the repugnant slave practice. Because such commercial sustaining activity was a key economic driver, lawmakers got into the act by backing such bonds with state credit. The Civil War, although influenced by arguments over states' rights and driven by the clash of the industrialized North and the agrarian cultured South, had at its core a philosophical division over slavery, which is a human rights issue.

As business ventures moved around the world in both ancient and present times, the treatment of those who had encountered the commercial ventures of business institutions suffered. Many native populations in numerous areas of the world were and are still today pressed into the service of multinational enterprises whether by economic choice or necessity. This remains a negative aspect of the globalization phenomenon.

CHAPTER 7

Mediums of Exchange and Financial Instruments

Money Makes the World Go Around

The cumulative manipulative power of commerce on the world is perhaps best illustrated by a song from the multiple-award-winning musical *Cabaret* that opened on Broadway in 1966, was made into a movie in 1972, and, after its revival on stage in 1987, garnered its second Tony award. Set in Berlin at the beginning of the Third Reich, the story follows the romance of an English cabaret performer and an American writer. Through its songs the audience witnesses the political changes taking place in Germany against the backdrop of the global economy of such a period. One of the memorable songs performed by the emcee, as joined by the female chorus line in international designated costumes with each nation's currency clearly delineated, is usually referred to as *The Money Song* although its original title was *Sitting Pretty*. The lyrics by Fred Ebb tell a universal tale: "Money makes the world go around ... of that we can be sure."[1]

There is no other worldwide physical object nor shared language or political dogma as expressed in philosophy or religious beliefs that unites all the peoples of the globe like money. Money is a medium of valued exchange as accepted by societies for their trading activities. It acts as a respected intermediary that further supports the commercial imperative, always retaining its intrinsic value: a dollar is a dollar, but what it receives in return—products or services in the marketplace—fluctuates. The importance of creating a designated value conciliator changed, united, and propelled civilization forward. Under the traditional barter system, if one party only had an apple to trade, he had to find those who wanted an apple and hoped what they had he also desired. This arrangement deeply limited the trading process especially between parties who were not acquainted with the fruits of the labors of distant lands. My own son at age six understood the marvel of money as a flexible instrument to enable one to get what he or she really sought. When asked what he wanted for his birthday, he replied, "Don't give me a present as it may not be what I want; give me money instead so I can go to the store and buy what I want." The development of a medium of exchange provided freedom of choice, thereby liberalizing and expanding the trade process. It fueled early commercial venturing, allowing for greater integration of people into the system, and thereby propelled the development of civilization.

Whatever the current denominated local currency unit or the value assigned to historic bartered items, a fundamental understanding and appreciation of a medium of exchange to enable parties to transfer ownership between them permeates all cultures. Aphra Behn, author of the play *The Rover* (1677), best expressed such a concept with the line "Money speaks sense in a language all nations understand."[2] The development of such an exchange tool grew out of the basic need of all human beings to trade with each other. Whether money is defined as metal coinage or paper currency backed by a governmental obligation or expressed as the intrinsic value in gold, silver, or some other mutually recognized intermediary material of accepted denomination from wampum shells to bricks of salt, its conceptual use is universal and the principle exists in all societies.

Economic textbooks describe money according to its three basic functional or operational characteristics. First, it is of value unto itself when used as a standard of evaluation in asset or wealth determination. Second, it has value as a measured unit of account or counting in exchange transactions. Third, it has value as a medium of exchange with potential value determined by the things or services it can purchase in return, thereby carrying a variable value determinable through agreement based on an exchange event. Perhaps the oldest forms of money were physical things based on the fruits of one's labor via agriculture and land use—the farming of grain and the herding of domesticated animals, predominantly cattle. Transactions based on such early physical embodiments of value were cumbersome or awkward to transport and difficult to accurately gauge before uniform weights and measures were introduced. Out of such a need the use of numerous other, more portable commodities as mediums of exchange, with their physical properties varying throughout history, was born. While precious metals—like gold, silver, and rare stone gems—are the most well known of the accepted value mediums, many others were used over mankind's history in the exchange process. The Aztecs of Mesoamerica used chocolate as money. The cacao beans served as a way to calculate value and round out the exchange computation in a basic barter system. They even used *quachtli* (cotton cloaks), beads, shells, and copper bells to shape their commercial transactions.[3] The use of ordinary commodities was also assigned a socially acceptable value of exchange in ancient times. The reliance on salt, due to its precious characteristic as a life-sustaining mineral, made it an intermediary denomination in China, North Africa, and the Mediterranean (see Chapter 5). During different periods, such necessary products to assist in life were granted value exchange status (e.g., rice to *zappozats* [decorated axes], eggs to nails). Rare and exotic items also took their places as intermediary value substitutes (e.g., amber, jade, ivory, shells [wampum, used by northeastern American Indians, and cowrie, a shell found off the coast of China]).

The first metal coins, made from an amalgam of gold and silver, by most archeological accounts, were invented in the Kingdom of Lydia around 560 BCE.[4] The concept, sometimes referred to as representative money, was adopted in nearby civilizations (e.g., the Persians) and used in many of the early Greek states. The victory of Alexander the Great over the Persians provided the Greeks with a large amount of mined gold and silver along with the ability to mint more coins. His insistence on a standard exchange rate between gold and silver—a 10:1 ratio—sustained trading confidence in the newly introduced coinage system while enabling his administration to control important commercial activities thereby providing economic stability to war-ravaged territories. The Romans furthered the use of coins after years of relying on heavy, cumbersome bronze bars while the expansion of their empire unified vast conquered areas with a common medium of exchange, itself contributing to the intercontinental trading process, an essential element to Romans' existence and maintenance of the empire. The engravings on ancient metal coins featured a variety of symbols and reliefs of emperors and kings. The Roman government even recorded messages, essentially propaganda, they wanted to get across to their citizens. The use of coins was an invention quickly implemented by many regimes in the ancient world as it provided a fair, predictable, and easily portable method of exchange as opposed to the old barter system that required the weighing or measurement—which was always questionable—of bulky and at times perishable intermediary commodities whose values fluctuated with market conditions.

Recently, scientists at McMaster University in Canada have found a method to use ancient coins to map trade routes and shed light on the early economic patterns as exemplified by commercial dealings in the Mediterranean region.[5] Probing their metal content, researchers have discovered trace elements that allowed them to determine the geographic origins and in turn the circulation of these initial mediums of exchange. The wide territorial acceptance of these precious metal pieces containing gold, silver, bronze, and copper (along with adulterating elements of tin or lead, indicative of economic troubles) exemplify the early spread of merchant trade based on common values across and between civilizations—the roots of globalization.

Markings on ancient coins often depicted the faces of territorial rulers as insurance of recognized acceptance in their kingdoms, but such engravings primarily were used to promote the sovereigns' public image. The true value of these early mediums of exchange was the inherent weight of the rare metal used in the forging process. An innovative change in the coinage-denominated value occurred during the reign of Cleopatra in Egypt.[6] Coins struck during her reign had varying denominations inscribed on them, a quantified face value, thereby negating value based on the precious ore content. This revolution in the prescribed value of intermediary mediums of exchange served as a precursor to the introduction of paper money and began the movement away from prized metal determining the value of money to state-backed acceptable currency.

Fiat money or paper currency does not have an inherent value like commodities, gold, or silver coinage. Its declared worth or value is derived from its authorization by a sovereign government or kingdom as legal tender for payment of all debts to be declared acceptable for the settlement of both public and private debt in the territories under the rule of such institutions. The first use of paper money (also referred to as bank or promissory notes of exchange) was attributable to the Song dynasty in China back in the seventh century, which imprinted the image of the emperor. Banknotes appeared in Europe in the mid-1600s issued by Stockholms Banco. It should be noted that the use of fiat money was tied throughout history to a gold standard wherein such paper notes were technically convertible to preset quantities of gold; hence, backed by the holdings of the sovereign state of the physical precious metal. The Bretton Woods Conference in 1944 was history's first example of a fully negotiated monetary order intended to govern currency relations among sovereign states. Signatory countries pegged their currencies to the U.S. dollar, which in turn was fixed to gold. However, in 1971, the United States revoked the U.S. dollar's conversion to gold and many countries suspended their currency's tie to the U.S. dollar. Since then. the principle of a government-backed legal tender has remained in practice.

This notion of representative money by governmental fiat has produced some very troublesome events. Ask yourself what would the currency in one's bank account be worth if you could find no one to accept such government-marked paper in return for the receipt of goods or services? Millions of hardworking thrifty German consumers during the administration of the Weimar Republic of Germany in late 1923 found almost overnight that their life's savings were worthless as a valued medium of exchange in the marketplace. It took 50 billion marks to purchase a postage stamp and 200 billion to buy a loaf of bread. Home owners quickly realized that it was cheaper to burn mark notes in their kitchen stoves than to use them to buy firewood. Hyperinflation (i.e., when prices increase rapidly and the nation's currency loses its value) can result in some ridiculous face values of bank notes. At the height of inflation, U.S.\$1 was equivalent to 4 trillion German marks. The Reichsbank during this period issued a denomination of 100 trillion marks, which was worth U.S.\$25. Throughout history, the loss of trust in government-issued mediums of exchange caused chaos. Whether it be the Roman emperors debasing their metal coinage, the French revolutionary regime printing a flood of useless *assignats*, or the U.S. Continental Congress issuing money until the phrase "not worth a Continental" was born, the danger of reliance on what Lewis Lapham calls our "secular religion,"[7] our spiritual-like reverence that places the public trust in such instruments, has always been a danger. This analogy is reflected in American currency with the words "In God We Trust" printed on dollar bills. Perhaps, such references echo the words of Voltaire, the French philosopher, who wrote that "When it is a question of money, everybody is of the same religion." The need, however, for nations to erect a common unit of exchange often accompanied by a shared measurement system (mutually accepted weights and measures) has helped societies throughout history to unite their people and bring social order; hence, giving credence to the idea that money is akin to a civil religion, a unified belief system as Lapham refers to it.

Paper money, as evidence of value, has moved beyond the scope of a nationally recognized currency. Commercial bank money, checks, or bank drafts are acceptable documents in the exchange process today. Bonds, letters of credit, wire transfer authorizations, and credit or debit cards all evolved to enhance and make more efficient the trading imperative, propelling mankind and the evolution of civilization. However the word *money* is defined and its value or worth measured, it is key to the socialization process of mankind. As observed by Lapham, "Money ranks as one of the primary materials with which mankind builds the architecture of civilization."[8] While it is a tool for living, the Latin phrase *radix malorum est cupiditas* (greed is the root of all evil) reminds us that it is not money that causes trouble but rather the use of money in a votive ritual as a pagan ornament with no redeeming social value or, worse, its utilization in a socially destructive or harmful manner. Jack Weatherford paints a rather stunning portrait of money in society when he states,

> Money constitutes the focal point of modern world culture. Money defines relationships among people, not just customer and merchant in the marketplace or employer and laborer in the workplace. Increasingly in modern society, money defines relationships between parent and child, among friends, between politicians and constituents, among neighbors, and between clergy and parishioners. Money forms the central institutions of the modern market and economy, and around it are grouped the ancillary institutions of kinship, religion, and politics. Money is the very language of commerce for the modern world.[9]

While Weatherford injects the term *modern* into his observation, the author would submit that money defined as a medium of socially acceptable value in the exchange process has been important throughout human history as an identifier and classifier, even a definitive measurement and structuring device in mankind's relationship with his fellow man. An American colloquial term, "Keeping up with the Joneses," signifies the desire to compare one's lifestyle with neighbors. Its theme, however, is universal as wealth accumulation in many cultures is a social conditioning mechanism to convey status and respect. Whether it is the number of chickens in a yard, the size of a cattle herd, gold jewelry anointing one's body, an expensive sports car in the driveway, or a platinum credit card, such material objects serve as the social symbolism of value attainment. On the other hand, an altruistic lifestyle that delivers peace, tranquility, and harmony is also to be envied but the former measurement device seems to permeate most societies.

The emergence of the commercial trade process in the world was the essential ingredient in the development and progression of societies or in some instances their demise. In the modern era, the system it created is known as globalization but the roots of its current format can be traced to the dawn of man on this earth and his interaction with his fellow men. The invention of money was an essential component to the basic exchange process. It eliminated the difficult barter system, which required the cumbersome transportation of physical objects offered for trade. It allowed for smoother and more efficient business transactions to be conducted.

Raise of Capital Instruments

While money in various forms was used as a medium of exchange in transactions, its intrinsic value as a thing unto itself allowed it to be used and exchanged as a capital asset and thereby fund commercial activities. The idea of loaning money has been recorded throughout time. It is evidenced in ancient stone and clay tablets describing such arrangements. Its use as a thing to be exchanged with payment back in the form of interest has been noted in religious texts with many doctrines attacking the concept as usury (an exorbitant rate of interest in excess of reasonably acceptable social conditions or the legal set rate). In the Hellenistic east, third century BC, commercial loans carried a legal interest rate of 24 percent and the practice was severely limited. In ancient Egypt and throughout the Middle East, the percentage was only 8 percent, as money was commonly viewed as an acceptable resource to fund long-distance trading expeditions. While around the world the use of money as a capital instrument varied, its real rise on the global stage as an influential financial tool was in the form of the government bond.

Government Bond

The development of the bond, a formal contract to repay a borrowed amount with interest at fixed intervals, was a step beyond the traditional singular relationship of debtors and their bank for a loan. It enabled the issuers to broaden their credit base to alternative sources of funds in the general public while at the same time created an instrument that unto itself could serve as a portable medium of exchange that was also of transferable value. Like money in its initial numerous physical forms from engraved tablets to forged metal to wampum, this new embellishment of trusted value was another step in the expansion of the economic system and the globalization of finance.

As originally used to raise funds for the independent city-states in northern Italy around 1200 CE, the government bond was primarily a financial tool to provide money to wage war and hence it is associated with hostile conflicts between royal houses. The idea of the issuance of bonds rose out of the need by regional and later national feudal kingdoms to go beyond the repugnant property tax system and institute a reward-like mechanism for its landed gentry whose support was required to maintain political allegiance and authorized control. While the bond was an investment vehicle as it paid periodic interest to the holder, in reality, its true value was literally a gambling chip—a bet placed on the outcome of its use. As the tides of war changed—battles won or lost—the value of the bond fluctuated, much like the present-day corporate bond or stock that moves in relationship to the quarterly success of the issuing company. It should be noted that the doctrine of the Catholic Church, a dominant force during the early period of the bond's introduction, prohibited usury, the charging of interest on a loan. Such religious-based prohibition was circumvented by not calling such instruments a loan or *mutuum*. Instead, they were constructed in contracts of purchase as a census or as they have come to be known an annuity—funds deposited with another for a future stream of periodic payments. The bond fit this definition perfectly.

In the 1200s, the banking house of Rothschild added a new wrinkle to the bond instrument. By placing family members in branches throughout the great cities of Europe, an integrated financial banking network was established. Previously, the bond market was limited to the sovereign territory and currency of the issuing state with interest paid domestically. But with the power and prestige, and also the shared intelligence of the Rothschild family, pressure was bought on bond issuers to denominate their value in a pan-European acceptable currency—sterling. In the capacity of an underwriter, the Rothschild family acted as its own syndicate, buying an entire issue of bonds from the issuer and reselling them to investors. This allowed bonds to be sold across and between national territories with interest payments available locally. The portability and expanded universality of the bond market was established. Today the pioneering activities of the Rothschild bank allows for national governments to place their debt securities on a global scale.

Although bonds were originally used as capital financing instruments to raise funds for military preparedness and to wage war, such specific designations were not adopted by countries until the United States did in World War II. During World War I, they were referred to as Liberty Bonds; then around 1935 a more exacting name was introduced, calling them Defense Bonds. The designation was officially changed to War Bonds with issuance of the E series after the attack on Pearl Harbor on December 7, 1941. The government with private interests launched a massive national advertising campaign for their sale. From attention-grabbing posters to radio and movie commercials to public bond rallies with Hollywood celebrities, a strong emotional promotional program was launched.

Apart from governmental use, the bond also played a significant part in early commercial transactions as well as historically raising investment capital for private commercial investments. In ancient times, such instruments were in the form of surety bonds or third-party promissory notes. However, within the bond family, such financial instruments are issued by one on behalf of another, guaranteeing that if the principle does not fulfill the contractual obligation, then the one owed the commitment can look to the bond for satisfaction. The term *surety bond*, a document evidencing an enforceable monetary obligation under specific circumstances, works like an insurance policy, and hence the term is often used in such commercial situations today requiring an event to trigger payment of the bond. The idea is not new, however. Stone tablets have been discovered in archeological sites dating back to 2400 BCE in Mesopotamia (Iraq) during the Babylonian era. Scribed by professional artisans of the period, such pieces described the guaranteed reimbursement if the principal failed to make timely payment for grain. Attested by witnesses who impressed their seals onto the tablet, this functional debt instrument served as a binding legal agreement between all parties. Historians tell us that the concept of business insurance as an endeavor entered into on a regular commercial basis probably originated under the term *bottomry*, an orientation toward the safe movement of merchant cargo stored in the hull or *bottom* of the ship. Recorded evidence of merchants entering the field of insurance for seafaring carriers via payments of *securitas* (Latin for security as well as the name in Roman mythology for the goddess of security of the empire and a veiled reference to a surety bond) is found in commercial documents of 14th-century Italy due to the ocean trading endeavors of the Venetian and Genovese city-states. These instruments insured against acts of God and other perils encountered outside of the control of the ship's captain and the crew; today the concept is acknowledged under force majeure clauses of contracts.

Perhaps the greatest use of the private commercial bond was by the Dutch East Indies Company (Vereenigde Oost-Indische Compagnie, or VOC). Their bond issuance in 1623 further propelled the company to global trading dominance. In 1669, it was the richest private company in the world with assets of 150 merchant ships, 40 war shipments to protect cargo from sea raiders, and a standing army of 10,000 to control and administer their land expeditions tied to Dutch colonial ambitions. More than 50,000 people worked for them making them the world's largest private employer in the 17th century.

Joint Public Stock Company

As world exploration in the 15th century yielded new sea lanes to support the East Indian trading initiative, the tiny Dutch nation, by European standards, rose to prominence as a globally induced commercial party to challenge the Portuguese and Spanish dominance of global trade. (Note that, between 1580 and 1640, these two nations were joined under one ruling royal house.) Due to the numerous hazards in sailing halfway around the world and back again, merchants pooled such one-off ventures to spread the financial risk of the numerous individual entities. Such an investment principle was not new as tradesmen in ancient times formed commercial partnerships to fund singular land trading excursions to traverse the Middle East. The Dutch experience improved on such a historic concept by merging these companies into a solitary unit to formally create a nationally charted monopoly on this lucrative trade route. Originating in 1602, the VOC introduced a model on which modern public corporate entities are based even though it was a government-sponsored enterprise. Not only was their structure a template for future companies to administratively and operationally construct their activities and legal formation but it also opened this investment vehicle to a wider public audience to participate in while also creating a trading system for shareholders to exchange their certificates of ownership, the forerunner of the contemporary stock exchange.

Subscription to the offering was open to all residents of the nation provinces, thereby allowing the public in general to participate in what was historically an exclusive elitist wealth-creating mechanism. Such expansion of the opportunity also helped to unite the country's citizens in pursuit of a national economic agenda with global implications. As with the trade partnerships under the agreement called *naruqqum* under the Assyrians and Babylonian kingdoms, as previously described, the company had a fixed period of operation (21 years), but shareholders could withdraw their investment after 10 years. Even the money needed to acquire an interest in the company could be paid in periodic installments via purchase warrants, a financial vehicle used in funding initial stock offerings today. The actual ownership instrument was called *apartijen*, also referred to as *actien* (which literally translates to *a piece of the action*), a veiled reference to the gambling nature of the entities' ventured activities. No actual stock certificates were issued but a receipt for monies received was issued and the name of the shareholder was entered on the company's ledger, thereby entitling them to dividends. Perhaps the most appealing and legally interesting principle established in the use of the stock offering was that of limited liability. A board of directors was established to control operations but within the tradition of hierarchical reverence in the society at such a time when these overseers were known as Lords. Initially, such Lords were appointed for life but later this term was limited to three years.

To act as a check and balance on the maintenance of the company's accounts, the use of independent auditors was also introduced. One of the key aspects of this capital funding system was the principle of limited liability—stockholders only risked their investment and could not be held liable for debts or losses that exceeded the subscription price. Their potential loss was restricted. The initial trading expeditions of VOC to set up operations in foreign markets were no easy task, and with many new commercial entities the venture was not immediately successful. Nervous investors could not withdraw their funds notwithstanding the potential liquidation of the company, so their options were limited. Out of such a situation emerged a new concept, a financial paper marketplace for the exchange of shares in a company, the stock market. As the trades were only officially registered periodically, the idea of forward purchases or futures was also created. Another interesting economic principle that came out of the public stock offering was the use of shareholding values being considered a recognized tangible asset that could act as collateral against which loans could be procured. The effect of such recognition was the expansion of credit opportunities as previously hard assets, usually land, livestock, or warehoused merchandise, were the only accepted form of guaranteed security for a loan.

Although the Dutch East Indian Company was initially charted to pursue trading activities in the Far East, one of its best known expeditions targeted North America. In 1609, the *Halve Maen* (Half Moon) captained by Henry Hudson, attempting to find a northwest passage for the VOC to the East Indies, sailed into what is today the New York Harbor. The area he explored was first developed and administratively operated by private commercial concerns primarily interested in the lucrative beaver felt pelts prized in Europe for the manufacture of waterproof hats. The region was later designated a colony of the Dutch Republic as a provincial entity in 1624 and, two years later, Peter Minuit created a deed with the local Indian tribe for the island of Manhattan, which eventually became New York City.

Congruent with the establishment of the VOC was the English joint stock company that came to be known as the British East Indian Company, which was also formed to pursue trade with the East Indies but focused more specifically on the Indian subcontinent and China. While initially created by Elizabeth I in December 1600, a greater privileged position was granted to the company in 1708 when a rival firm caused the original one to be merged into a singular entity. While the trading activities of the firm grew, its regional influence morphed into a semigovernmental arm of the British Empire as it came to rule large areas of India, exercising military control and administrative functions and eventually moving away from its original commercial activities.

Like bonds, shareholdings expanded a new base of credit and monetary value that helped to revolutionize the economic systems of societies and helped to propel civilization forward. These financial instruments—like their predecessors, the coinage of money and paper currency—expanded the mediums of exchange. Such documentable, easily transferred portable stores of value dramatically altered the commercial landscape, contributed to the trading initiative, and were fundamental to mankind's progression. Paraphrasing the ideas of Jacob Bronowski, Niall Ferguson said that "the accent of money (and all its revolutionary instruments) has been essential to the ascent of man." Such "financial innovation has been an indispensable factor in man's advancement .... The evolution of credit and debt was as important as any technological innovation in the rise of civilization."[10] The bond and the stock certificate can also be considered as social reengineering instruments.

Before the introduction of these instruments, wealth was defined by a prime tangible appreciable asset, land, which could itself generate increased value based on its ability to produce extracted or supported resources through agricultural crops, a natural sustenance for farm-bred and wild animals, as well as mining operations for precious metals. While gold and silver were certainly valuable, they mainly served as an intermediary measurement for the transfer of other assets. When used on their own as investment capital with a return received for their use, they had value unto themselves, like a physical asset. As with the ownership of land, bonds and stock could generate an ongoing return via interest and dividends as well as increase in value themselves. Their one great advantage over property is that they were portable transferable wealth—land could not be moved. One could now move his or her wealth around, creating a more mobile society. Working capital created a new aristocracy as opposed to the historic landed gentry. And as the general public began to participate in the marketplace for such securities, they began to accumulate wealth, a privilege traditionally associated with landownership. Society was presented with a vehicle that allowed for a new class of citizens to emerge to challenge the elite landlords of the past. The societal system that had previously created a large gap between the rich and the poor was presented with an initial building tool to bridge the chasm of economic and social separation. It should be noted that bonds and stocks were not the only mechanisms to have a social impact. The rise of a merchant class and valued craftsmen or artisans also propelled social change in medieval times but it was these groups that gravitated to the use of bonds and stocks more quickly than the average laborer or commoner; so it provided additional fuel for their social accent. Primarily devised to aid the commercial trading imperative, these financial instruments combined to help shape the course of global human affairs and contributed to the development of civilization on earth.

PART IV

Collateral Influences on Global Commercialization

While the merchants of numerous historic societies were directly involved in the commercial globalization of the world and the ancient products they transacted affected its growth and expansion across territories as enhanced and supported by the social infrastructures that arose around them, other influences contributed to the phenomenon taking place. Religion and government were strong collateral players. They both nourished and directed, allowing the early roots of globalization to take form. The philosophical doctrines of religions recognized the need to provide for announced expected ethical behaviors with respect to the exchange process and its by-product (i.e., wealth), reacting to a social mandate from their followers. The rulers of ancient lands began to see that their involvement in, no less control of, foreign commercial venturing was a new stepping stone outside of war to gain power, prestige, and enrich their kingdoms. Out of these two influential institutional vestiges the need for secular social laws and regulations with respect to property and the right of private transfer was born. The legacy of religion and government intervention still permeates the modern era of globalization.

CHAPTER 8

Religion and the Exchange Process

Spiritual belief doctrines and the systems built around them are collectively known as religion. The Latin word *religio* comes from the verb *religare*, meaning to bind, while the word relation is rooted in *referre*, to refer and create a link to provide orientations for guidance. The term *religion* therefore refers to ties or binds to principles that define our relationships with fellow human beings, as well as revered deities and the environment. The exchange process, and its mature descendant the commercial trade system, is a natural fundamental social relationship required by people to survive and hence a subject worthy of a religion-based determination. It is therefore valuable to include a series of introspections from the major religious teachings to better understand their effect on the commercial process and its collateral undertaking the accumulation of wealth using a profit motive.

Prior to the first millennium BCE, the dominant form of religious belief throughout Eurasia and the rest of the world was polytheism. Each separate community worshipped its own individual supernatural beings who physically manifested themselves in celestial, natural, and even human forms. Along with the national empires of the ancient world emerged a number of major religious sects, each characterized by the dispensing of a single doctrine to their followers with a common claim to universality. These spiritual organizations replaced the multitudes of widely dispersed cults but innumerable other creeds survived without making the transition to world religions, a widely shared belief in a single spiritual reality, the right way to live. Most of the dominant world religions spread along the trade routes, diffused by the merchants themselves, the administrators of the commercial process, the soldiers guarding safe passage, and the missionaries and travelers who often booked passage with money-making caravans transporting products. There is little doubt, due to massive evidentiary materials, that the emergence of organized religion contributed to the growth and cohesiveness of civilizations. Their teachings provided order in society by creating uniform principles of acceptable and punishable behavior—the ethical and social responsibility mandates that included references to the behavior of societies in respect to the commercial exchange idea, an acknowledged necessity to living life. The development of larger, more centralized states adopting specific religious doctrines and the increased intercontinental trade across and between them acted as the prime agents for the growing universality of the ancient major religious orders.

Not to be overlooked is the simple fact that spiritual indoctrination and practice also accounted for disturbances, even leading to armed conflicts in and between societies. Throughout history, minority religious orders were often persecuted for their beliefs, while in certain societies they were tolerated due to their ability to contribute to the valued exchange process. Foreign merchants whose beliefs were alien to many of the territories they traveled across were given permission to continue to practice their religion as the benefit provided the local commercial system outweighed prejudicial concerns. Whereas, in other societies, their skills in providing capital for financial transactions allowed them to exist in a controlled environment. Many early religious philosophies were critical of the profit side of the commercial initiative as they preached charity and fair treatment in the exchange process, while others distained material gain itself. In some cases, such as Islam, their doctrines forbid specific practices such as usury, the charge of interest on loans, and operating a commercial enterprise in areas considered as offering products or services considered unclean and damaging to society. In Christianity, the money changers were harshly criticized for their transactions, while in many Far Eastern religious orders, the accumulation of material wealth was a path filled with destruction. Due to such prohibitions, certain marginal religious sects often emerged to handle transactions that the majority could not participate in.

In spite of such objections to commerce as a skeptical undertaking, it was through the roadways constructed by merchants that religious observation in fact spread from region to region. The incense trade in the Arabian corridor not only "catalyzed the birth of Islam" but was instrumental in broadening its influential reach in Asia, Europe, and Africa: "Riding on a rising tide of global trade along the land and sea routes of Asia, Islam came to dominate the continent's spiritual as well as commercial life."[1]

During the era of European exploration, the Church, in conjunction with the royal court and commercial interests, became a willing participant in the colonization of barbarian lands. The Church, alongside those in search of valued resources in foreign territories, was charged with missionary work and the conversion of alien societies to the Christian belief system. The prologue to the king and queen in the *Journal of the First Voyage* of Christopher Columbus in 1492 depicts well his religious, indoctrinated, and strategic mindset. Christianity served as the spiritual inspiration for this exploratory imperative as the religious order was missionary in its attempts to convert the heathen natives and later an impetus for exploration in South America. Such a concept well suited the economic policies of the period and not only contributed to the trade policy of the European nations but also offered a spiritual blessing for their activities. The integration of religion and the exchange process has accrued throughout history. A review of the great religious doctrines of the world and some of the commercial events they participated in demonstrate well, the connection of these two forces and how their special relationship affected the world and contributed to the development of civilization.

Pagan Worship

Ancient social groups placed their beliefs in the natural environment around them as they exhibited control and influence over their daily lives. As sun and the night's darkness—as well as wind and rain—altered their physical environment, nature in its entirety became the often unseen and unknown guardian of their lives and hence forces they gave reverence toward. Numerous collections of gods have been found around the world, as all civilizations practiced some form of religious tolerance. Some of them were endowed with the ability to affect aspects of the exchange or trade initiative.

According to the Egyptian *Ritual of Judgment*, after death, the deceased must come before a court of gods overseen by Osiris to essentially argue for the salvation of one's soul and be granted the right to move on to the afterlife. A series of declarations regarding one's behavior during life must be satisfied. These are testaments to exhibiting self-righteousness, purity of the soul, or in a more modern religious context providing evidence of the absence of sin. A number of these personal proclamations revolve around property rights and commercial activities. Included in the list are declared statements such as:

I have not defrauded the poor of their property.
I have not added to or stolen land.
I have not encroached on the land of others.
I have not diminished the bushel when I have sold it.
I have not added weight to the scales to cheat buyers.
I have not misread the scales to cheat buyers.

The maintenance of societal order in ancient societies was deeply associated with the exchange process. If either party in a transaction misled or cheated, the other relationships could be compromised and the community disrupted. It is therefore understandable that tenants directing one to be mindful of their ethical behavioral obligations in the commercial arena would find their way into faith oriented principles as directed by higher deities.

Other ancient societies have intertwined religious deities with the commercial imperative. The early Chinese recognized T'Shai-Shen, a deity who represented wealth or good commercial fortune and appeared as a majestic figure robed in exquisite silks, was itself a symbol of endowed riches. Even today, he has taken on a popular secular pop culture personality. Originally portrayed as a symbol of material attainment to assure a valued outcome in commercial ventures even atheists have adopted a desire to be blessed by him in all endeavors of material advancement from employment and promotion to gambling success.

For centuries, various Mesoamerican tribes acknowledged *Ek Chua*, the God of traders and the protector of their chief commodity cacao.

Across Micronesia, the first merchants traveling the seas to ply their trade prayed to *Aluluei*, the God of knowledge and navigation, and they continue to do so today. He is depicted as having two faces, one to see where he is going and the other to see where he has been. This characterization is an ode not only to his course plotting skills but as a reminder that all journeys have a beginning and an intended end. Early traders also acknowledged that it is intended to make them mindful of the last transaction with the party they wish to conduct future business with so that a commercial harmony of the past and future is maintained.

In Japan, Chimata-No-Kami was considered the deity overseeing the good fortune of travelers on roadways. Since merchants were the main users of this infrastructure, they prayed to him to guide their way as they moved from village to village on their trading expeditions. The public symbol used to honor this god was a phallic carving, placed at intersections to allow the voyager a blessed movement around the country. In native Mesoamerica, the God Ek-Chuah was called on to bless merchants and assure cacao growers of a good harvest and value in the marketplace.

The practical unification of a Godlike system interconnected with major and minor deities, which are recognized both in literature and in related architecture through places of organized worship with organized social leadership roles, may be attributable to the Greek civilization. Within this religious type order, the lower God, Hermes, the son of the top god Zeus, was considered the patron of merchants as he protected travelers who in those days were mostly traders gathering and selling their wares across the land along with seamen. As such, he was also referred to as the God of abundance in the commercial exchange venue. The tale of Hermes is also interesting as he is said to have stolen some of Apollo's cattle. When confronted with the theft, his defense before his father was so skillful and spirited that his criminal offense was dismissed with the decree that a friendly settlement of the matter be arranged between the brothers. Hence he also became known as the spirit of the spoken word and oratory. He is also the voice of good reason when men had disagreements, therefore becoming the messenger of the Gods and the intermediary with mortals. Such characteristics also contributed to his being considered the founder of the contract in commerce to signify that language in such documents should be precise and exact to insure that the correct meaning of agreements be conveyed between parties. It is ironic, however, that Hermes is also considered a friend to thieves, perhaps a veiled reference to the untruthfulness or untrusting of those engaged in commercial dealings.

The Romans adopted many of the spiritual networks of the Greeks, replacing Hermes with Mercury and anointing their God with the same basic traits—the overseer of trade, profit, merchants, and travelers. Some linguists believe that the name Mercury comes from the Latin word *mercari*, meaning "having to do with deals or trade," while others relate it to the Latin term *merx*, or merchandise, but both believe it signals a relationship to the business function or the exchange process in social settings. Mercury is portrayed with wings on his sandals and hat, indicative of swiftness, and holding a caduceus (a staff with two intertwined snakes) and a purse or money bag, indicative of his connection with commerce. He is celebrated during a festival known as the Mercuralia on May 15, a day when merchants sprinkled their heads and their goods with water, requesting a favorable return on their business activities. Even in antiquity, commercial events warranted spiritual intervention and blessings.

As other organized religions began to emerge around the world, their doctrines contained rules of engagement for societies that included directives and guidance on relationships between men that recognized the importance in their lives of an exchange imperative, the need to trade in an honest and meaningful manner.

Western-Based Religious Orders

Judaism

The Old Testament speaks of Moses receiving the hallowed Ten Commandments about 1300 BCE. From such basic rules of life emerged the Law of Moses that not only began the regulation of every aspect of Jewish life including commerce and property rights but also influenced the doctrines of Christianity and Islam. While little is known of the early life of Moses—apart from his adoption in the reeds by the pharaoh's sister and then a biblical jump to his witnessing of a Jewish slave being beaten, his killing of the Egyptian overlord, arrest, escape, and wandering in the desert before his return to free his people—certain assumptions might be made about his time in the royal court about 40 years prior to such events. Moses, being part of the pharaoh's household, would have had access to tutors who educated him in all aspects of Egyptian life. He would have been taught that revenue generation for the kingdom came not only from war but also from taxation of local commercial dealings as well as foreign trading expeditions as administered under the royal decree. Egyptians, in the time of Moses, plied the King's Highway, using it as the prime route for its merchants as they traded with its neighbors. In exchange for the rich agricultural products grown in the Nile River basin, the prized resources in alien territories were imported into the realm. Exotic spices along with unique crafted items of foreign craftsmen made their way into the household of the pharaoh and then on to the general public.

Moses would therefore have been instructed in the value of trade by his mentors and educated in its basic principles. He would also have understood well the need for laws regulating property rights across the empire as such rules promoted civil peace and sustained the pharaoh's kingdom. It could be concluded that such exposure instilled in Moses a deep respect for an orderly process to be presented to his birth brethren as he led them to a new life and presented them with a set of divine laws to live by.

The influence of ancient Jewish religious direction has been used to form principles reflected in modern commercial codes and even specific provisions of the Uniform Commercial Code. The legal tenet requiring compensation to be exchanged in order for a contract of purchase to be valid as well as morally correct could be traced to a biblical story. When King David in 1006 BCE purchased the Temple Mount and founded the city of Jerusalem, he paid Aravna the Jebusite:

And the King said unto Aravna, Nay: but I will surely buy it of thee at a price; neither will I offer burnt offerings unto the Lord my God of that which doth cost me nothing. So David brought the threshing floor and the oxen for 50 shekels of silver.[2]

One aspect of Mosaic Law was the use of the undisputed affidavit for the arrival of judgment in commerce. Under Hebrews 6:16–17, any proceeding in courts, tribunal, or arbitration forum consisted of a contest, or a duel of commercial affidavits wherein the points remaining unrebutted in the end stand as the truth and the matter to which judgment of the law is applied.

As to the exchange process, Leviticus 25:14 provides the following teaching, "If you sell ... or buy ... you shall not wrong one another." The Old Testament instructs shopkeepers to point out to customers, regardless of their creed (reference to treat all equally regardless of their faith, nationality, race, etc.) the defects in your merchandise. The Melkita, to Exodus 15:26 states, "To be honest in business is to fulfill the whole Torah." Dr. Caron H. Varner Jr., in his paper presented at the Midwest Business Administation Association Regional Convention, remarked that after studying biblical references he concluded that the Old Testament is the religion of commercial people. That business, trade, and money were a central part of the lives of the ancient Jewish people and that secular success was admired and encouraged. However within this context, dire punishment awaits those who forget the majesty and central place of God and the law of God in their lives, such is prized above material wealth.[3]

International commerce is carried out between nations and hence across the territories of sovereign governments. Foreign investment, be it direct or indirect, in many cases requires governmental approval. The interplay between commerce and those in public administrative offices is as old as trade itself. From the ancient Egyptian pharaoh's approval of private merchants to traverse the King's Road, to European royalty's monopolistic license bestowed on companies in the 1600s to conduct trade with foreign territories, and on to U.S. legislators' chartering of public companies, governmental authorities have always been involved. The potential for abuse of the public office by taking bribes to allow such commercial activities has, however, been recognized over thousands of years ago. Exodus 23:8 declares, "And thou shall take no bribe" as such an action "blindeth them that have sight" while perverting "the words of the righteous." In modern times, numerous local national laws have echoed this ancient religious teaching. The United States in 1977, with the enactment of the Foreign Corrupt Practices Act, extended such illicit actions to American-based firms, their overseas subsidiaries, branches, agencies, and foreign-operating multinational corporations (MNCs) in this country. The law makes it a crime to bribe foreign governmental or administrative officials, an extraterritorial governmental reach affecting global operations.

Christianity

Varner also deduces that "the New Testament is more difficult" with respect to analyzing meaning: Both biblical texts speak of charity and the pursuit of piety for the poor, but the New Testament is more critical of the commercial process in respect to the accumulation and use of wealth:

> In the New Testament, one finds in Luke 18:24 Jesus looking at him saying, "For it is easier for a camel to go through the eye of a needle than for a rich man to enter the Kingdom of God," or Paul writing in Hebrew 13:5, "Keep your life free from love of money, and be content with what you have."[4]

It would seem that while business is not condemned per se, the potential of wealth to corrupt the mortal soul and bring about a non-Christian lifestyle is addressed. However, the Bible in Leviticus 25:37 makes a seemingly specific reference to commercial activities, commenting on usury and the prime commercial incentive (i.e., profit) when it proclaims, "You shall not give him your money at interest nor lend him food at a profit." The interpretation, however, is often seen as closeted in the principle of basic humanity with the announced directive referring to the offering of charity to those in need as opposed to commenting on equitable transactions in an everyday commercial environment. Because reference to this passage is too often reduced to the common phrase "Neither a lender nor a borrower be," it thereby misleads someone to think it is anti-business when the full quote is really housed in directing one to acts of kindness to the less fortunate, the needy, and especially those who cannot feed themselves. In the New Testament, Christ is portrayed as casting out the merchants from the Jewish Temple with a whip, crying "Take these things hence; make not my Father's house a house of merchandise," according to John 2:16. While proclamation is aimed at insulating the sanctity of a house of worship from commercial dealings, it does not prohibit or curse the practice—only serving to make sure it does not disrupt the holiness of a revered sanctuary devoted to God.

Jesus, the architect of Christianity and its belief system, was born into the family of Joseph and Mary. His father's commonly accepted occupation is that of a carpenter but other interpreters of the translated word "tecton," as the Bible refers to his profession, feel it refers to a stone mason. Given this definition, Joseph may have been involved in mosaic work placing him in a valued artistic circle that included traders, merchants, and craftsman, all of whom made up the middle class in the economy of first-century Israel.[5] As it was the practice of the day that sons would learn the profession of their fathers, Jesus was probably skilled in such arts and participated in business dealings with the patrons desirous of engaging such services. There is also speculation that Joseph of Arimathea, a rich metals merchant, referred to by the Romans as "nobilis decurio," or minister of mines to the Roman government, and one of the wealthiest men of the times, was the uncle of Mary, mother of Jesus.[6] While the Bible states that the body of Jesus after the crucifixion was entrusted to Joseph and that Jesus was interred in the tomb meant for him some scholars of the period infer that the two previously had a long-standing relationship. Beyond being a follower of his teachings, Joseph may have taken the young Jesus on business trips, both in the region as well as to Europe and perhaps India. Jesus could therefore have been introduced to the nuances of the commercial world from his father's occupation or perhaps influenced by his great-uncle's trading activities he observed.

Wealth accumulation from commerce, even if such activities were questionable within the Christian doctrine, certainly provided the force for development of civilization. A prime example were the Medicis, the richest family in Europe in the 1430s. Their money was made from banking, which included lending out money and charging interest for doing so—usury in the eyes of the Catholic Church. To atone for such sins, they sponsored, basically "bankrolled," a wide range of religious and charitable works—building and remodeling chapels and constructing hospitals and libraries. In the process of their contributions, they brought together in Venice and Florence (as profiled earlier) the best artisans of the period in architecture, sculpture and painting while employing the great minds of the day to work on translations of ancients manuscripts of and the collective works of wonderful writers, poets, and scholars. Many of their creations were in the service of the Church but funded by rich commercial families. Their actions, which sparked the Renaissance and moved civilization forward, had at their heart a religious repentance for their business activities. Although considered a negative pursuit and therefore worthy of redemption, the influence of commerce did produce a positive outcome. The faith-induced benevolent indulgences of the Medicis were perhaps the root of today's corporate social responsibility, which is bathed in a religious pursuit but activated by the commercial imperative.

Islam

By 500 CE, the ancient lands of Arab dwellers were drawn into contact with those practicing Judaism and Christianity due to the cross-commercial venturing of all parties. Back then established religious orders "often taunted the Arabs about their polytheistic beliefs and their lack of an overarching creed and an afterlife."[7] Perhaps, out of this environment rose the Islamic religious order, a desire for a belief system to call their own and to combat those of others.

The Prophet Muhammad in his youth (circa 585 CE) traveled with the caravans, which traded between Mecca and Syria. Prior to pursuing his religious enlightenment as the founder of Islam, his chosen vocation was a trader[8] or merchant[9] and he became one of the most prosperous businessmen in the region. His first wife, Khadijah, was also a successful trader. Muhammad ibn 'Abd Allah lived in Mecca, the most important thriving settlement in Arabia due to the commercial activities of its residents. Mecca itself was not a provider of valued raw materials or skilled craftsmen. Its commercial attribute may have been possible through its geographical positioning, as it is midway on the Arabian Peninsula; hence, a stopping point for the lucrative incense trade carried on by caravan merchants. Beyond such consideration, and even before its designation as the prime holy city for Islam, Mecca was visited by pilgrims (precursor to the later sacred hajj journey) as it contained the Kaaba stone and black stone, shrines of ancient desert gods, which the nomadic tribes revered and prayed to.

Capitalism in the form of barter transactions made Mecca, in 610 CE, a center of trade and high finance; hence, a regional economic power. This was a new endeavor for its habitants and the newfound wealth "saved them from the perils of the nomadic life."[10] Muhammad, some believe, felt that such an emerging "cult of self-sufficiency built on personal fortunes [led] to egotism and greed" with the potential result of destroying traditional Arab tribal collectiveness and the ingrained morality to take care of others, especially the weaker ones.[11] The recognition of the loss of interdependency based on old tribal values and the creation of economic classes within the society may have prompted Muhammad to seek a new communal spirit. Perhaps the recognition of the inherent danger of material processions becoming the dominant driving force in the lives of his people inspired his search for a better balance in life and influenced his own prophetic calling. Accordingly the economic principles set down in the Koran speak of free enterprise and of earning legitimate profit through trade and commerce as long as such activities do not exploit others to one's own advantage:[12] "The Koran teaches respect for private property, business contracts, and trade."[13] One might posture that the exposure of the prophet to varying cultures and thinking via his trading activities may have provided him with an education that influenced his teachings in later life. The ideals of living up to contractual obligations, keeping one's word, and abstaining from deception are parallel concepts exhibited in business transactions he observed and valued in his teachings. It is noteworthy that according to Muslim history Abraham's son Ishmael, the forefather of Islam, was himself a textile merchant. Abraham is the patriarch of both Islam and Judaism although such ascription of Ishmael is not part of Jewish teachings. Even "Muhammad's immediate successor, the cloth merchant Abu Bakr, was also a trader."[14] The prophet's initial Islamic teachings began as sermon-like pronouncements in the commercial marketplaces of Mecca and were directed to merchants who later would carry his words in the Koran to the far reaches of the globe during their trading expeditions.

An inspection into Islamic laws as related in the basic Shariah principles and still used today reveals that language steeped in commercial antiquity.[15] A prime tenet in the Koran directed to commercial activities advises the faithful to conduct themselves ethically stating, "O you who believe! Do not devour your property among yourselves falsely, except that it be trading by your mutual consent" (Sura 4:29). Other sections are devoted to specific guidelines in establishing and conducting contracts with others, as is the case in Section I.

Basic Shariah Principles or Fiqh-al-Muamalat of the Islamic Business Contracts

(a) *Gharar* or Dubiousness in Contract:

The Shariah determined that in the interest of fair and transparent dealing in the contracts between the parties, any unjustified enrichment arises out of uncertainty or undefined of the essential pillars of contract is prohibited. *Gharar* originated out of deception through ignorance by one or more parties to a contract. Gambling is also a form of *gharar* because the gambler is ignorant of the result of the gamble. There are several types of *gharar*, all of which are *haram*. The following are some examples:

1. Selling goods that the seller is unable to deliver;
2. Selling known or unknown goods against an unknown price, such as selling the contents of a sealed box;
3. Selling goods without proper description, such as shopowner selling clothes with unspecified sizes;
4. Selling goods without specifying the price, such as selling at the *going price*;
5. Making a contract conditional on an unknown event, such as when my friend arrives if the time is not specified;
6. Selling goods on the basis of false description; and
7. Selling goods without allowing the buyer to properly examine the goods.

In order to avoid *gharar*, the contracting parties must (a) ascertain that both the subject and prices of the sale exist, and are able to be delivered; (b) specify the characteristics and amounts of the counter values; (c) define the quantity, quality, and date of future delivery, if any.[16]

Contracts following Islamic religious principles always close with the phrase *Enshalla* (If Allah wills it), a reference invoking his blessing for the proposed relationship while noting that as all life is in his hands. The solemn promises of the parties are still subject to his force and overall determination. It is interesting to note that a similar type of consideration using the Greek phrase *force majeure* is found in common law principles to recognize acts of God, or a superior or irresistible force, not contemplated by the contract parties and usually covered by specialized insurance, that negates the obligations and responsibilities annunciated in the agreement.[17] While a direct connotation is difficult to empirically sustain between these two legal concepts, the religious and the secular, they do seem to have the same intent as to the extent of contractual obligations on mutual parties.

It is important to appreciate that Islam promotes the integration of the faith into all aspects of life. It does not separate the spiritual from the secular everyday lives of its followers. There are no distinguishing adaptations between the religious and the secular worlds such as the well-known Christian verse pronounced by Jesus, "Render to Caesar the things that are Caesar's, and to God the things that are God's."[18] All is prescribed, with guiding doctrines of how to conduct oneself, via Sharia law. Therefore, the Koran contains very precise instructions on the conduct of commercial activities and financial transactions. The key to understanding these guidelines revolves around the position of capital in society and its use in the commercial system. Money itself is not a business nor is it an asset. It is merely an instrument, a collateral medium of representational value that is used in the exchange process. It facilitates, and therefore it is not an end in itself, trade between buyers and sellers of tangible property, be it real or personal. Fundamentally Islam does not allow money to be made from money. Philosophically one might think of money as a farm tool. By itself it produces nothing. Only when it is put to use, to plow the earth and dig holes for plant seeds that produce a crop for harvesting, does it produce a value to society. The idea is that humanity benefits when tangible assets, real things that are owned, are sold. In the process profits are allowed.

Two overriding principles govern Muslim commercial and related business activities:

Impermissible Investments (*Haraam*)—Muslims cannot invest in any venture that is considered unlawful or impermissible. Falling within such definition are industries, and therefore businesses, connected to the handling of pork, alcohol, tobacco, weaponry, as well as those engaged in pornography, prostitution, gambling, and in the modern world many forms of Western entertainment or advertising. Moreover, because of the prohibition against usury, one cannot invest in businesses that operate on interest payments like major Western banks and mortgage providers.

Interest payments or usury (*Riba*)—The notion of interest payments in conventional banking is not permissible because it is considered usury and is therefore unjust. Usury is prohibited by Sūrah 2:275 of the Koran, "Those who devour usury will not stand except as stand one whom the Evil one by his touch hath driven to madness." The practice is viewed as exploiting those in weaker bargaining positions, permitting unjustified profit and enrichment, and encouraging speculative or risky (as noted earlier—gharar) transactions. In place of interest (fee for loaning money), Islamic finance is based on ownership of assets and the sharing of risk. These two concepts (*Musharakah* and *Mudarabah*) distinguish the Islamic financing process from Western finance, which is largely based on principles of interest, debt, and risk transfers. An Islamic bank or investment group that provides funding to a business will have an agreed share in the profit or loss generated from the money it provides. This negates the need for separately set periodic interest payments regardless of the success of the venture capitalized. It places the invested funds in a mutually shared risk pool created jointly by the capital provider and the business. It should be noted that usury is also prohibited in Christianity which defines the term as an exorbitant amount or rate of interest. However under Islamic laws usury is synonymous with interest of any kind and in any form whether the quantitative figure is reasonable or not.

In the seventh and eighth centuries, Muslims ruled the seas with large fleets of merchant ships and marauding pirate ventures dispatched by powerful rulers that followed the faith. On land they controlled the caravan trade with China and the Far East as it passed through northern India ending at the eastern Mediterranean shore line. Islam followers had subjugated territories that bordered the southern coast of Spain, the entire northern coast of Africa, the Arabian Peninsula, and all areas presently designated as the nations of Iraq, Iran, and Turkey. Effectively, they controlled transnational commerce over the then known world. Devoted Muslim merchants became standard bearers of the faith wherever they traveled. They always paid homage to their religion's directions while interweaving commercial dealings into their lives as faithful servants of Allah's commands. Trading partners would often depart after concluding their business by reciting, "May your hajj be acceptable, your sins forgiven and your merchandise not remain unsold."

The influence of Islamic principles on world business principles is too often overlooked and thereby underestimated. This third spiritual belief system to come out of the Levant has 2.1 billion followers today, who are spread around the world, a testament to the historic commercial activities of their ancient merchant brothers. Although not as large as the 7.1 billion who distinguish themselves as Christians, they outnumber the 1 billion who adhere to Hinduism and the 350 million Buddhists.

Eastern Spiritual Teachings

The spiritual teachings of the East—Confucianism, Buddhism, Hinduism, and Taoism—which many believe are more lifestyle guidelines for attaining internal happiness as opposed to formal religious orders, mention that one should be free of ambition when it comes to material desires. To engage in harmless occupations that do not take advantage of another in the bargaining and trading process is often stressed. Harmony with nature and the instruction not to bend such forces to human needs request one to be respectful of the environment.

Confucianism

Confucius was the Roman identification or label given by 17th-century Jesuits to a sage whom disciples knew in the fifth century BCE as Kong Fu-Zi. He championed a highly ordered society and many of his ideas on how one should live life in a good way—always behaving with humanity and courtesy while working diligently toward such goals—have survived in the form of sayings. Confucius was a member of the impoverished nobility, as his parents were not wealthy but belonged to a superior class, the *shi*. He was orphaned at a young age and therefore grew up poor in the feudal state of the time. As a young man, he was hired out as a servant to a noble family where he was exposed from a distance in the maintenance of material indulgence and the production of wealth from commerce. Some historians have concluded that he may have spent time as a minister of the state and as an overseer of granaries, the chief commercial crop of the day. It is generally believed that he rebelled against the motivational beliefs of the landed gentry to acquire wealth that came from the riches of the trading imperative, having concluded that learning that knowledge and virtue trump material gain.

Basically a philosopher and not a religious leader, Confucius wrote about social order and its dependency on sustaining human relationships. He did not object outright to the drive for commercial profit and resultant wealth accumulation per se, just that such a pursuit might disrupt the balanced harmony between people, injuring their relationships. Such temptations could cause one to mistreat others by practicing dishonesty or fraud in order to gain a material advantage. It was not the concept of exchange that bothered him, it was that the system encouraged deceitful wrongdoing. In essence, Confucius was an Eastern moralist whose ideas are comparable with the Western Greek philosophers like Socrates who referred to such principles as ethics. Two basic tenets of Confucianism directly influenced commercial dealings: They are the Chinese designations *Li* and Shu. *Li*, which stands for *profit, gain, advantage*, is described as a set of improper motives affecting others; again, a relationship-based principle and often used as a disparagement of commerce and industry or the capitalistic imperative. *Shu* refers to relationship reciprocity, the duty to treat others righteously, and is the basis for a modern term used in Chinese (and even Japanese) business dealings referred to as *guanxi*. While the word *guanxi* itself refers to *good connections* or the benefit from networking arrangements, it more closely resembles the Western notion of nepotism but in a wider social context than just the family. Chinese managers are inclined to make decisions based on social ties and obligations as opposed to objective indices. Hence, a better deal from one outside their collective environment would be dismissed in favor of one offered from inside their social circle or relationship network. The Japanese, borrowing from Confucian teachings, practice an organizational arrangement called a *keiretsu* (network of affiliated companies or businesses normally with interlocking ownership). It is usually a vertically integrated group of companies that cooperate, working closely with each other to provide a cross variety of goods and services that in the end are delivered to end users or consumers—essentially, a network of integrated suppliers in the value chain. Many members of a *keiretsu* may also be bound together by interlocking ownership, long-term contractual commitments, financing arrangements, and interconnected directorships—all tied to special social relationships. In South Korea, the term *chaebols* (conglomerate of business enterprises usually owned and controlled by a single family) describe firms that are organizationally and structurally indicative of the Confucian influence. These extensive family-owned conglomerates, many of which have become large multinationals, are built on extended commercial relationships across and between industries. They exert great economic and social power in the country due to their shared collective agendas.

Western firms have begun to replicate but not exactly follow the Confucian relationship principle as they have begun to develop global joint venturing under a variety of international alliances even with competing firms. Whether the method uses a direct contractual association or just shared intelligence transnational companies are increasingly promoting borderless relationships. The go-it-alone historic attitude (as exhibited by American multinational firms in post–World War II) and the traditional marked desire to pursue independent international programs have given way to relationship building around the world. Given the increased use of global communication technology this new managerial direction is sometimes referred to as the *virtual corporation*. Also known as *virtual relationships*, the concept is "defined as networks of companies that come together to exploit fast-changing opportunities and share costs, skills and access to global markets."[19] While the Confucian philosophy instructs one to be ever mindful of a profit motive that when wrongly practiced may destroy relationships. It also serves as an influential guide to the benefits of relationship building as fundamental to the social order and attainment of mutual commercial goals.

Buddhism

Buddha was a contemporary of Confucius and they died two years apart. He was the son of a Sakya king and thereby destined for a luxurious life, as he was surrounded by material comforts from birth. He was educated in state affairs, which included commercial trade and the distribution of wealth that it produced. Such material self-indulgence deeply disturbed Buddha and he sought a new enlightened path, or the middle way, to achieve life's true existence. His teachings presuppose universal laws called dharmas, which govern human existence—the intertwined relationship of all things.

Buddhism does not denounce the accumulation of wealth; it only states that it be obtained lawfully and that all should benefit from its use. This Eastern philosophy concerning the affairs of commerce and the material world it creates are found in the Diamond Sutra, which depicts it as having a fleeting value such as that in the example of a flash of lightning in a summer cloud or a flickering lamp. Both references are meant to advise one to dispose of wealth as soon as it is received as it is of no lasting importance. It should be used to promote social harmony, perhaps a statement on the social responsibility of commercial enterprises, a modern topic that MNCs find themselves dealing with today. The writings of Buddha note five benefits that can be obtained from wealth, the end product of one's "efforts and enterprise amassed through the strength of the arm and piled up through the sweat of the brow, righteous wealth righteously gained."[20] Wealth gives pleasure and satisfaction to (a) oneself and his household consisting of his family, servants, slaves, and (b) to friends and associates. It (c) affords protection from nature's unpredictable events as well as the unscrupulous activities of thieves, governments, and hateful heirs. It keeps men safe from forces beyond one's control. It allows them to (d) fulfill their charitable obligations to all their encounter and specifically (e) toward priests and contemplatives whose vows prohibit them from indulging in material possession. Those who follow such wealth distribution are considered noble with their actions leading them to a heavenly repose. In essence, wealth is to be used to promote human good and the right livelihood for mankind. The fundamental principle directs followers to develop an attitude of compassion, develop a social conscience, and promote the profit of commerce through wealth and the assurance of *maitri* (i.e., true friendliness toward others). It instructs one to not waste money on extravagant pleasures but to promote the social good. A forerunner of entrepreneurial social responsibility or in today's terminology: corporate social responsibility. Companies in modern-day India are obligated by the legal environment as influenced by Buddhist concepts to portray a strong social commitment in the activities they perform. The idea of a common benefit being derived from their operations permeates the commercial culture and forms the strong undercurrent of socialism in the country as echoed by the federal and local law makers and the administrative bodies enforcing such regulations.

Hinduism

Hinduism is representative of a conglomeration of religious beliefs having no central founder or core group of prophet-like characters who advanced its principles and decreed ceremonial worship systems. Its proclamations are derived from sets of stories, poems, and other literary works as opposed to the singular biblical books of Islam, Christianity, and Judaism. Its basic tenet is that individuals should not be judged by their attainment of material achievements but rather their spiritual improvement. One should strive for eternal bliss, a condition of nirvana, a purified state, and a process that is interrupted by pure material pursuits. An ascetic lifestyle is therefore preferred as one goes through a continuous cycle of birth, death, and rebirth on the pious road to salvation. During each life experience, however, one is expected to work hard but accept his or her fate, which may negate receiving any justified reward. Such accepted doctrine sometimes produces apathy in seeking measured material achievement as karma decides what one receives in life and not one's activities. One aspect of Hinduism that affects the managerial process is the idea that people are divided into a social system of labor. A caste system is embedded in the traditional Hindu religion with four different society classes or varnas. Brahmin is composed of priests, scholars, or bureaucratic (leadership) groups. This is followed by the Kshatriya, the protector or warrior sect. On the third level are merchants and artisan tradesmen called Vaishya. At the bottom of the social ladder are the Sudras, whose skill sets do not rise above manual labor. Movement between such prescribed echelons is difficult; people are asked to accept their destiny with dignity as the next life will offer a greater reward. People, therefore, know their place and that of others around them. Asking one to lower his or her social status by working on an equal basis of shared responsibility or authority with an underclass individual or pushing one into a group above his or her birth station can create embarrassment and friction in an organizational structure.

Taoism

As founded by Lao Tzu, a contemporary philosopher of Confucius as well, Taoism is primarily based on finding the Tao or *the way* in life. The search for this enlightened path by exercising the three jewels; compassion, moderation, and humility while practicing self-control and letting things take their normal course. An example of accepting the natural essence of life is that spring comes and grass grows of itself, hence to plan or try to alter nature's self-designed pace goes against the Tao. Accomplishment does not necessarily require effort as long as one attunes himself or herself to the rhythms of life and maintains harmony. Balance in life is represented by the Taijitu symbol (yin and yang), admonishing one to acknowledge the duality of all things, elemental pairs always connected. Such a philosophy directs one to see both sides of issues and to base decision making within the context of the whole issue.

The "actual precepts of Taoism do not bear down unfavorably upon businessmen and traders" and the "official scriptures do not portray merchants in a negative light."[21] Unlike the monolithic or Abrahamic singular God found in Judaism, Christianity, and Islam, multiple spiritual deities are worshipped in Taoism (and Buddhism). Two heavenly beings watch over the world of commerce in Taoist doctrines. *Chenghuang* (God of the town) maintains peace and protects the inhabitants in the daily exchange activities while *Caishen* (God of wealth) brings good fortune and prosperity to individuals and the institutions they serve. A statue depicting Caishen is often placed in one's home or business to invite good commercial success into the establishment. Temples reserved for Caishen are in many areas surrounded by commercial buildings and shopping plazas as proximity to the deity helps bring good joss or luck to businesses placed near them.

A Shared Regional Belief System

A common thread connecting Asian–Indian cultural values, as influenced by these religious teachings, is the importance of relationships and the responsibility owed to those within one's social circle. Nepotism is routinely practiced and its virtues trump the more objective measurement values that Western societies use in the hiring and even firing of personnel. Family members and friends are more often hired as they come with an inherent sense of loyalty and reciprocal duty that negates them from ever leaving the company to secure better opportunities elsewhere. Although they may not come with the required practical skills needed for a specific job, it is argued that such proficiencies can always be taught. Dismissing one is also more difficult as— the failure of one to adequately perform is visited on the one in charge with the notion that one must be properly instructed and supervised. The burden is on the manager and not the employee to see that the job is done right. This attachment to social and economic solidarity in Asian–Indian societies permeates the commercial activity. It has its roots in religious doctrines of the region that stress the importance of long-term relationships. The idea is often expressed in cross-cultural managerial textbooks as Eastern collectivism or group orientation as opposed to Westernized focus on the individual.

The Protestant Directive

It was not until the Reformation in the early 1500s and the emergence of Protestantism under the tutelage of Martin Luther that a religious order moved to embrace aspects of the commercial system and the creation of wealth as a tool to facilitate the betterment of man. Although Martin Luther was born to a historic farming family—hence his characterization as originating from peasant stock—such a depiction of his background is misleading. It was Hans, Luther's father, who was raised on an extensive parental farm, the inheritance of which bypassed him to his younger brother. Hans therefore was pressed to seek his fortune not through agriculture but as a miner. By the time Luther entered the world, his father was the owner of a small but initially prosperous smelting business at a time when demand across Europe was high for this industry.[22] Such occupation and status as a melting master coupled with marriage to a woman from a higher social class allowed the family to be integrated into the upper strata in Germany—such was the environment into which Luther was born. Luther never lived on a farm but dwelt all his life in towns and cities. His maternal cousins were all professionals coming from a highly educated urban family. When Luther entered as a student at Erfurt his family was considered wealthy, and he was doing exactly the kinds of things, that is, studying law, that were expected of a member of a rich, high-achieving, confident bourgeois professional family in Renaissance Germany.[23] The early life of Luther was tied to material wealth accumulation and his writings years later were reflective of such heritage. However it took the writings of German sociologist Max Weber in 1904 to propose a linkage between Protestant ethical doctrines and the spirit of capitalism. He argued that Protestant teachings stress the value of hard work and wealth accumulation for the glory of the creator and that such principles are compatible with the practice of individual abstinence from material pleasures even if such returns are used to expand the general welfare of society; hence the creation of the Protestant work ethic. Such recognition of the work ethic to produce a kind of charity for others resulted in the doing of God's work. The idea sparked the expansion and development of business enterprises and certainly helped to unify what had for centuries been at odds—religious practice and the commercial imperative.

Direct Intermingling of Religion with World Trade and Business Principles

The teachings of the world's major religious sects recognized the need to promote social order, which necessitated prescribed behavior in respect to commercial dealings among their followers. However, it was the Catholic Church that not only used its influence to promote and underwrite trading expeditions, as previously noted, but was directly involved in organizing and regulating global commerce. During the Crusades in 1139 CE, a papal bull, *Omne Datu Optimum*, first endorsed the Order of the Poor Knights of Christ and the society known as the Temple of Solomon, known by their historic name, Knights Templar. This decree, issued by Pope Alexander VI and followed by Celestine II's *Milites Templi* in 1144 and Eugenius III's *Militia Dei* in 1145, bestowed on the Knights Templar exceptional rights and privileges. Out of the remnants of the first crusade for the holy city of Jerusalem by European armies, a most unique group developed. The Knights Templar acted as guardians for pilgrims making the hazardous journey to pay reverence to the birth place of the Christian religion. This warrior and lay religious order, however, also placed their mark on the commercial development of the landscape during their time. Besides offering protection for tourists, they created the first international banking system with the use of a rudimentary travelers check so visitors would not have to carry valuables that bandits could easily rob. Their protection of and assistance to pilgrims visiting the Holy Land developed the precursor to the modern-day letter of credit. Not disposed to carrying money with them as they journeyed to Jerusalem for fear of being robbed on the way, they were encouraged them to leave funds on deposit in a Templar-type bank account. As they traveled they could draw down—take portions of their money—from geographically placed Templar offices en route using a secret withdrawal code. Using cryptic encoded written documents the Templar society allowed such instruments to be safely cashed once destinations were reached by the customers of their service. This early cross-territorial financial system is similar to carrying a credit card today. It later evolved into the previously noted letter of credit, the most widely used secured method of payment in international financial transactions and an instrument that propelled more efficient modern-day global trade.

In recognition of their devotion to the faith in the protection of pilgrims to the Holy Land, they were excluded from tithes and taxes and were granted extraordinary property ownership liberties. A key provision of the grant was they were promised all spoils of war from the

Muslim conquest, which essentially gave them exclusive trading rights to the Middle East region. This commercial monopoly enabled the Knights Templar to create perhaps the first multinational company as their trading opportunities between Christian Europe and the regional Muslim territories propelled them into the leading financial position in the world at such time.

Their merchant fleet, extensive warehouse infrastructure across all of Europe, and their ability to act almost as a sovereign untouchable economic entity produced great wealth and power for their brethren. Their knowledge of complex financial transactions coupled with their skills in the creation of cross-territorial banking procedures were the basis for today's modern global networks. The Templars were patrons of the first craft guilds to be independent of the Church and nobility. Called *Compagnons du Devoir*, this trade brotherhood was responsible for Templar building projects across Europe. Originally, this association of journey men was primarily associated with cathedral construction and other edifices underwritten by the landed elite gentry. The Templar initiative took them out of the historic control of such institutions and made them more independent, creating in their wake a new societal class between the rich and poor. Even after the demise of the Templar sect it has survived with some sections evolving into the Masonic Order, itself possessing by some accounts specialized knowledge. Today the Masons are still active as is the original trade association.

Many years later, the royal houses of Europe—primarily by the French king—who were in debt to the Knights Templar, accused the Templars of heresy, and with papal blessing their order was disbanded and their properties and fortune confiscated. Their commercial global trade domination was therefore created and destroyed by the Church. Their historic economic impact on the region ended abruptly on Friday the 13th when the combined forces of the King of France and his aligned religious leader the pope destroyed the order. While many fictitious works, like the bestseller *The Da Vinci Code*, make veiled references to their possession of many secrets regarding the birth of the Catholic faith, there can be no doubt of their influence on the maintenance of civilization in 1096 via their commercial activities and the contribution to modern global financial transactions. The Knights Templar was at one time considered too big to fail but their accumulation of wealth and power, however, led to their collapse; a lesson that equally domineering MNCs would be wise to consider in today's world.

The Church's influence on world commercial dealings also extended to other parties during the 1100s. The papacy, under the Third Lateran Council (1179), excommunicated Christians who supplied the heathen Saracens with weapons, iron, timber, and all measure of personnel support on their seagoing vessels in an indirect attempt to deprive them of money flowing from their commercial activities. To further such policy, a letter was sent to the City of Venice in 1198 (whose economic sustenance was based on its extensive extraterritorial trading associations) expressly forbidding its citizens to aid the Saracens by directly selling them, exchanging with them, or indirectly providing the means by which they could obtain iron, flax, pitch, sharp instrument, rope, weapons, galleys, ships, and timbers in either raw or finished form. This pronouncement was in reply to an appeal by Venetians, whose survival relied on shipping and commerce, as they are not agriculturally based people. While trade with Saracens was prohibited, the Church did temper its declaration by allowing merchandise trade with Egypt to continue while also requesting commercial dealing with the province of Jerusalem to improve.

As noted earlier, the influence of the Church on global trade reached its zenith three centuries later with the publication of the *Inter Caetera*, a papal bull issued by Pope Alexander on May 4, 1493. It divided the New World, the non-European foreign territories, between the Portuguese and the Spanish, in essence settling the first global trade issue. The decree divided the two major oceans of the world via a meridian moving east and west thereby conferring the lucrative trade in such lands via the routes such waters touched.

Creating royal monopolies of trade yielded great wealth to these sovereign nations. From the East Indies rare spices, prized silks, unique woods and ivory along with Chinese porcelain fed the insatiable demand in Europe for exotic consumer products, while from the Americas flowed gold, silver, precious stones, furs, and eventually tobacco—the historic mainstays of material wealth. The massive traffic between Europe and the colonies not only created a new merchant class in society but insured the continued funding of the state via the levy of the *quinto*, the monarchy's 20 percent tariff on goods transiting the trading ports. It also helped to solidify the power of the Church as an architect of world economic affairs. The division was unequal due to Spanish influence in the Vatican (*note*: Pope Alexander VI himself was of Spanish heritage), as it precluded Portugal from Asia. As a remedy to this injustice the Treaty of Tordesillas was signed between the two nations in 1494. The document itself is a precursor to international trade legacy agreements and the collateral creations of systems regulating and promoting global trade.

As the papal bull excluded other monarchs, both the British and Dutch (a Protestant nation) were jealous rivals, and the leaders of both countries encouraged the raiding of galleons on the demarcated merchant transport lanes. In the late 1500s, English ships were especially active attacking ships returning from the Western Hemisphere as Spain would not allow her majesty's commercial agents to trade with their American colonies. King Philip of Spain was well aware that Queen Elizabeth I supported such pirate adventures of her sea dogs, or privateers as they came to be called, while she gave her tacit approval to their rival gangs, the Huguenot corsairs and Dutch buccaneers. He called upon the Church once more for assistance. The Pope, then Pius V, could not outwardly condemn such events. Instead, he issued a bull excommunicating Queen Elizabeth I for her supposed actions by extricating the English Church from the mother Roman Catholic Church, while also accusing her of causing the persecution of its members in Britain. The declaration was in reality a backhanded punishment for the disruption of Spanish trade flowing back to Europe.

Outside of the European theater, Chinese explorers were also bestowed with an equal passionate ethereal religious-based directive, as noted earlier. The great Star Fleet was assembled in China in 1421 to circumvent the world and open cross-trading initiatives with new territories as well as offer the protection of the empire for tribute was endowed with a third initiative—to acquaint potential subjects with the Confucian doctrine and hopefully spread its message of enlightenment.

A century later, during the age of discovery, when European nations sought to mine the valuable riches of China, one of the prime arguments by counselors to the emperor to affect the closing of harbors and limit contact with European merchants was the danger of Christian religious contamination in the country. Chinese administrators were well aware that such commercial ventures were sanctified and influenced by the Christian Church while observing firsthand that missionaries routinely accompanied such trading ventures into their lands. Their preaching corrupted Confucian principles while also undermining the supreme power of the emperor and his pronounced secular laws for those of a higher authority, the Christian god.

Beyond these mergers of interests, organized religion recognized the need to both incorporate commercial relationships in their doctrines and perhaps borrow trade rules of conduct in constructing their venerable laws concerning relationships between people. Beyond the prime religious order direction to sanctify their prescribed deity and address family issues, many early teachings dealt with exchange of property and contracts between parties. But the mix of religious doctrine with the commercial profit incentive and accumulation of wealth has caused debate over the ability of the two programs to properly assimilate. Putting aside this scholarly question and the interpretation of scriptures as to the merits of the commercial imperative on the construction of the faith-based directive, an inspection of biblical references does indicate that such activity was addressed in the scriptures of many religious teachings as previously presented.

When analyzed closely, the influence of the ancient commercial exchange process on the construction of faith-based teachings is relevant. The seeds of thought, reflection, and enlightenment provided by all of the aforementioned spiritual prophets might have been founded to a degree on their association with the commercial environment of their times and the material wealth such activities produced. While the ancient forms of limited capitalism were treated as a corrupt negative value for most religious leaders in the formation of their principles, it is interesting to note that Chinese exploration via the Star Fleet and the European initiative in the new world included a religious element in the commercial acquiring of new lands for respective national sovereigns. While religion may not have condoned such wealth accumulation practices, it has learned to ally with commerce when the overall goal of both institutions was in sync. Nevertheless, all the great prophets of the world's major religions learned from their exposure to the commercial imperative, and perhaps used such experiences to frame their respective outlooks on how men should live. In ancient economies the focus was on wealth accumulation based on use of land and manual labor, the two most value-producing elements. Life was hard and turning to the spiritual for the promise of non-material heavenly rewards after death in Western religious teachings or finding an individual state of peaceful euphoria in eastern doctrines was the only respite that offered relief to the average person.

Roots of Religion: The Wealth Fable Connection

It is most interesting to note that the backgrounds of many of the world's most respected religious inspirational leaders, and in most cases the man on whom the sect is constructed, always tell the adventure of a wayward prince who leaves his castle (metaphor for material wealth and a high secular social structure), begins to see his world as composed of a corrupted or false environment, takes a vow of poverty or attains some form of spiritual enlightenment, and walks among the common people. It is the classic hero as told through the eyes of so many societies. This unique personality abandons the familiar and safe, confronts the specter of his special status, confronts dangers and challenges on his new journey, and returns home with altered insight to better the world around him. Sometimes he leads people against a wicked oppressive force in their lives or provides those he encounters with a new direction, a divine or inspirational message to live their own lives, in spite of their transgressions, with redeemed purpose that forges a bridge between the spiritual and secular worlds. He recognizes that the material advantages arising from the natural exchange process are intertwined with the behavioral direction of society. Therefore his early initial exposure to wealth accumulation acted as a catalyst for his later inspirational and enlightening directed message to those that heeded his teachings and formed religious-like orders.

Ethics in the Commercial World

There has been a marked resurgence questioning the ethical conduct, and its collateral issue corporate social responsibility, in respect to the decisions and operational activities of global corporations. Companies are desirous of positioning themselves as complying with, and in many instances promoting, acceptable moral standards around the world as the era of modern globalization brings them into contact with a larger more diverse audience than ever before. Numerous differences in social structures, cultural values and regulatory infrastructures has made the job of constructing global codes of conduct for transnational companies a most difficult process. These issues are addressed in this author's book on the subject titled, *A Strategic and Tactical Approach to Global Business Ethics, Second Edition.*[24] The influence of religious principles based on ancient spiritual practices is noted in this managerial guide.

It is noteworthy to remember that the interplay of commercial transactions and ethical concerns was reflected in the early teachings of religious groups as they well recognized the importance of such maters on maintaining and fostering secular social harmony in their respective societies. This concern is still valid today as the process of exchange, in is numerous modern forms, continues to impact the world. The lessons offered by ancient religious practitioners remains as an important contribution to understanding the roots of globalization and business principles.

CHAPTER 9

The Influence of Government on Global Trade and Ancient Secular, Commercial, and Legal Regulations

Government and Global Trade

The responsibility of societal administration overseers or government in all forms is to stay in power by providing for the economic sustainability and growth of their domain. Such consideration was perhaps best exemplified by the simple statement of the U.S. President Calvin Coolidge in a 1925 speech before the American Society of Newspaper Editors, when he proclaimed "The business of America is business."[1] While the quote is reflective of a conservative, capitalistic, free-market economic model, its relevance to the broader commercial imperative as a driving force in the construction and maintenance of societies is true for both the modern and the ancient worlds. For nations to grow and prosper, wealth needs to be created to support the needs of its citizens, although not always in an equal distribution system. As noted earlier, outside of war, trade, the extension of the exchange process, is the greatest creator of prosperity for a kingdom or a country. A balanced or positive trade with others is a better vehicle for sustaining life than a negative one. Autocratic regimes or governments early on in history recognized, therefore, that the promotion of trade was a beneficial element in the maintenance of their domains.

The involvement and influence of an authoritative body in the construction and preservation of the commercial endeavor were as evident in ancient times as they are today. Initially, the ruling bodies of independent

regions controlled cross-territorial trade using court-appointed trade emissaries who worked on behalf of the state with all wealth or profits from
their transactions accruing to the coffers of the monarchs. As previously
noted, the initial cross-territorial trading expeditions of the Egyptians
and Chinese were conducted under the auspices of counselors, pharaohs,
and emperors. The funds flowing from such ventures were used not only
to sustain the opulence of such rulers and to fund their armies but also
to provide financing for public use, projects, and other administrative
services deemed necessary for the control of their constituents. As
long-distance commercial venturing increased, the use of private parties
began to emerge. Rulers realized that while they might not be in absolute
control of these traders, letting them operate on their own did not require
an investment of the ruler's state funds. If they could still participate in
the rewards of trade that such independent merchants produced they still
benefited. Out of this consideration royal charters were begun, bestowing
the right of merchants to trade privately on behalf of the kingdom. In
return for the privilege in some cases, a license-like fee was paid up front
or a tax was collected when goods were imported—the tariff principle, in
which the monarch participated as a noncapital partner with guarantees
of revenue from the trading venture. The idea of the state receiving a
constant flow of revenue from the trading exercise was very appealing and
hence governments naturally partnered with businessmen in the pursuit
of their jointly beneficial commercial endeavors.

As presented earlier, even ancient tribal regimes, normally an extended
family or clan with a chieftain, operating in and therefore controlling
a specific territory, recognized that they could extract a toll from those
crossing their region. Such a transit fee, ensuring safe passage for a merchant and his commercial caravan, was the forerunner of the modern-day
import tariff. This tax was for many governments the chief revenue-
generating mechanism. It is noteworthy that the first federal tax enacted
by the fledgling U.S. Congress was an import duty.

The involvement of the state or royal regimes in the exchange
process began in antiquity and is still evident in the modern era of
globalization. The regulation of trade both within its own borders as
well as the commercial crossing of its borders is a prime objective of

the administration of societies—a governmental imperative. Not only did it serve to enrich the state, but the exercise of control over their societies ensured the economic prosperity of its citizens, which was paramount to assure those in power remained in power. Chapters 3 and 4 provided a profile of the influence of governing bodies on the commercial imperative, underscoring the importance of such interaction. From the Pax Mongolica of Genghis Khan providing safe passage for merchants in lands under his domain, to provisions in the Magna Carta recognizing the importance of foreign traders in the English kingdom, and on to the free-trade argument made in the Declaration of Independence, governments have always recognized the inherent need to intermingle the affairs of state with the commercial imperative. While at times such determination was shared with religious forces, as noted in Chapters 4 and 8, during the age of discovery, the effect on the advancement of global trade has always required a partnership between government and the private commercial sector.

The government drivers of globalization are just as evident today as they were in antiquity. The initial privatization of cross-border trade and the influence in degrees of regulatory governmental control began in ancient times. Today this process is evident in reverse as former communist nations transferred the factors of production from state ownership and control back to the private sector. The shift in modern times to capital or freer market economies and away from the mercantile policies of the 15th century as recounted in Chapter 4 continue to be influenced by the early social economic writings of Adam Smith in 1776[2] and the competitive advantage theories of foreign trade advanced by David Ricardo in the 1800s.[3] The use of tariffs and other trade domestic restrictions especially as to the rights of foreigners to engage in commerce has always been practiced by governments.

In the modern era, following World War II, national governments have influenced and fostered the growth of globalization beginning with the General Agreements on Tariffs and Trade (GATT) initiative in 1947 that called for new or in essence more liberal trading agreements among the signatory nations to promote open and freer trade in the world. The intent was perhaps best expressed by President Ronald Reagan just before the progressive Uruguay Round of GATT discussions in 1986 urging the participants to open their markets from domestic protectionist policies and "treat American products as they treat their own."[4] While such reference to equal treatment was targeted to investment opportunities by foreign corporations in today's world, it reflected and echoed the often prejudiced treatment of alien citizens in the domestic commercial circles of ancient regimes, as well as the recognition of the importance of foreign trade in the development of the world. The GATT provisions were primarily aimed to reduce historically high restrictive tariffs (import duty percentages) on foreign products. The effect was to open markets to other countries. For example, India moved from a former rate of 71 percent to 32 percent while the United States dropped from 7 percent to 3 percent. While the emerging nations like India had larger percentage rate reductions, the developed countries took a larger monetary loss in tax revenue. Replaced by the World Trade Organization (WTO) in 1975, the continuing pressure to lower national tariffs and the liberalization on national foreign direct investment regulations by governments have helped global commercial trading and investment to record new levels in the modern era. The basis for such a direction was the global economic learning curve that began with the ancient practice of barter and progressed as the roots of globalization took hold over centuries of intercontinental trade.

Regional territorial trading blocks, like the European Union (EU) and North American Free Trade Agreement, are reminiscent of ancient lands trading with their contiguous territories. Many of the global governmental economic trading associations are directly traceable to these practices in ancient times, as the traditional commercial relationships continue to be used. Overall, the more recent reestablishment of East–West trade and the rise of China (in 2010 the second largest economy after the United States) and India have brought global trade back to days initially built on the spice and incense trade as well as the Silk Road.

Governments have always worked with the commercial sector to achieve mutual goals. In the ancient world, the marriage of national political agendas with cross-border trade resulted in a unification of goals as their economic fortunes intertwined.

Protection of High-Seas Trade

As previously noted, the Roman Empire was so concerned with the interruption of their shipping lanes for imported grain that they dispatched army legions to protect such precious routes, knowing fully their importance in the maintenance of their civilization. Emperor Julius Caesar rose to public prominence when he was proclaimed a national hero for his valiant victories over pirates in the Mediterranean.

European sovereign rulers many centuries later not only dispatched their own military forces but also hired privateers along with rival buccaneers to attack and plunder the lucrative resources of the newly explored worlds in both the East and the West. During this era of mercantilism, the survival of the country depended on the free, unencumbered movement of resources back to individual nations to enrich their kingdoms. In 1801 to 1805, reminiscent of the problem that plagued Rome, the Barbary States of North Africa supported pirates plundering seaborne commerce as their ancestors had before them. They demanded tribute money, seized ships, and held crews for ransom or sold them into slavery. To combat these outrages, the United States sent maritime regiments into the Mediterranean. With the U.S. Navy blockading the enemy's coast, bombarding their shoreline defenses and engaging pirate ships on the sea, a contingent of seven marines along with 300 Arab and European mercenaries descended on Tripoli. The free and unencumbered movement of commercial trade on sea as well as land routes has always been a global priority for nations. Such unity of purpose, transnational alliances, outside of allying in war may be rooted in an economically based imperative. A joint recognition of mutual need and support for free trade still motivates governments to act in unison. In modern times, the pirates of Somalia off the coast of East Africa have begun to duplicate the historic scenarios that have interrupted essential global trade routes. The fundamental need to protect international shipping lanes is recognized by national governments of the world. Again one sees their united efforts to support and foster the global exchange principle. Even emerging nations like China, new to the world economic system, have joined this endeavor. Chinese admirals have reportedly stated that "they want warship to escort commercial vessels that are crucial to the country's economy" and secure their interests in the resource-rich areas of the world, wanting to position them in an ocean stretch from the Persian Gulf to the Strait of Malacca just south of the Asian continent.[5]

Trade: The Political Tool

In the 19th century, as the United States grew in commercial importance to the world, its chief exportable commodity ended up not only dividing the nation but also sending ripples across the Atlantic and affecting other nations. The Civil War began in 1861 between the industrialized North and the agriculturally bound South. The overt sentiments were about the moral ideology of slavery and the division, but the conflict was in reality grounded in economic principles that had international ramifications. Without the use of slave labor imported from Africa, the production of cotton, the key to the Confederate economy and its largest cash crop, doomed the region to commercial disaster. But even in that day, this U.S. domestic issue had extraterritorial trade implications. The British textile industry, the mainstay of the Victorian industrial complex, was beholden to imports from the American South, as the area accounted for 80 percent of the raw material. In consideration of such recognition, the Confederacy tried to use its global advantage to force England to support its position in both deed and financial assistance using economics as a financial foreign policy tool, a principle used today in international politics. The Confederacy first placed an embargo on shipments to the port of Liverpool, the chief cotton-receiving facility in England. Such an action not only drove up the price of cotton but also severely impacted the plight of textile workers, resulting in the phrase "the cotton famine." Knowing well the value of this specialized commodity, the Confederacy used the resource as collateral for cotton-backed bonds to finance the war as they controlled its price and hence the value supporting the bonds. As Niall Ferguson rightly points out, this two-pronged financial mechanism might have worked and strengthened the South's ability to win the war if it were not for the fact that the key port of New Orleans, the embarkation point for cotton shipments to England, was seized in April 1882 by Union naval forces, effectively eliminating the South's commercial trump card to force other nations to join their cause.[6] The fall of the valued Southern port destroyed the South's ability to control cotton shipping and hence its pricing along with the destruction of the financial security backing the bonds was eliminated and their cause was dismissed by other trading nations. The disruption in foreign ocean trade led to the South losing its political economic strength and with it one of the key financial backing instruments, contributing to the loss of the war with the North.

In his book *1434: The Year a Magnificent Chinese Fleet Sailed to Italy and Ignited the Renaissance*, Gavin Menzies[7] proposes that a delegation of the commercially inspired Star Fleet of the great Chinese explorer Admiral Zheng visited Florence, then an independent state. Menzies further hypothesizes that during an audience with Pope Eugenius IV and his advisers, the knowledge (via books, research papers, instruments, and maps) gathered by Chinese merchant travelers was bestowed on the Italians, resulting in the beginning of a revival movement—the Renaissance. While the notion that the Chinese ignited the Renaissance is certainly challengeable, what is interesting is that this meeting may have been the first official globally based trade discussion between governments. If the conferences did take place it was a historic occasion setting the precedent for international trade cooperation and an important step toward globalization driven by a government-to-government initiative. It may have been a precursor to trade agreements as well as the grandfather of GATT and the present WTO. As noted previously, Florence was an independent state while the Catholic Church was considered a semipolitical entity. (Today the Church operates as an independent state—the Vatican—and has diplomatic relationships with governments around the world.) Although the meeting has been challenged by scholars, the European circumnavigation of the world that followed is a substantiated fact testified to by the travels of Christopher Columbus, Ferdinand Magellan, Vasco da Gama, and the others that followed. Perhaps, although it is a conjecture, the idea that such new routes did in fact even exist may have been realized through the information and techniques given to the Europeans. The globalization imperative to reach out to new lands, engage with new people, and trade with them may have been one of the Chinese legacies that enabled separate regions of the world to grow with a common human endeavor. The great period of European exploration that followed may owe a debt to the Chinese government's political initiative if Menzies's contentions become widely accepted. However, some historians believe that Christopher Columbus possessed ocean maps and navigation guides, like the compass that the Chinese invented, that he got from early Arab traders who in turn had procured them from Indian and Chinese sources during their own trading expeditions to the Far East.

Trade has always existed as a political tool of governments. Countries have cut off trade with foreign nations to punish them or signed lucrative trade deals coupled with special loan conditions to further their political and economic influence around the world. Countries offer the most favored status with tariff exceptions or reduced rates to further their global policies. Both in antiquity and today such practices abound. On the other hand, the relative strength of multinational corporations (MNCs) in modern times has begun to offset the historic authority of nations to influence global trade. The ability to monitor, no less control, the private worldwide commercial moves of MNCs has diminished the influence of governments to a degree. With more and more freedom to roam the globe and place their value chain activities in the emerging countries of their choice, those offering them the best deals to operate within and without their borders will receive the benefit of MNC financial investment. The future ability of major industrialized nations to force commercial enterprises to abide by their domestic-oriented policies does not carry the same weight as historical examples would indicate.

Emergence of Ancient Commercial Secular Laws

While the belief in the supernatural and the emergence of organized religions had interpretive doctrines to suit the needs of their followers within the realm of the everyday exchange of goods and services (the commercial process and wealth attainment), it was also left to the secular government authorities to compose the rules of commercial transactions. The state, in the historic guise of supreme rulers, also recognized that it was essential to preserve harmony (thus their continued dominance in their kingdoms) and to ensure the economic welfare of their citizens through regulations pertaining to the exchange process. Records of such laws have been maintained and are revered in the same manner as religious teachings, as they provided guidelines for the construction and interpretation of many of our modern secular commercial laws.

Code of Hammurabi

Since the commercial process was so important to early civilizations, one of the first recorded rules of civil conduct, around 1700 to 1880 BCE, the Code of Hammurabi, contained vast passages on business transactions along with those devoted to family and land transfers. All records of commercial transactions were required to be kept on tablets as legal documents in case of discrepancies.

The concept to write down a deed of agreement between parties was created. This idea allowed people to have a say over their affairs provided the actions required did not violate the Code. So sacred was this legal provision that it was prescribed to be drawn up in the temple by a notary public and confirmed with an oath by the parties to it that it would be carried out as if made with *god and the king*. It was publicly sealed and attested to by professional eyewitnesses, as well as by collaterally interested parties. The transparent manner in which it was executed may have provided sufficient guarantees that it would be abided by. If a dispute arose, the judges would first consult the agreement to see if it coincided with the Code as it still remained the overriding instrument of prescribed justice. While one could appeal the court ruling to the king, in most cases, the king returned the case to the judges with orders to decide in accordance with the Code.

A growing way of conducting business was for a merchant to entrust his goods or invested capital in a traveling agent (as noted previously) who would then seek markets via a series of trade transactions and, in the process, produce operating revenue. In recognition of this commercial system the code insisted that such an agent should precisely inventory and offer a receipt for all he received in every transaction in order to account for all losses and profits from the business activities entered on behalf of principles. Such commercial principles further noted,

Even if the agent made no profit he was bound to return double what he had received, if he made a poor profit he had to make up the deficiency; but was not responsible for loss by robbery or extortion on his travels. On his return, the principle must give a receipt for what was handed over to him. Any false entry or claim on the agent's part was penalized three-fold. In normal cases profits were divided according to contract, usually equally.[8]

The caravan, or common carrier in ancient times for those merchants using intermediary agents, required a receipt for the consignment and a receipt upon delivery. This is the basis for the two prime principles of the modern bill of lading. Even the warehousing of grain was granted regulatory outlines as the warehousemen took all risks and paid double for shortages evidenced by a properly witnessed receipt first given while being granted one-sixtieth of the stored value for his services—state-instituted price guidelines.

Prior to the Code of Hammurabi, archaeological evidence notes the existence of Urkagina's Code around 2350 BCE and Ur-Nammu's Code placed at 2050 BCE; both contained a legal reference that punished the unjust and those who dealt unfairly in trading activities.

Laws of Manu

The Laws of Manu, prescribed from 1280 BCE to 880 BCE, in the region known today as India, synchronized life's social obligations and became the cornerstone of the practice of Hinduism. Portions are devoted to business contracts and trade disputes with specific references to rules and practices governing the exchange of merchandise, shipping, and even port dues, another forerunner of the tariff or duty systems employed today. Such laws transcended a vast territory as "India is more than a country. It is a subcontinent."[9] Such proclamations with a commercial ingredient influenced the way of life of vast populations across large stretches of land mass and the traders who traversed such routes. They followed many centuries later the origin of codes of behavior for the region as proclaimed in the *Arthashastra*, as previously noted.

Draco's Law

The Greeks via Draco's Law in 621 BCE touched on debtor's obligations, providing for enslavement for those whose status was lower than that of their creditor. Issuance of these very dogmatic rules evolved into the term draconian to exemplify unyielding and inflexible, strict policies and decrees. Romans using the 12 Tables prescribed in 450 BCE also handled the problem of debtors, as noted in Table III:

Aeris confessi rebusque iure iudicatis XXXdies iusti sunto.
[A person who admits to owing money or has been adjudged to owe money must be given 30 days to pay.]
Post deinde manus iniectio esto. In ius ducito. Ni iudicatum facit aut quis endo eo in iure vindicit, secum ducito, vincito aut nervo aut compedibus XVpondo, ne maiore aut si volet minore vincito. Si volet suo vivito, ni suo vivit, qui eum vinctum habebit, libras faris endo dies dato. Si volet, plus dato.
[After then, the creditor can lay hands on him and haul him to court. If he does not satisfy the judgment and no one is surety for him, the creditor may take the defendant with him in stocks or chains 15 pounds in weight, he may not restrain him in greater but if he wishes in less. The debtor may live where he wishes. If he does not live on his own, the creditor must give him a pound of wheat a day. If he wants to he may give more.]
Tertiis nundinis partis secanto. Si plus minusve secuerunt, se fraude esto.
[On the third market day, (creditors) may cut pieces. If they take more than they are due, they do so with impunity].[10]

Japan's Feudal Labor Practices

The Seventeen Article Constitution of Japan (640 CE) may have contained the first nationally mandated labor law regarding employment practices and set the stage for modern state intervention in such matters:

XVI. Let the people be employed (in forced labor) at seasonable times. This is an ancient and excellent rule. Let them be employed, therefore, in the winter months, when they are at leisure. But from Spring to Autumn, when they are engaged in agriculture or with the mulberry trees, the people should not be so employed. For if they do not attend to agriculture, what will they have to eat? If they do not attend to the mulberry trees, what will they do for clothing?[11]

Law of Justinian

The Law of Justinian, circa 483 CE, has a section that can be considered as the originator of the legal theory recognizing intellectual proprietary rights—which were later applied to copyrights, patents, and trade-marks—in a section titled "Different Kinds of Things." It speaks of things and personal property rights that are accrued from altering basic elements found in natural raw materials as well as recognizing the capacity of man to adjust them and create new things. It is the precursor for the protection of inventions and work that changes the original structure of materials or how they are used together:

In the preceding book we have expounded the law of Persons: now let us proceed to the law of Things. Of these, some admit of private ownership, while others, it is held, cannot belong to indi-viduals: for some things are by natural law common to all, some are public, some belong to a society or corporation, and some belong to no one. But most things belong to individuals, being acquired by various titles, as will appear from what follows.

Thus, the following things are by natural law common to all—the air, running water, the sea, and consequently the sea shore. No one therefore is forbidden access to the seashore, provided he abstains from injury to houses, monuments, and buildings generally; for these are not, like the sea itself, subject to the law of nations.

On the other hand, all rivers and harbors are public, so that all persons have a right to fish therein.

The sea shore extends to the limit of the highest tide in time of storm or winter.

Again, the public use of the banks of a river, as of the river itself, is part of the law of nations; consequently everyone is enti-tled to bring his vessel to the bank, and fasten cables to the trees growing there, and use it as a resting place for the cargo, as freely as he may navigate the river itself. But the ownership of the bank is in the owner of the adjoining land, and consequently so too is the ownership of the trees which grow upon it.

Wild animals, birds, and fish, that is to say all the creatures which the land, the sea, and the sky produce, as soon as they are caught by any one become at once the property of their captor by the law of nations; for natural reason admits the title of the first occupant to that which previously had no owner. So far as the occupant's title is concerned, it is immaterial whether it is on his own land or on that of another that he catches wild animals or birds, though it is clear that if he goes on another man's land for the sake of hunting or fowling, the latter may forbid him entry if aware of his purpose.

Fowls and geese are not naturally wild, as is shown by the fact that there are some kinds of fowls and geese which we call wild kinds. Hence if your geese or fowls are frightened and fly away, they are considered to continue to be yours wherever they may be, even though you have lost sight of them; and anyone who keeps them intending thereby to make a profit is held guilty of theft.

When a man makes a new object out of materials belonging to another, the question usually arises, to which of them, by natural reason, does this new object belong—to the man who made it, or to the owner of the materials? For instance, one man may make wine, or oil, or corn, out of another man's grapes, olives, or sheaves; or a vessel out of his gold, silver, or bronze; or mead of his wine and honey; or a plaster or eye salve out of his drugs; or cloth out of his wool; or a ship, a chest, or a chair out of his timber. After many controversies between the Siabinians and Proculians, the law has now been settled as follows, in accordance with the view of those who followed a middle course between the opinions of the two schools. If the new object can be reduced to the materials of which it was made, it belongs to the owner of the materials; if not, it belongs to the person who made it. A vessel can be melted down, and so reduced to the rude material—bronze, silver, or gold—of which it is made: but it is impossible to reconvert wine into grapes, oil into olives, or corn into sheaves, or even mead into the wine and honey of which it was compounded.

Writing again, even though it be in letters of gold, becomes a part of the paper or parchment, exactly as buildings and sown crops become part of the soil. Consequently if Titius writes a poem, or a history, or a speech on your paper or parchment, the whole will be held to belong to you, and not to Titius. But if you sue Titius to recover your books or parchments, and refuse to pay the value of the writing, he will be able to defend himself by the plea of fraud, provided that he obtained possession of the paper or parchment in good faith.

Where, on the other hand, one man paints a picture on another's board, some think that the board belongs, by accession, to the painter, others, that the painting, however great its excellence, becomes part of the board. The former appears to us the better opinion, for it is absurd that a painting by Apelles or Parrhasius should be an accessory of a board which, in itself, is thoroughly worthless.[12]

Throughout the development of the rule of law, a commercial imperative based on dealings of men and the property they wish to control is shown in the history of codified codes. The influence of the trading process is intertwined with the growth of civilization and the advancement of human society as exemplified by the state's desire to create rules of social conduct. So important to the conduct of life was commerce that through ancient times its regulation was placed in both secular and religious documents.

History of Proprietary Rights

Mankind has always harbored his personal items and has gone to great lengths to protect his belongings. From hiding them in caves, to placing them in the ground, to storing them in a series of inaccessible or fortified surroundings, the desire to safely conceal valued things that one has acquired has always been an activity practiced by human beings. It may be one of the traits we share with other species on earth. Perhaps, most valued of our possessions are the things we create ourselves, as opposed to finding them naturally in our surroundings, as they came to identify us as unique and special individuals. We refer to such property as proprietary rights.

Patents

Although developing in a communal setting for one's survival, mankind, according to Maslow's hierarchy of needs, shows that he has always desired to be individualistic, striving for a higher level of attainment and personal recognition for his accomplishment along with an economic reward for such proprietary actions. Individual victory in battle was probably the primeval equivalent of such desire, as the spoils went to the winner. But within a peaceful environment individual contest was also practiced with the Greek origination of the Olympic games in 776 BCE and the crowning of champions on the physical athletic field. Recorded history tells us that somewhere between 600 and 500 BCE, city administrators in the Greek colony of Sybaris granted exclusive right of use to citizens producing worthy new things. Specifically, "encouragement was held out to all who should discover any new refinement in luxury, the profits arising from which were secured to the inventor by patent for the space of a year."[13] Some historians suggest that the first recipients were annual competitive creators of unique culinary dishes, according to the records of Athenaeus.[14] Such an authorized public designation was not so much a law as a grant of recognition by the local authority. In England around 1330, recognized endowments in the form of *letters patent* were issued by the sovereign to inventors petitioning the crown. In Latin, *literae patentes* meaning *letters that lie open* referred to the fact that a seal hung from the foot of the document proclaiming, "To all to whom these presents shall come." Such an announcement was symbolic of a public town crier addressing the masses, advising them to come forth and hear the proclamations of their liege lord as opposed to a private communication between parties or *letters closed* and addressed to a specific person who would have to break a seal in order to read its personal content. Such a document was usually posted on the door or wall of an establishment so that all who entered would be aware of the special dispensation given to the owner. The use of such early documents was really to raise money for the royal house and in essence granted a monopoly to those who could afford payment. During this period, patents were given to companies of common goods, such as salt, which outraged the population as it limited competition and hence fair market pricing.

This economic abuse of the crown's power was stopped by James I, who revoked all prior letters of patent and under the Statue of Monopolies, the Parliament restricted the king's grant to inventors of original work. Years later, during the time of Queen Anne, a more systematic procedure for the governmental issuance of patents was inaugurated with the requirement of a written description of the invention having to be submitted with a formulized review process and other legal protections for the prescribed owners. In France, a similar system evolved with submitted patents also reviewed by the *Maison du Roi* (household of the king) and the Parliament of Paris, often in conjunction with academies of learning. The Republic of Florence in 1421 recognized the patent idea following the financially induced petitioning of Filippo Brunelleschi for a barge with hoisting gear to load and unload marble along the Arno River. In the 12th century, Venice granted special protected privileges to inventors of the silk-weaving process, as silk at that time was a prized luxury item. Exporting silkworms and the knowledge of the procedure from China is prohibited and punishable by death. A Venetian statute of 1474 was passed primarily to protect economies of the city's glass makers, who, as they emigrated, demanded similar protections in their new homelands, thereby expanding the concept. The inducement for the legal rights for patents may have started in individual recognition and as the first Patent Act of the U.S. Congress in 1790 recognized "an Act to promote the progress of useful Arts" for "useful and important" discoveries,[15] but its historic development had a decidedly financial motive.

Copyrights

The historical protection of literary works was not developed so much for the legal rights of authors as in its modern usage but as an ancient device to regulate and control the output of printers, the public dissemination of ideas, and information that those in power deemed such circulation dangerous to their authority.

Very early written forms of communication in antiquity were limited to record keeping, a historical account of events. The symbolic pictorial storytelling as found in cavemen's drawings, Egyptian hieroglyphics, and the petroglyphs of American Southwest Indians were limited in circulation as they were carved in stone. As movable parchment-type surfaces like animal skins, papyrus, and later paper developed, the main users of such devices were merchants to make lists of transactions and inventory, as the preceding text has evidenced. Reproduction of writing was later entrusted to the work of scribes, many of whom were literate slaves during the Roman era. The ancient Chinese dynasties used the services of religious order monks in monasteries as imperial scribes. However, most works remained cloistered in the houses and institution of their benefactors, as copying by hand was an arduous task and hence expensive to employ. Furthermore, only a small percentage of the ancient populations was literate and capable of reading. The technology of the printing press in the 15th and 16th centuries was welcomed by the state and the church in Europe with Johannes Guttenberg's invention of the movable type, although the original process is attributed to Chinese ingenuity. Such development also occurred during the first global expansion of mercantile trade by major European nations, which in turn resulted in the appearance of secular universities that were producing a new educated bourgeois or middle class as opposed to the previous royalty and their aligned landed gentry elite. The publishing industry was encouraged and tolerated as a tool for the wider dissemination of Bibles and governmental information to keep societies in check. Therefore, little leeway was allowed for authored dissents and criticism of such institutions. Consequently, sovereign states, as encouraged by the Church, established controls over printers with the need for licenses to produce particular approved and authorized books for a fixed period while prohibiting the import of foreign printed works. Under the English Licensing Act of 1662, a monopoly was granted to members of the Stationery Company, who acted most diligently in their selection of books so as to not offend the license grantor, the sovereign, and their alliance partners in the realm, the Church. The act lapsed in

1695 and was followed 11 years later by the Statute of Anne, whose proper title was *An Act for the Encouragement of Learning, by Vesting the Copies of Printed Books in the Authors or Purchases of Such Copies, during the Times Therein Mentioned.*

This statute was the originator of the modern copyright law, containing a provision that first recognized the legal right of authorship works as a form of intangible property, giving it equal status to the more traditionally recognized physical estate and other personal tangible assets; hence, it was subject to financial penalties if misappropriated by others (one penny for every page, split between the author and the crown). It required a copy of the book to be placed on deposit with the King's Library (a predecessor to the modern practice of the U.S. Library of Congress) as well as the educational institutions of Oxford and Cambridge. It granted protection rights for an initial period of 14 years (grandfathering 21 years for books already in print form) with a renewable 14-year term if the author was still alive. What is interesting is that while the statute was still a draft, it was debated in the House of Lords that the legal theory behind the enactment was that the right of the author was proclaimed as a natural law recognized by all mankind and that the added statutory grant of a limited (time) monopoly was to protect and insure such a universally accepted proposition. Intellectual pursuit—the dissemination of knowledge via its resulting physical embodiment, the written work itself—was raised to a unique altruistic status. However, in *Piracy: The Intellectual Property Wars from Gutenberg to Gates*, author Adrian Johns relates that intellectual property rights (i.e., patents, copyrights, trademarks) are rooted in theories of economics and trade as well as the needs of civilizations.[16] He argues that the noble idea of disseminating knowledge, quoting John Stuart Mill in his protest that the abolishment of patents would "enthrone free stealing under the prostituted name of freed trade," would leave "men of brains" defenseless "before men of money-bags," or the unscrupulous and motivated entrepreneurs who make money off the ideas of others without giving reasonable compensation to them. Johns is describing piracy, the unauthorized financial enrichment of one to the financial detriment or loss of another. While Johns's book also focuses on the more modern dissemination of information via digital networks, he underscores the mutual relationship between creativity and commerce with the exchange imperative (i.e., trade), the handmaiden and protector of the intellectual process, and the agent of the development and progression of civilization.

Trademarks

As related in the preceding text, the use of marks to identify and distinguish one's property is as old as mankind's presence on earth. The basis for such use was rooted in an economic motivation to resolve ownership disputes, aid in public identification or advertising, and to signify quality of workmanship. Archaeologists feel that cave drawings as early as 5000 BCE not only were intended to describe events, as noted earlier, but represented ownership of them by the drawer. Distinctive markings are also evident on primitive pottery and tools, indicating that they belonged to a specific party, family, or clan. In the Mesopotamian period (circa 3500 BCE), as well as the area of Cnossos on Crete, cylindrical seals in stone were used to identify daily traded commodities. In the first dynasty in Egypt, ownership symbols were placed on bricks, quarry stones, and roof tiles to identify the craftsmanship of stonecutters and fashioners of these architectural structures. Potter's marks have been found on clay and ceramic containers in almost all societies in the ancient world. The markings of property outside the workmanship of artisans appeared on animals allowing the early farmer, rancher, or lord to distinguish his livestock in open grazing pastures and to identify them when they went to market. Blacksmiths of the Roman world placed marks on their metal armaments while in medieval England the requirement to place a distinguishing mark on the construction of swords was not so much to publicize quality workmanship but to identify defective weapons so that the maker could be punished for causing injury on the battlefield to its user.[17] As goods moved in transit across more extensive geographical territories, the use of a merchant's mark on goods in the 10th century was primarily to provide a way of identifying ownership rights of goods lost in transit to shipwrecks, pirates, and other disasters on route.

The earliest known trademark laws were not intended to protect the rights of product makers against those appropriating their name, but it was for the benefit of the buyer. The English Bakers Marking Law in 1266 governed the use of stamps of pinpricks on loaves of bread for health considerations while a similar requirement in 1363 pertaining to silver-smiths was aimed at ensuring quality and integrity. It was not until the 15th century with the emergence of craft guilds that trademark-like symbols and logos began to be used as marketing techniques to represent the quality of products and to promote the goodwill of collective artisan groups housed in specialized towns or regions. These guilds used distinctive markings to promote the collective unified tradesmen as opposed to particular indi-viduals. Membership in the guild was restricted and those members who manufactured defective or poor products were held accountable in order for the reputation to be upheld. Bell makers were among the first artisans to use this practice and they were followed by paper makers with water marks to identify sheets of paper. The first recorded case involving trade-marks, *Southern v. How*,[18] was brought under English common law prin-ciples in 1618 that allowed for remedies in respect to fraud and improper use of marks known then as "passing off." A high-quality cloth manufac-turer brought a claim of improper appropriated use against a competitor who made inferior quality products while placing the marking reserved for the superior quality on his goods. The first law on the subject was passed in 1862 and titled The Merchandise Marks Act focusing on deceptive indications or fraudulent activities. Thirteen years later, the registration of trademarks was incorporated with the first one made by the Bass Red Triangle of the Bass Brewery, a company established in 1777.

Universal Conventions

Nations, by becoming signatories to universal conventions for the cross-border legal protection of trademarks, copyrights, and patents, have helped to further drive globalization in the modern era. While not directly involved in the international trade process as active partners in transactions as in ancient times, their consolidated efforts to recognize the importance in the commercial arena of shielding proprietary rights on a global stage has greatly assisted the promotion of globalization.

Countries have banded together to create the Paris Convention, first signed in 1883, for the protection of industrial property. To date, it has been signed by more than 170 countries. Its prime provision allows a trademark owner to *backdate* in a foreign country to the date of initial filing in his home country if an application for registration is made in another treaty country within six months of the first filing at home. What is so important about this extended time frame, the *backdate* allowance, is that it has the effect of stopping *trademark pirates*. The phrase describes those unscrupulous parties who wait to see the filings in major countries by large multinational organizations and then rush abroad to register them and then attempt to sell them back to the true owners, who are at some point wished to enter such markets but upon filing found their trademarks already owned by others. This practice in the past prevented global firms from enlarging their business via the marketing of a universal brand name without paying off those who hijacked their trade names. In some instances, as the author has experienced firsthand, such dishonest parties resort to international blackmail. As part of the price to transfer a trademark back to the original owner, they demand a hefty fee as well as their appointment as the local distributor or licensee for products, services, or both, bearing the valued trademark. Some even threaten to put on the market, using their country or multiple country registration rights, an inferior version of the trademarked product thereby damaging the quality and reputation of the brand with consumers in these markets destroying the ability to enter them in the future. They further intimidate the true owner by threatening to dump substandard merchandise at less than the established prices in the home countries as well, thereby damaging an existing market. Besides the Paris Convention, the Madrid Protocol allows a national of a member country who has an application pending or has been granted trademark registration in his home country to file a single application with the World International Property Organization (WIPO) for all other countries covered by the protocol. Such a procedure eliminates the need to file in numerous independent jurisdictions, a timely and costly process. The Community Trade Mark system allows, from the onset, no prior country application or registration needed, a single filing to cover all EU countries at once. The previously noted Paris Convention also applies to patents. Like the provision of the right to claim priority for trademarks, when one files in any of the member states his or her right is preserved for one year (*note*: trademark is within six months) to file in other member nations and still retain the original filing date in such additional countries. The ability to centralize patent filing is provided under the Patent Cooperation Treaty covering 140 countries and is administered by WIPO. The European Patent Convention grants a similar procedure: one filing for the members of the European Patent Organization (EPO) while equal provisions are available for groups of African countries and the current nine member states that formed the Eurasian Patent Organization (EAPO).

Within the area of copyrights, the Berne Convention for the Pro tection of Literary and Artistic Works, first originating in 1886, covers authored materials. Under the Berne Convention, copyrights for creative works automatically come into force and are protected upon their creation. They do not have to be asserted or declared nor do they need to be registered nor applied for in signatory countries to the convention. As soon as a work is *fixed*—that is, written or recorded on some physical medium—its author is automatically entitled to all copyrights in the work and to any additions or derivative works based on the original, unless and until the author explicitly disclaims them or until the copyright expires. Foreign authors are accorded equal rights and privileges for their copyrighted works. They are treated just like domestic authors in any of the countries that adhere to the convention. Under the convention, all works are protected from being copied or infringed on for a minimum of 50 years with member countries having the right to extend such a period. Related to the Berne Convention and reared to copyrights are the Universal Copyright Convention and specific sections of the Trade-Related Aspects of Intellectual Property Rights declaration as formulated under the WTO.

Piracy, in respect to copyrights and patents, is not so much the appropriation of a proprietary right or name stealing as with trademarks, but internationally takes the form of counterfeit merchandise that uses the work of authors and inventors in the products they offer to consumers. While the aforementioned agreements under unified governmental action have helped strengthen globalization, the problems of misappropriating someone else's intangible property still remains.

Back to the future

Historical economists looking back a thousand years, and using the standards of the times, have determined using gross domestic product (GDP) as the measurement value of a country, that for over 800 years from 1000 to 1820 China and India together accounted for almost 54 percent of the world's GDP.[19] The swing, beginning in the 19th century and attributable to the embrace of the Industrial Revolution in the West, moved Europe and US, to a combined 62 percent a century later in 2004. Latest 2014 GDP, in current price figures, shows China as the second largest economy with the US in the top position. But if GDP is adjusted for purchasing power parity (PPP) China is number 1 followed by the US and India.[20]

The projected world economic structure as a percentage of global GDP for 2050 indicates that the world is moving *back to the future*. Economists predict that China and India would again attain their dominance with a collective 45 percent while the EU and US would be at a united 41 percent. Globalization seems to be at work again altering the global economic environment returning it to those ancient civilizations that birthed the commercial imperative. However this time the world is more interconnected and more interdependent as opposed to centuries ago when nations were remotely linked. Improvements in high-tech communication and rapid efficient transportation have shrunk the globe while commerce has united it.

The world tends to be transfixed on the vast amount of technological advancements in the 20th and 21th centuries. This fascination with the present tends to distract from the fact that most of the basic inventions and discoveries upon which the modern world is based, and in fact still used, as well as the creation of modern marvels originated in the ancient world. It is interesting to note that most scholars suggest that more than half of human histories innovative breakthroughs originated in old age China. The world is also deeply beholden to antiquated India and the civilizations of the Islamic regions of the Levant for the scientific foundations the modern world takes for granted. A list of breakthroughs and advancements afforded global society by the ancestors of these areas would take up many pages in this book.

It should be well noted that cross regional trade allowed original inventions and ideas as well as their ongoing enhancement to be carried abroad. They made her way around the world carried by merchant tradesmen, both those visiting foreign lands from the regions of initial development and those coming into those areas. It could be said that even the motivational inspiration for their initial creation and continuing upgraded innovation was and still is the commercial value that flows from their use.

Contemporary packaging for products or systems carries the attention getting moniker 'new and improved' while advertising for them touts the familiar phrase as a competitive advantage. This declaration is a common recognized purchase motivator seen and heard by consumers around the world. It existed in ancient times and continues in the modern era as the present always reflects elements of the past.

Although scientific historians do credit specific countries with these aforementioned numerous advancements their wide dispersal, being copied, borrowed and improved upon as they made their way around the world, makes it difficult to specifically assign a geographical origination point. Today with the explosion of modern globalization new technological improvements tend to be a composite, the combined input of centers of excellence located around the world. This process is fueled by semi-closed nations embracing more open capitalistic programs as countries like China and India are again becoming centers of research distinction, again another example of moving *back to the future*. Global civilization continues to be enhanced and global commercialization energies the process.

As his book goes to press, a TV commercial by one of America's larger fast food hamburger chains, *Jack in the Box*, debuted. The spot, titled "*Spice Trade*," is inspired by the deserts of Mongolia and chronicles the beloved Jack big head character's pursuit to acquire an irresistible spice to use in his next craveable burger dubbed the *Black Pepper Cheeseburger*. The voice over informs the viewer that a legendary quest was undertaken by him across the globe for an ingredient that was coveted by royalty. After endless searching, he comes across a wise spice trader who gives him exotic black peppercorns, and in exchanges Jack barters his most beloved precious procession a motorcycle. The last frame is of Jack riding a camel laden with the spice and the merchant trader on the bike. In the modern era, the idea of a valued imported spice is revisited as is the age old method of exchange, the simple barter process. The marketing and trading principles still applies even as globalization matures. Today, like centuries ago, basic spice ingredients that add flavor and therefore richness to food is still relevant. Around the world pepper and salt continue to be essential kitchen components and are placed on the tables of restaurants. Not much has changed as the first global products, as introduced in Chapter 5, endure as to their impact on global consumers and world trade. The phrase *back to the future* still resonates.

Also, as the book manuscript is prepared for publishing, the influence of religion on globalization as covered in Chapter 8 also continues. Pope Frances, the head of the Catholic Church, is critical of global capitalism calling it a "subtle dictatorship" that "condemns and enslaves men and women."[21] His Eminence even mentions the crimes of the Roman Catholic Church during the period of Spanish colonialism (see Chapter 4); presumably the clergy's acquiescence to the harsh treatment of indigenous people used as forced labor to acquire the resources of the colonized territories for economic gain. He acquaints such historic period with the unfairness and inequity that destroys the livelihood of the poor by the current beneficial agents of global capitalism. The past seems to always echo into the future.

Final Reflections

Parallel and embedded in the movement of ancient innovative advancements that the modern world tends to take for granted were also the fundamental tenets of business principles—trade practices and supportive infrastructures that are still in use today. As the reader may recall the book's Introduction opened with a personal recollection of a young naïve international executive from the US venturing out into the world. His overseas associates to ease the transition would often remark, "As you Americans are fond of saying, let's get down to business"; like the idea was the sole invention of my native country. Such prompting was to offer some degree of comfort to a nervous fledgling American businessman. Although, in retrospect, it could be interpreted as having been delivered in a *tongue-in-cheek* manner by the speaker it was their way of easing the initial restraint or awkwardness of a first meeting, a social breaker for a juvenile international businessman. As previously explained tongue-in-cheek is an English language idiom, a figure of speech. It implies that a statement is humorously or otherwise not seriously intended, and should not be taken at face value. A way of saying something that is untrue in a way that amuses you, but you want the person you're speaking to to believe it. You brace your cheek with the tip of your tongue, to keep yourself from laughing; hence tongue-in-cheek.

As I recall their kind empathetic pronouncement, I am embarrassed, ashamed of my ignorance. I did not know that barter the forerunner of trade that begot the commercial initiative is simply a human trait. It developed everywhere and began in antiquity. Its origin cannot be traced to a particular society identified by geographical location, ethnicity or belief system. It has produced both good and bad results as have all social engineering instruments and the institutions that utilize them. It was and still is a contributing factor to the development of civilization around the world. It is a common characteristic of all people, a shared bridge that connects us. My valued associates were going *back to the future* echoing a historic relationship connection based on the most standard of human interaction—the ancient process of exchange that first brought people together. Universally understood and practiced by all. As I look back today I marvel at the wisdom of my friends that uttered the aforementioned statement even if it was uttered tongue in cheek. Today, we refer to the process as globalization but in fact the practice has always been with us.

In the Introduction section of the book, the natural propensity to exchange the valued results of one's special knowledge and/or applied physical skills was noted as a trait found only in human species. A recent article sustains this proposition, recognizing it a sociological mechanism in the evolution of mankind.[22] Professor Marean, offering an explanation of how humans conquered the planet, concludes that it is due to a generically encoded feature embedded in H. sapiens he calls *hyperprosociality*. The term describes a proclivity to engage to an extraordinary degree "in highly complex coordinated group activities with people who are not kin to us and who may even be complete strangers." This predisposition toward an extreme brand of cooperation with those outside of one's family, territorial clan or regional tribe helps explain the motivational onus for cross border trade beyond the general search for basic survival resources and need fulfillment, both instinctive characteristics in all living creatures. The ancient barter process was a natural extension of the ingrained cooperative activities of human beings. Over time such exchanges progressed to organized commercial trade across and between wider geographical destinations; and globalization was born.

Clearly the often quoted line from the play *The Tempest* by Willian Shakespeare (Act 1, Scene 1) "What's past is prologue" reminds us that history helps to set the stage for what exists today and what may occur in the future. Global business managers should appreciate and understand the roots of globalization and business principles as they influence their modern activities.

Notes

Prologue

1. Cornell (1995).
2. Seymour-Smith (1998).
3. Friedman (2008).
4. McLean (1971).
5. O'Sullivan and Graham (2010).
6. Brooks (2010).
7. Brooks (2010).

Introduction

1. Donne (1624).

Part I

1. Diamond (1999; 2005).

Chapter 1

1. Bernstein (2008).
2. Tucker (2010).
3. Tucker (2010).
4. Chang (2008, 83). For those interested in the great debate on which economic model is best, see the following authors: Chang (2008) and Stiglitz
   (2006).
5. Levitt (1983).
6. Friedman (2005).
7. Beattie (2009).
8. Greenwald (2009, 238–243).
9. Greenwald (2009, 233–238).
10. Greenwald (2009, 238–243).
11. Greenwald (2009, 238–243). Angell's ideas first presented in a pamphlet
    in 1909 called *Europe's Optical Illusion* and then published in book format
    in 1910. His main thesis was the emergence of the independent nature of
    trade and finance with decreased dependence on countries to influence such
    factors.

12. Rodrik (2011, 23, 310).
13. Friedman (1999).
14. Hill (2007); Wild (2006); Wood (2001); Rugman and Hodgetts (2000). All these authors take a similar approach to describing the onset of globalization in the opening chapters of their respective works.
15. Ball et al. (2004).
16. Griffin (2005); Hodgetts (2006, 8): Box insert inserted titled *Roots of Globalization* written by Lawrence A. Beer in Hodgetts (2006).
17. Peng (2009, 12).
18. Peng (2009, 12).
19. Peng (2009, 12).
20. Friedman (2005).
21. Beattie (2009).
22. Giridharadas (2010).
23. Rugman and Oh (2008).
24. Rostovzeff (1926; 1959).
25. Bernstein (2008, 14).
26. Morris (2010, 144).
27. Morris (2010, 97).
28. Diamond (2005).
29. Everett (2003).

Chapter 2

1. Figueira, Brennan, and Sternberg (2009, ix).
2. Aristotle, *Economics*, quoted in Figueira, Brennan, and Sternberg (2009, 86).
3. Euripides, as quoted in Figueria, Brennan, and Sternberg (2009, 140).
4. Hesiod, "Works and Days," 303, 306–313, quoted in Figueira, Brennan, and Sternberg (2009, 155).
5. Epictetus, *Discourses*, as quoted in Figueria, Brennan, and Sternberg (2009, 118).
6. Xenophon, *The Household Manager*, 20.27–28, quoted in Figueira, Brennan, and Sternberg (2009, 132).
7. Plato (360 BCE).
8. Boesche (2003).
9. Michaelson (2001); Krause (1999); Jay (1967).
10. Pillai (2007).
11. Boesche (2003).
12. Boesche (2003).
13. Chow (2007, 13).
14. Chow (2007, 13).

15. Chow (2007, 24).
16. Ghazanfar (2000).
17. Ghazanfar (2000).
18. Ghazanfar (2000).
19. Ghazanfar (2000).
20. Ferguson (2008).
21. Roberts (2004, 68).
22. Dunning (2003).
23. McEvilley (2001).
24. McEvilley (2001, 141).
25. Curtin (1994, 2).
26. Curtin (1994, 3).
27. Chadwick (2006).
28. Bergreen (2007, 295).
29. Ferguson (2008).
30. Ohmae (1990).
31. Von Daniken (1999).
32. Donne (1624).
33. Darwin (1859).
34. Pieterse (2003).
35. Cowen (2002).
36. Ridley (2010).
37. Ridely (2010).
38. Ridley (2010).
39. Arthur (2009).
40. Tapscott and Williams (2008).
41. Robertson (2003).
42. Bernstein (2008).
43. Jensen and Meckling (1976, 305–360).
44. Diamond (1999, 14).
45. Diamond (1999, 25).
46. Diamond (2005).
47. Diamond (2005).
48. Diamond (2005).
49. Boyce (2003).
50. Boyce (2003).
51. Dunning (2003, 17).

Part II

1. Wheeler (1916).
2. Wheeler (1916).

3. Sting (1987).
4. Confucius (n.d.).
5. Churchill (n.d.).
6. All sources indicate this quote is from Plutarch's *Of Banishment*; see http://www.greekstudies.pdx.edu/Quotes.htm

Chapter 3

1. Isle of Wight wheat DNA points to ancient trade (2015).
2. Whallon (2012).
3. Tykot (2002).
4. McLachian (2011).
5. Griffins (2015).
6. Did warfare fuel the birth of advanced civilization? (2011).
7. Keita (2003).
8. Keita (2003).
9. Roberts (2004).
10. Dunn (2010).
11. Lichteim (1975).
12. Ancient Egypt: Domestic Trade (2014).
13. Solomon (2010).
14. Karam (2007).
15. Cahill (2003).
16. Abatino, Dari-Mattiacci, and Perotti (2009).
17. Santa Clara County v. Southern Pacific Railroad Company (1856).
18. Pliny the Younger, *Letters* 1.24, in Figueira, Brennan, and Sternberg (2009, 98).
19. New York University (2009, December).
20. Smith (1776).
21. Young (2001).
22. Menzies (2002).
23. Menzies (2008).
24. Menzies (2008).
25. Brook (2008).
26. Wee (2001).
27. Byong-Kuk (2003).
28. Yoshino (1988).
29. Yoshino (1988).
30. Weatherford (1997).
31. Chocolate Seen as Ancient Trade Offering (2011). http://www.upi.com/Science_News/2011/03/17/Chocolate-seen-as-ancient-trade-offering/UPI-52621300412957/

32. Holsten (1996).
33. Dell'Amore (2011).
34. Diamond (2005).
35. Pringle (2012).
36. O'Neill (2001).
37. Pratt (2011).
38. Yule (1998).
39. Bernstein (2008, Ch. 6, 130–151).
40. Bernstein (2008, 140).
41. Silver Coins Testify to Ancient Global Trade Reaching Northern Germany (2010).

Chapter 4

1. Blasford-Snell and Snailham (2000).
2. Bergreen (2003).
3. Menzies (2002).
4. LaHaye (2010).
5. Mun (1664).
6. Magnusson (2003).
7. Yule (1918).
8. Bergreen (2007).
9. Viorst (1994, 159–163).
10. Viorst (1965, 173).
11. Bergreen (2007).
12. Brook (2008, 44).
13. Grann (2009).
14. Translated from Latin in Mogoffin (1916, 3, 4, 8).
15. Murray (2005).
16. Murray (2005).

Chapter 5

1. Johnson (1989).
2. Mrdonn.org (2010).
3. Bergreen (2007).
4. The work of Xavier Guichard in his book *Eleuis (Alaises)*, published in the 1930s, is referenced in Butler and Dafoe (1999).
5. Edwards, Gadd, and Hammond (1969).
6. Lynch (1984).
7. Herbert (2005)

8. Bergreen (2007).
9. Silk History (2010).
10. Becket (2015).

Chapter 6

1. Pierce (1968).
2. Diamond (1999, 215).
3. Civilization (2009).
4. Butler (1999, 19).
5. Aravantinos (1999, 45–78).
6. Roberts (2004, 68).
7. Van Doren (1991).
8. Van Doren (1991).
9. Diamond (1999, 234).
10. Tablets (2010).
11. Ajram (1992).
12. Pumin (2014).
13. Menzies (2002, 26).
14. Stopford (1997).
15. Saylor (2007).
16. Madrick (2014).
17. Schanberg (1996).
18. Lalami (2014).
19. de Balzac (1835).
20. Exod. 21:16.
21. Tim. 1:8-10.
22. Miller (1981).
23. Thomas (1997).
24. Thomas (1997).
25. Grant (1982, 30).
26. Bradley (1994).
27. Van Drehle (2011).

Chapter 7

1. Ebb and Kander (1966).
2. Behn (1677).
3. Weatherford (1997, 19, 21).
4. Reid (2003).
5. Boswell (2010).

6. Schiff (2010).
7. Lapham (1988).
8. Lapham (1988).
9. Weatherford (1997, 11).
10. Ferguson (2008, 3).

Chapter 8

1. Bernstein (2008, 66).
2. 2 Sam. 24:24.
3. Varner (1989).
4. The word "tecton" is rooted in *architecton*, the Greek word for "architecture," and its use in early biblical accounts describing the occupation of people at that time was often used as a common term for all those artisans involved in the specialized and professional construction of building foundations.
5. JesusCentral.com (2008).
6. AllAboutJesusChrist.org. (2009).
7. Bernstein (2008, 68).
8. Hill (2003).
9. Becker (2003).
10. Armstrong (1993).
11. Armstrong (1993).
12. Hill (2003).
13. Becker (2003, 26).
14. Bernstien (2008, 71).
15. Sarker (2007).
16. Sura 4:29.
17. Force majeure (1957).
18. Mark 12:17.
19. Neuborne (2003, 20).
20. Bhikkhu (1997).
21. LCCA (2009).
22. Brecht and Schaaf (1985).
23. Mullett (2004).
24. Beer (2015).

Chapter 9

1. Coolidge (1925). The statement comes from a speech called "The Press Under a Free Government," given on January 17, 1925. The quote is really "After all, the chief business of the American people is business." However,

Coolidge did go on to say that "of course the accumulation of wealth cannot be justified as the chief end of existence."

2. Smith (1776).
3. Ricardo (1817).
4. Reagan (1986).
5. Wong (2010).
6. Ferguson (2008).
7. Menzies (2008).
8. Johns (1911).
9. Nayak (2007).
10. Debt (2010).
11. Shotoku (640 AD).
12. Anthon (1841, 1273).
13. Frumkin (1945, 143).
14. MacLeod (2002, 11).
15. Patent Act (1790).
16. Johns (2010).
17. Tabber's Temptations (2010).
18. Southern v. How (1618).
19. Gupta and Wang (2009).
20. World IMF Economic Outlook (2015).
21. Yardley and Appelbaum (2015).
22. Marean (2015).

References

Abatino, B., G. Dari-Mattiacci, and E. Perotti. 2009. "Early Elements of the Corporate form: Depersonalization of Business in Ancient Rome." http://ssrn.com/abstract=1526993 (accessed June 10, 2010).

Ajram, K. 1992. *The Miracle of Islam Science*. 2nd ed. New York: Knowledge House.

AllAboutJesusChrist.org. 2009. Joseph of Arimathea. http://www.allaboutjesuschrist.org/common/printable-joseph-of-arimathea-faq.htm (accessed July 15, 2009).

Ancient Egypt: Domestic Trade. 2014. June 2014. http://www.reshafim.org.il/ad/egypt/trade/internal_trade.htm (accessed June 14, 2014).

Anthon, C. 1841. *A Classical Dictionary: Containing an Account of the Principle Proper Names Mentions in Ancient Authors, and Intended to Elucidate All the Important Points Connected with the Geography, History, Biography, Mythology, and Fine Arts of the Greeks, and Romans Together with an Account of Coins, Weights and Measures, with Tabular Values of the Same*, p. 1273. New York: Harper & Bros.

Aravantinos, V. 1999. Mycenaean Texts and Contexts at Thebes: The Discovery of New Linear B Archives on the Kadmeia. In *Floreant Studia Mycenaea: Akten Des X Internationalen Mykenologischen Colloquiums in Salzburg*, eds. S. Deger-Jalkotzy, S. Hiller, and O. Panagl, pp. 45–102. Vienna: Verlag der Osterreichischen Akademie der Wissenschaften.

Armstrong, K. 1993. *A History of God*. New York: Gramercy Book.

Arthur, W.B. 2009. *The Nature of Technology: What It Is and How It Evolves*. New York: Free Press.

Ball, D.A., W.H. McCulloch Jr., P.L Framtz, M. Gewringer, and M.L. Minor. 2004. *International Business*. 9th ed., p. 8. New York: McGraw-Hill Irwin.

Beattie, A. 2009. *False Economy: A Surprising Economic History of the World*, p. 218. New York: Riverhead Books/Penguin Books.

Beck, U. 2000. *What Is Globalization?* Cambridge, UK: Polity Press.

Behn, A. 1677. *The Rover*. London, UK: Author.

Becket, S. 2015. *Empire of Cotton: A Global History*. New York: Alfred A. Knopf

Beer, L. 2015. *A Strategic and Tactical Approach to Global Business Ethics*. 2nd ed. New York: Business Expert Press.

Bergreen, L. 2003. *Over the Edge of the World*. New York: HarperCollins Publishers.

Bergreen, L. 2007. *Marco Polo, from Venice to Xanadu*. New York: Alfred A. Knopf.

Bernstein, W. 2008. *A Splendid Exchange: How Trade Shaped the World*. New York: Grove Press.

Bhikkhu, T. 1997. "Wealth and the Right Livelihood." http://www.hinduwebsite. com/buddhism/wealth.asp (accessed July 21, 2008).

Force majeure. 1957. *Blanks Law Dictionary*. 4th ed. St. Paul, MN: West Publishing.

Blasford-Snell, J., and R. Snailham. 2000. *Kota Mama: Retracing the Lost Trade Routes of Ancient South American Peoples*. London, UK: Headline Books Pub. Ltd.

Boswell, R. 2010. "Canadian Scientists Using Ancient Coins to Map Trading Routes." *Post Media News*, December 7. http://www.canada.com/story_print. html?id=3941054&sponser=hp-storytoolbox (accessed December 17, 2010).

Boesche, R. January 2003. "Kautilya's Arthasastra on War and Diplomacy in Ancient India." *The Journal of Military History* 67, no. 1, pp. 9–37.

Boyce, A. 2003. "Early Anthropological Economic Theory by Karl Polanyi." http://www.mnsu.edu/emuseum/history/trade/karlpolanyi.htm (accessed March 3, 2010).

Bradley, K. 1994. *Slavery and Society at Rome*, New York, NY, Cambridge University Press

Brooks, D. 2010. "History for Dollars." *New York Times*, June 7. http://www. nytimes.com/2010/06/08/opinion/08brooks.html (accessed June 8, 2010).

Brecht, M., and J. Schaaf. 1985. *Martin Luther, His Road to Reformation: 1483—1521*. Philadelphia, PA: Fortress Press.

Brook, T. 2008. *Vermeer's Hat: The Seventeenth Century and the Dawn of the Global World*. New York: Bloomsbury Press.

Butler, A., and S. Dafoe. 1999. *The Knights Templar Revealed*. New York: Barnes and Noble.

Byong-kuk, K. 2003. "[New Horizon] Feasibility for Korea-Japan Free Trade Area." http://www.koreatimes.co.kr/kt_op/200107/t20010725155923348110.htm (accessed May 18, 2009).

Cahill, T. 2003. *Sailing the Wine-Dark Sea: Why Greeks Matter*, p. 10. New York: Doubleday.

Chadwick, A. 2006. "Interviews: Lake Titicaca's Lost Civilizations." *National Public Radio*. http://www.npr.org/templates/story/story.php?storyId=4079710(accessed October 17, 2009).

Chang, H. 2008. *Bad Samaritans: The Myth Offree Trade and the Secret History of Capitalism*, p. 83. New York: Bloomsbury Press.

Chocolate Seen as Ancient Trade Offering. March 17, 2011. United Press International Website. http://www.upi.com/Science_News/2011/03/17/ Chocolate-seen-as-ancient-trade-offering/UPI-52621300412957/ (accessed May 20, 2011).

Chow, G. 2007. *China's Economic Transformation*. 2nd ed., p. 13. Malden, MA: Blackwell.

Churchill, W. (n.d.). "Quotations." http://jpetrie.myweb.uga.edu/bulldog.html (accessed October 21, 2009).

Cohen, R., and P. Kennedy. 2000. *Global Sociology*. London, UK: Macmillan.

Confucius. (n.d.). Quote. http://www.quotationspage.com/quotes/confucius (accessed October 21, 2009).

Coolidge, C. January 17, 1925. "Remarks Made before the American Society of Newspaper Editors." Washington, DC. http://www.presidency.ucsb.edu/ws/index.php?pid=24180 (accessed April 5, 2011).

Cornell, T.J. 1995. *The Beginning of Rome: Italy and Rome from the Bronze Age to the Punic Wars (c.1000 to 264 B,C.)*. New York: Routledge

Cowen, T. 2002. *Creative Destruction: How Globalization is Changing the World's Clture*. Princeton, NJ: Princeton University Press.

Curtin, P. 1994. *Cross Cultural Trade in World History*, pp. 2–3. London, UK:Cambridge University Press.

Darwin, C. 1999. *The Origin of Species by Means of Natural Selection, Reissue edition*, New York, NY, Bantam Classics.

De Balzac, H. 1835. *Lepere Goriot*. Paris, France: Werdet Publishing.

Debt. 2010. In *Wikipedia*. http://en.wikipedia.org/wiki/Debt (acccessed July 1, 2009).

Dell'Amore, C. 2011. "Prehistoric Americans Traded Chocolate for Turquoise." http://news.nationalgeographic.com/news/2011/03/110329-chocolate-turquoise-trade-prehis (accessed March 18, 2011).

Diamond, J. 2005. *Collapse: How Societies Choose to Fail or Succeed*. New York: Viking-Penguin Group.

Diamond, J. 1999. *Guns, Germs, and Steel: The Fate of Human Societies*. New York: W.W. Norton & Company.

"Did Warfare Fuel the Birth of Advanced Civilization?" 2011. http://io9.com/5824875/did-warfare-ful-the-birth-of-advanced-civilization/ (accessed July 27, 2011).

Donne, J. 1624. *Devotions Upon Emergent Occasions and Seurall Steps in My Sickness—Meditation XVII*. http://www.online-literature.com/donne/409 (accessed January 10, 2010).

Dunn, J. 2010. "The Wonderful Land of Punt." http://touregypt.net/featurestories/punt.htm (accessed January 15, 2010).

Dunning, J. 2003. *Making Globalization Good*. Oxford, UK: Oxford University Press.

Ebb, F., and J. Kander. 1966. The Money Song [Song from the musical *Cabaret*]. On *Cabaret* [CD]. Santa Monica, CA: Hip-O Records.

Edwards, I.E.S., C.J. Gadd, and N.G.L. Hammond. 1969. *The Cambridge Ancient History*. Cambridge, UK: Cambridge University Press.

Everett, D. 2003. *Don't Sleep, There Are Snakes*. New York: Pantheon Books.

Farhad, S. (Producer), and M. Gibson. (Producer, Director). 2006. *Apocalypto* [Motion picture]. United States: Icon Productions.

Ferguson, N. 2008. *Ascent of Money: A Financial History of the World*. New York: Penguin Press.

Figueira, T., C. Brennan, and R. Sternberg. 2009. *Wisdom from the Ancients: Enduring Business Lessons from Alexander the Great, Julius Caesar, and the Illustrious Leaders of Ancient Greece and Rome*. New York: Fall River Press.

Friedman, T. 2008. *Hot, Flat, and Crowded*. New York: Farrar, Straus and Giroux.

Friedman, T. 2005. *The World is Flat*. New York: Farrar, Straus and Giroux.

Friedman, T. 1999. *The Lexus and the Olive Tree*. New York: Anchor Books.

Frumkin, M. March 1945. "The Origin of Patents." *Journal of the Patent Office Society* 27, no. 3, p. 143.

Ghazanfar, S. 2000. "The Economic Thought of Abu Hamid Al-Ghazal and Thomas Aquinas: Some Connective Parallels and Links." *History of Political Economy* 31, no. 4, p. 857.

Giridharadas, A. 2010. *India Calling*. New York: Times Books/Henry Hold& Co.

Grann, D. 2009. *Lost City of Z*. New York: Doubleday.

Grant, M. 1982. *From Alexander to Cleopatra: The Hellenistic World*. New York: History Book Club.

Griffins, S. 2015. "Britain's Ancient Connection to Carthage." http://www.dalymail.co.uk/sciencetech/article-3038594/Britain-s-anicnet-connection-Carthage-2-300-years-old-coin-reveals-Mediterranean-trade-route-dating-Oron-Age.html (accessed May 14, 2015).

Hegre, H. January 2001. "Trade as a War Deterrent." *Paper Presented at Den Nasjonale Fagkonferansen i Statsvitenskap*, Bergen, pp. 10–12.

Hill, C. 2007. *International Business*. 6th ed., p. 10. New York: McGraw-Hill Irwin.

Hill, C. 2003. *International Business*. 4th ed., p. 100. New York: McGraw-Hill Irwin.

Holsten, M.J. 1996. *Civilization Lost—the Conquest of the Incas*, p. 12. New York: Advantage Press.

Isle of Wight Wheat DNA Points to Ancient Trade. 2015. http://www.bbc.com/news/uk-england-hampshire-31647440 (accessed February 26, 2015).

Jay, A. 1967. *Management and Machiavelli*. New York: Holt, Rinehart and Winston.

Jensen, M.C., and W.H. Meckling. 1976. "Theory of the Firm: Managerial Behavior Agency Constraints and Ownership Structure." *Journal of Financial Economics* 3, pp. 305–360.

JesusCentral.com. 2008. "Life of Jesus: First Century Context of Palestine (Israel)." http://www.jesuscentral.com/ji/historical-jesus/jesus-firstcenturycontext.php (accessed on May 14, 2009).

Johns, A. 2010. *Piracy: The Intellectual Property Wars from Gutenberg to Gates.* Chicago, IL: University of Chicago Press.

Johns, C.H. 1911. "The Code of Hammurabi." *The Avalon Project at Yale Law School/Babylonian Law.* http://avalon.law.yale.edu/subject_menus/hammenu.asp (accessed August 17, 2009).

Johnson, H. 1989. *Vintage: The Story of Wine*, pp. 35–46. New York: Simon and Schuster.

Karam, C.C. 2007. "Phoenicians in Brazil." http://phoenicia.org/brazil.html (accessed August 28, 2009).

Keita, M. 2003. "Rise of Civilizations and Empires in Mesopotamia, Egypt and the Indus Valley." http://history-world.org/rise_of_civilizations.htm (accessed February 5, 2008).

Krause, D. 1999. *Musashi's Classic: The Book of Five Rings for Managers.* London, UK: Nicholas Brealey Publishing Limited.

LaHaye, L. 2010. "Mercantilism." *The Concise Encyclopedia of Economics.* http://www.econlib.org/library/Enc/Mercantilism.html? (accessed June 21, 2010).

Lalami, L. 2014. *The Moor's Account.* New York: Pantheon Books.

Lapham, L. 1988. *Money and Class in America: Notes and Observations in Our Civil Religion.* New York: Grove Press.

LCCA. 2009. "The Tao of Commerce." http://www.lcca.co.uk/new.php (accessed March 7, 2009).

Levitt, T. 1983. *The Globalization of Markets.* Boston: Harvard Business Review, http://www.lapres.net/levit.pdf (accessed May–June 1983).

Lichteim, M. 1975. *Ancient Egyptian Literature: The Old and Middle Kingdoms*, vol. 1. Berkeley, CA: University of California Press.

Lynch, D. 1984. *Dune* [movie]. Los Angeles, CA: Universal.

MacLeod, C. 2002. *Inventing the Industrial Evolution: The English Patent System, 1660—1800*, p. 11. Cambridge, UK: Cambridge University Press.

Maddison, A. 2003. *The World Economy: Historical Statistics.* Paris: OECD Development Centre.

Madrick, J. 2014. "Our Misplaced Faith in Free Trade." *New York Times*, Sunday Review, October 5, p.5.

Magnusson, L. 2003. *A Companion to the History of Economic Thought.* Malden, MA: Blackwell.

Marean, C. August 2015. "The Most Invasive Species of All." *Scientific American* 313, no. 2, pp. 32–39.

McLean, D. 1971. "American Pie." On *American Pie*. [Vinyl.] Century City, CA: United Artists.

McEvilley, T. 2001. *The Shape of Ancient Thought: Comparative Studies in Greek and Indian Philosophies.* New York: Allworth Press.

McLachian, S. 2011. *Ancient Port Discovered in Egypt* http://www.gadling. com/2011/07/30/ancient-port-discovered-in-egylt/print/ (accessed July 30, 2011).

Menzies, G. 2008. *1434: The Year a Magnificent Chinese Fleet Sailed to Italy and Ignited the Renaissance.* New York: William Morrow/Harper Collins.

Menzies, G. 2002. *1421: The Year China Discovered America,* pp. 26–27. New York: William Morrow/Harper Collins.

Michaelson, G. 2001. *SunTzu: The Art of War for Managers.* Avon, MA: Adams Media Corporation.

Miller, J. 1981. "Mortality in the Atlantic Slave Trade: Statistical Evidence on Causality. *Journal of Interdisciplinary History* 11, no. 3, pp. 385–423.

Mogoffin, R. 1916. *Greek and Roman Documents.* New York: Oxford University Press.

Morris, I. 2010. *Why the West Rules—for Now: The Patterns of History, and What They Reveal About the Future,* pp. 3–6. New York: Farrar, Straus and Giroux.

Mrdonn.org. 2010. "Trading Gold for Salt and Spices and Other Luxury Goods." http://africa.mrdonn.org/goldandsalt.html (accessed April 21, 2010).

Mullett, M. 2004. *Martin Luther.* London, UK: Routledge.

Mun, T. 1664. *England's Treasure by Foreign Trade.* http://history.hanover.edu/ courses/excerpts/111mun.html (accessed May 30, 2010).

Murray, J. 2005. *Bruges, Cradle of Capitalism, 1280—1390.* Cambridge, UK: Cambridge University Press.

Nayak, S. 2007. "Globalization—Indian Experience and Perspective." *Global Economy Journal* 7 no. 2. http://www.bepress.com/gej (accessed January 15, 2009).

Neuborne, E. December 2003. "The Virtual Relationship." *Sales and Marketing Management* 155, no. 12, p. 20.

New York University. 2009. *The Lost World of Old Europe: The Danube Valley, 5000-3500 BC* [Museum exhibit]. New York: New York University.

Ohmae, K. 1990. *The Borderless World.* New York: Harper Business.

O'Neill, J. 30 November, 2001. "Building Better Global Economic BRICs." Global Economics Paper No: 66, New York, Goldman Sachs.

O'Sullivan, M., and M. Graham. 2010. "Moving Forward by Looking Back: Business History and Management Studies." *Journal of Management Studies* 47, no. 5, p. 775–90. http://www.interscience.wiley.com/journal/123276970/ abstract (accessed February 19, 2010).

Patent Act. 1790, April 10, 1790. *The Patent Act of 1790.* http://ipmall.info/ hosted_resources/lipa/patents/Patent_Act_of_1790.pdf (accessed on May 11, 2011).

Peng, M. 2009. *Global Business*. Mason, OH: South-Western Cengage Learning.

Pierce, J. 1968. *Science, Art, and Communication*. New York: Clarkson N. Potter Inc.

Pieterse, J.N. 2003. *Globalization and Culture: Global Melange*. Lanham, MD: Rowman & Littlefield.

Pillai, R. 2007. 7 Pillars of a Business. http://hinduism.about.com/od/script uresepics/a/businesspillars.htm (accessed October 2008).

Plato. 360 BCE. *The Republic*. Translation by Benjamin Jowett. http://classics. mit.edu/Plato/republic.2.i.html (accessed April 4, 2011).

Pringle, H. November 2012. "Vikings and Native Americans." *National Geographic* 222, No. 5.

Pratt, D. August. 2011. "The Ancient Americas: Migration." *Contacts and Atlantis*. http://davidpratt.info/amercicas1.htm (accessed March 17, 2015).

Pumin, Y. 2014. "A Second Wind for an Ancient Route." http://www.bjreview. com/print/txt/2015-02/02/content_666547.htm (accessed February 5, 2015).

Reid, G. 2003. "A Case for the World's First Coin: The Lydian Lion." http:// rg.ancients.info/lion/article.html (accessed April 20, 2009).

Reagan, R. July 17, 1986. "Remarks at a White House Briefing for Trade Associations Representatives on Free and Fair Trade." http://www.reagan. utexas.edu/archives/speeches/1986/86jul.htm (accessed April 5, 2011).

Ricardo, D. 1817. *On the Principles of Political Economy and Taxation*. London, UK: Author.

Ridley, M. 2010. "Humans: Why They Triumphed." *The Wall Street Journal* 22, May 22. http://online.wsj.com/article/SB100014240527487036918045752 54533386933138.html? (accessed May 22, 2010).

Roberts, J. 2004. *Ancient History*. London, UK: Duncan Baird.

Robertson, R. 2003. *The Three Waves of Globalization: A History of a Developing Global Consciousness*. London, UK: Zed Books.

Rodrik, D. 2011. *The Globalization Paradox*. New York: W.W Norton & Co.

Rostovzeff, M. 1926. *Social and Economic History of the Roman Empire*. Cheshire, CT: Biblo-Moser.

Rostovzeff, M. 1959. *A Social and Economic History of the Hellenistic World*. Oxford, UK: Clarendon Press.

Rugman, A., and C. Oh. 2008. "Friedman's Follies: Insights on the Globalization/ Regionalization Debate, Business and Politics." *The Berkeley Electronic Press* 10, no. 2.

Rugman, A., and R. Hodgetts. 2000. *International Business*. 2nd ed. Harlow, UK: Pearson Education Limited.

Sarker, M. 2007. "Islamic Business Contracts, Agency Problem and the Theory of the Islamic Firm." *International Journal of Islamic Financial Services* 1, no. 2, pp. 12–28. http://www.iiibf.org/journals/journal2/art2.pdf (accessed March 20, 2009).

Saylor, S. 2007. *Roman.* New York: St. Martin's Griffen.

Schanberg, S. 1996. "On the Playgrounds of America, Every Kid's Goal is to Score: In Pakistan, Where Children Stitch Soccer Balls for Six Cents an Hour, the Goals is to Survive." *Life Magazine,* June, pp. 38–48.

Schiff, S. 2010. *Cleopatra.* New York: Little, Brown and Co.

Seymour-Smith, M. 1998. *The 100 Most Influential Books Ever Written.* New York: Barnes & Noble Books.

Shotoku, T. 604 AD. "Shotoku's Seventeen Article Constitution of Japan." http://www.duhaime.org/LawMuseum/lawarticle-1182/604-the-seventeen-article-constitution-of-japan.aspx (accessed May 21, 2009).

Shamisastry, R. 2010. *The Arthashastra.* New York: Spastic Cat Press.

Silk History. 2010. InfoPlease.com. http://www.infoplease.com/ce6/society/A0861091.html (accessed May 10, 2010).

Silver Coins Testify to Ancient Global Trade Reaching Northern Germany. 2010. *The Local,* September 5. http://www.thelocal.de/politics/20100905-29625.html (accesssed September 6, 2010).

Smith, A. 1776. *An Inquiry Into the Nature and Causes of the Wealth of Nations,* book. 4, section 2, 12. Edinburgh: N.p.

Solomon, S. 2010. *Water: The Epic Struggle for Wealth, Power and Civilization.* New York: Harper.

Southern v. How. 1618. http://www.caslon.com.au/ipchronology.htm (accessed April 9, 2009).

Stopford, M. 1997. *Maritime Economics.* London, UK: Routledge Press.

Sting. 1987. "History will Teach Us Nothing [song]." In *Nothing Like the Sun*[album]. London, UK: A&M Records.

Stiglitz, J. 2006. *Making Globalization Work.* New York: W.W. Norton &Company.

Stiglitz, J. 2002. *Globalization and Its Discontents,* p. 2. New York: Norton Press.

Tabber's Temptations. 2010. "The History of Trademark Law." http://www.tabberone.com/Trademarks/TrademarkLaw/History/History.shtml (accessed March 5, 2010).

Tablets. 2010. "Tablets of 4,000-Year-Old Trade Agreement Found in Central Turkey." *Daily News & Economic Review.* http://www.hurriyetdailynews.com/n.php?n=0829142348237-2010-08-30 (accessed September 2, 2010).

Tapscott, D., and A.D Williams. 2008. *Wikinomics: How Mass Collaboration Changes Everything.* New York: Penguin Group.

Thomas, H. 1997. *The Slave Trade: The Story of the Atlantic Slave Trade: 1440-1870.* New York: Simon & Schuster Paperbacks.

Tucker, J. May 27, 2010. "Why Economic Exchange Sustains Us." *The Christian Science Monitor.* http://www.csmonitor.com/Business/The-Circle-Bastiat/2010/0527/Why-economic-exchange-sustains-us (accessed May 27, 2010).

Tykot, R. 2002. "Geochemical Analysis of Obsidian and the Reconstruction of Trade Mechanisms in the Early Neolithic Period of the Western Mediterranean." In *Archaeological Chemistry Materials, Methods and Meanings*, ed. K. Jakes. Washington, DC: American Chemical Society

Van Drehle, D. 2011. "The Civil War 1861-2011: The Way We Weren't." *Time*, April 18, pp. 40–51.

Varner, C., Jr. 1989. "Business: The Clergy Debate—Business and the Bible." *Presented at the MBAA Regional Convention, The Palmer House*, Chicago, Illinois. http://www.coursehero.com/file/4555849/The-Business-Clergy-Debate (accessed March 21, 2009).

Von Daniken, E. (1968) 1999. *Chariots of the Gods? Unsolved Mysteries of the Past*. New York: Bantam Books.

Weatherford, J. 1997. *The History of Money*. New York: Three Rivers Press.

Wee, C.H. 2001. *The Inspirations of Tao Zhu-Gong*. New York: Prentice Hall.

Wheeler, C. May 25, 1916. "Fight to Disarm His Life's Work, Henry Ford Vows." *Chicago Daily Tribune*, p. 10.

Whallon, R. 2012. "Excavations at Grotta S. Angelo." http//www.lsa.umich.edu/umma/research/robertwhallon (accessed August 1, 2014).

Wong, E. 2010. "Chinese Military Seek to Extend Naval Power." *The New York Times*, April 23.

World IMF Economic Outlook. April 2015. Knoema. http://knoema.com/nwnfkne/world-gdp-ranking-2015-data-and-charts (accessed May 1, 2015).

Wood, M. 2001. *International Business*. New York: Palgrave Macmillan.

Yardley, J., and B. Appelbaum. 2015. "In Fiery Speeches Frances Excoriates Global Capitalism." *New York Times*, July 12, p. 12.

Young, G. 2001. *Rome's Eastern Trade: International Commerce and Imperial policy 31 BC—AD 305*. London, UK: Routledge.

Index

OTHER TITLES IN THE INTERNATIONAL BUSINESS COLLECTION

Tamer Cavusgil, Georgia State; Michael Czinkota, Georgetown; and Gary Knight, Willamette University, Editors

We have over 30 books in this collection—here are just a few you may have an interest in...

- *Assessing and Mitigating Business Risks in India* by Balbir Bhasin
- *The Emerging Markets of the Middle East: Strategies for Entry and Growth* by Tim Rogmans
- *Doing Business in China: Getting Ready for the Asian Century* by Jane Menzies and Mona Chung
- *Transfer Pricing in International Business: A Management Tool for Adding Value* by Geoff Turner
- *Management in Islamic Countries: Principles and Practice* by UmmeSalma Mujtaba Husein
- *Burma: Business and Investment Opportunities in Emerging Myanmar* by Balbir Bhasin
- *Global Business and Corporate Governance: Environment, Structure, and Challenges* by John Thanopoulos
- *The Intelligent International Negotiator* by Eliane Karsaklian
- *As I Was Thinking....: Observations and Thoughts on International Business and Trade* by Michael R. Czinkota
- *A Strategic and Tactical Approach to Global Business Ethics, Second Edition* by Lawrence A. Beer
- *Innovation in China: The Tail of the Dragon* by William H.A. Johnson
- *Dancing With The Dragon: Doing Business With China* by Mona Chung and Bruno Mascitelli
- *Making Sense of Iranian Society, Culture, and Business* by Hamid Yeganeh

Announcing the Business Expert Press Digital Library

Concise e-books business students need for classroom and research

This book can also be purchased in an e-book collection by your library as

- a one-time purchase,
- that is owned forever,
- allows for simultaneous readers,
- has no restrictions on printing, and
- can be downloaded as PDFs from within the library community.

Our digital library collections are a great solution to beat the rising cost of textbooks. E-books can be loaded into their course management systems or onto student's e-book readers.
The **Business Expert Press** digital libraries are very affordable, with no obligation to buy in future years. For more information, please visit **www.businessexpertpress.com/librarians**. To set up a trial in the United States, please email **sales@businessexpertpress.com**.

CPSIA information can be obtained
at www.ICGtesting.com
Printed in the USA
LVOW13s1124260617
539398LV00005B/750/P